Admiral Albert Hastings Markham

By the same author

Valentine Baker's Heroic Stand at Tashkessen 1877:
A Tarnished British Soldier's Glorious Victory
(Pen & Sword, 2017)

Admiral Albert Hastings Markham

A Victorian Tale of Triumph, Tragedy and Exploration

Frank Jastrzembski

Pen & Sword
MARITIME

First published in Great Britain in 2019 by
Pen & Sword Maritime
An imprint of
Pen & Sword Books Ltd
Yorkshire – Philadelphia

ISBN 978 1 52672 592 9

Printed and bound in the UK by TJ International Ltd,
Padstow, Cornwall.

Pen & Sword Books Limited incorporates the imprints of Atlas,
Archaeology, Aviation, Discovery, Family History, Fiction, History,
Maritime, Military, Military Classics, Politics, Select, Transport,
True Crime, Air World, Frontline Publishing, Leo Cooper, Remember
When, Seaforth Publishing, The Praetorian Press, Wharncliffe
Local History, Wharncliffe Transport, Wharncliffe True Crime
and White Owl.

For a complete list of Pen & Sword titles please contact

PEN & SWORD BOOKS LIMITED
47 Church Street, Barnsley, South Yorkshire, S70 2AS, England
E-mail: enquiries@pen-and-sword.co.uk
Website: www.pen-and-sword.co.uk

Or

PEN AND SWORD BOOKS
1950 Lawrence Rd, Havertown, PA 19083, USA
E-mail: Uspen-and-sword@casematepublishers.com
Website: www.penandswordbooks.com

To my loving family, wonderful friends and the forgotten
men and women from history.

I thank God for giving me the opportunity and
ability to tell their stories.

Fortitudine Vincimus (By endurance we conquer).
The Antarctic explorer Sir Ernest Henry Shackleton's family motto

'England was made by her adventurers … and I believe, will only hold
its place by adventurers.'
Attributed to Major General Charles George 'Chinese' Gordon,
The Spectator, 1894

Contents

List of Illustrations		viii
Maps		xii
Foreword		xxi
Acknowledgements		xxv
Introduction		1
Chapter 1	A Son of the Ocean	5
Chapter 2	Anarchy in the Far East	13
Chapter 3	The Martyrs of Nukapu	38
Chapter 4	The Chosen Band	66
Chapter 5	Into the Arctic Unknown	90
Chapter 6	The American Frontier and Novaya Zemlya	113
Chapter 7	A Gentleman Adventurer	128
Chapter 8	The Fiend of Misfortune	148
Epilogue		170
Appendix I	*A Complete List of the Officers and Men of the British Arctic Expedition of 1875–76*	171
Appendix II	*Albert Hastings Markham's Books and Articles*	173
Bibliography		175
Index		189

List of Illustrations

1. Ships anchored at Macao. From Matthew C. Perry and Francis L. Hawks, *Narrative of the Expedition of an American Squadron to the China Seas and Japan, performed in the years 1852, 1853, and 1854, under the Command of Commodore M.C. Perry, United States Navy by the Order of the Government of the United States, Compiled from the original notes and journals of the Commodore Perry and his officers, at his request and under his supervision*, 1856. (*Courtesy of the Library of Congress*)

2. Charles Lennox Richardson's remains after his murder. (*Courtesy of Het Scheepvaartmuseum*)

3. Rear Admiral Sir James Hope (1808–81). From William Laird Clowes, *The Royal Navy: A History from the Earliest Times to the Death of Queen Victoria*, 1903.

4. Sir Clements Robert Markham (1830–1916) at 25 years old. From Albert Hastings Markham, *The Life of Sir Clements R. Markham, KCB, FRS*, 1917.

5. The Fleet defeated Yokohama in Japan's first cricket match. Markham is seated second from the left. From Geoffrey Rawson, *Life of Admiral Sir Harry Rawson*, 1914. (*Courtesy of the Alexander Turnbull Library, Wellington, NZ*)

6. Markham as a young lieutenant. He was said to have recommended the design that would become the national flag of New Zealand while serving in the Australia Station. Helen Lambert, Portraits of Lieutenant Frederic A. Sargeant, Lieutenant Albert H. Markham, and unknown naval officer, 1868–70. Albumen silver photograph, pen and ink, 27.9 x 23.5 cm. (*Courtesy of the National Gallery of Australia, Canberra*)

7. Bishop John Coleridge Patteson (1827–71). From E.S. Armstrong, *The History of the Melanesian Mission*, 1900.

8. HMS *Blanche*. From Halton Stirling Lecky, *The King's Ships Together With the Important Historical Episodes Connected with the Successive Ships of the Same Name from Remote Times, and a List of Names and Services of Some Ancient War Vessels*, 1913.

9. Native labourers on an Australian plantation. From Albert Hastings Markham, *The Cruise of the "Rosario" Amongst the New Hebrides and Santa Cruz Islands, Exposing the Recent Atrocities Connected with the Kidnapping of Natives in the South Seas*, 1873. (*Courtesy of the Cleveland Public Library*)

10. HMS *Rosario*. (*Courtesy of the Shipping Collection, Alexander Turnbull Library, Wellington, NZ*)

11. Missionaries and villagers at the landing place of Nukapu, Reef Islands, 1906. National Library of Australia, nla.obj–141117803, photographer John Watt Beattie. (*Courtesy of Dr Clive Moore*)

12. Markham's assault on Nukapu. National Library of Australia, CDC–10634971, *Town and County Journal*, 21 February 1872.

13. HMS *Alert*'s winter camp. From Edward L. Moss, *Shores of the Polar Sea: A Narrative of the Arctic Expedition of 1875–6*, 1878. (*Courtesy of the Cleveland Public Library*)

14. A photograph of the *Alert* in its winter quarters on Floeberg Beach. From George Nares, *Narrative of a Voyage to the Polar Sea During 1875–6 in H.M. Ships 'Alert' and 'Discovery'*, 1878. (*Courtesy of the Cleveland Public Library*)

15. Sailors building snow halls at Floeberg Beach. From Edward L. Moss, *Shores of the Polar Sea: A Narrative of the Arctic Expedition of 1875–6*, 1878. (*Courtesy of the Cleveland Public Library*)

16. Morning inspection and prayers on the *Alert*'s deck. From Edward L. Moss, *Shores of the Polar Sea: A Narrative of the Arctic Expedition of 1875–6*, 1878. (*Courtesy of the Cleveland Public Library*)

17. Sledge travelling in the Arctic. From Edward L. Moss, *Shores of the Polar Sea: A Narrative of the Arctic Expedition of 1875–6*, 1878. (*Courtesy of the Cleveland Public Library*)

18. Markham's most northern camp. From Albert Hastings Markham, *The Great Frozen Sea: A Personal Narrative of the Voyage of the 'Alert' During the Arctic Expedition of 1875–6*, 1878. (*Courtesy of the Archives & Rare Books Library, University of Cincinnati*)

19. Markham, Radmore, Joliffe and Maskell return to the *Alert*'s camp after seventy-two days. (*Illustration by Zsuzsi Hajdu*)
20. A ticket from one of Markham's lectures while in the United States. (*Courtesy of the 19th Century Rare Book & Photograph Shop*)
21. The Kiowa and Comanche Reservation near Fort Sill. (*Courtesy of the Clay County Historical Society, Inc*)
22. Camp Supply. From *Harper's Weekly*, 1869. (*Courtesy of the Library of Congress*)
23. A watercolour from Markham's journal showing him hunting buffalo. (*Courtesy of the 19th Century Rare Book & Photograph Shop*)
24. A modern view of Clements Markham's residence at 21 Eccleston Square. (*Courtesy of Robert B. Stephenson, The Antarctic Circle*)
25. Markham dressed in his travelling outfit during his Hudson's Bay expedition. (*Illustration by Zsuzsi Hajdu*)
26. Sir Henry Gore-Booth (1843–1900) and some of the *Isbjörn*'s Norwegian crew during Markham's trip to Novaya Zemlya. From Albert Hastings Markham, *Polar Reconnaissance: Being the Voyage of the "Isbjörn" to Novaya Zemlya in 1879*, 1881.
27. HMS *Triumph* in Esquimalt Harbour, Vancouver Island. City of Vancouver Archives, Out P303, photographer George W. Edwards.
28. The Battle of Miraflores. National Library of Chile, id Bnd: LE0000904, artist Ruperto Salcedo, available in Memoria Chilena/ Biblioteca Nacional Digital. (*http://www.bibliotecanacionaldigital. cl/bnd/631/w3-article-334181.html*)
29. Entry of General Baquedano's victorious Chilean soldiers into Lima, 17 January 1881. National Library of Chile, id MC: MC0002340, available in Memoria Chilena/Biblioteca Nacional Digital. (*http:// www.memoriachilena.cl/602/w3-article-98788.html*)
30. A modern aerial view of York Factory, Manitoba, established as a trading post by the Hudson's Bay Company in the seventeenth century. (*Courtesy of Parks Canada*)
31. A modern view of the Great Meteoron Monastery, Greece, established by St Athanasius of Alexandria in the fourteenth century. (*Courtesy of Visit Meteora*)
32. Markham climbing to the top of the Great Meteoron Monastery. From *Pearson's Magazine*, 1899. (*Courtesy of Herman B. Wells Library, Indiana University*)

33. Vice Admiral Sir George Tryon (1832–93). From William Laird Clowes, *The Royal Navy: A History from the Earliest Times to the Death of Queen Victoria*, 1903.

34. A) What should have happened on June 22, 1893; B) What happened; 3) What Markham thought Tryon intended. From *William Laird Clowes, The Royal Navy: A History from the Earliest Times to the Death of Queen Victoria*, 1903.

35. HMS *Victoria* moments after its collision with HMS *Camperdown*. (*Courtesy of Voyager Press Rare Books and Manuscripts*)

36. Theodora Chevallier Gervers Markham (1875–1962). (*Courtesy of the International Autograph Auctions Ltd*)

37. Admiral Sir Albert Hastings Markham (1841–1918). (*Courtesy of the International Autograph Auctions Ltd*)

38. Markham's retreat: Amat Lodge. (*Courtesy of the Tain & District Museum*)

39. Markham with his daughter, Joy Mary Minna (1900–35). From *The Sketch, A Journal of Art and Actuality*, 1904. (*Courtesy of the University of Minnesota*)

40. Markham's tombstone in Kensal Green Cemetery. (*Courtesy of the Henry Vivian-Neal, Kensal Green Cemetery*)

41. A close-up view of Markham's tombstone epitaph. (*Courtesy of the Henry Vivian-Neal, Kensal Green Cemetery*)

Maps

A nineteenth-century map of China. Markham was active in the South China Sea, running along the Chinese coast from Macao to Shanghai. The Taku Forts were situated in the Gulf of Pe-Chili (Bohai) at the mouth of the Peiho (Han) River leading to the Qing capital of Pekin (Beijing).

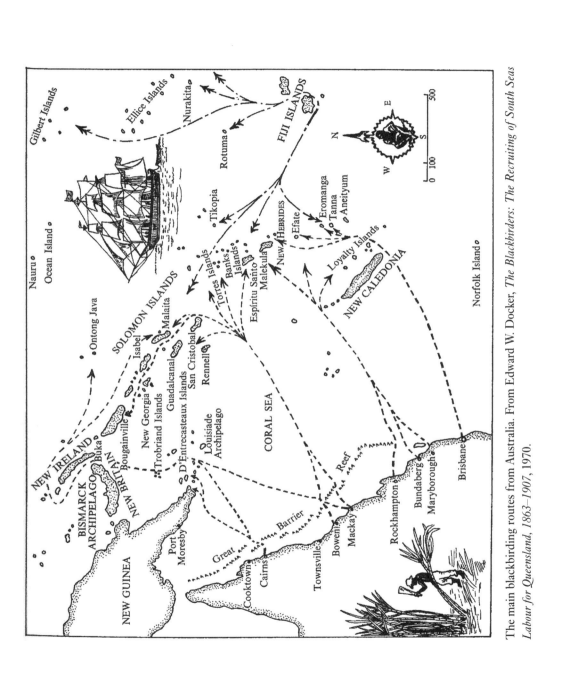

The main blackbirding routes from Australia. From Edward W. Docker, *The Blackbirders: The Recruiting of South Seas Labour for Queensland, 1863–1907*, 1970.

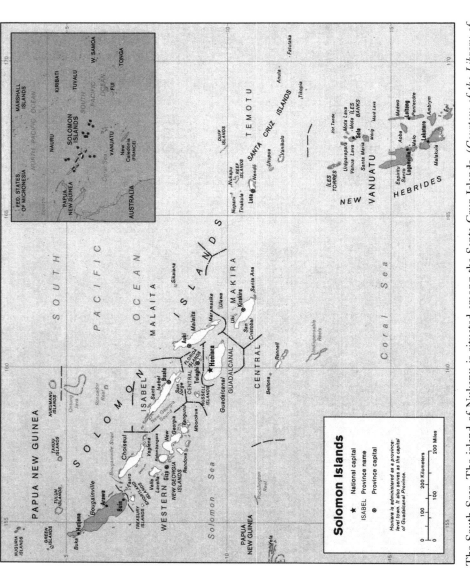

The South Seas. The island of Nukapu is situated among the Santa Cruz Islands. (*Courtesy of the Library of Congress, Geography and Map Division*)

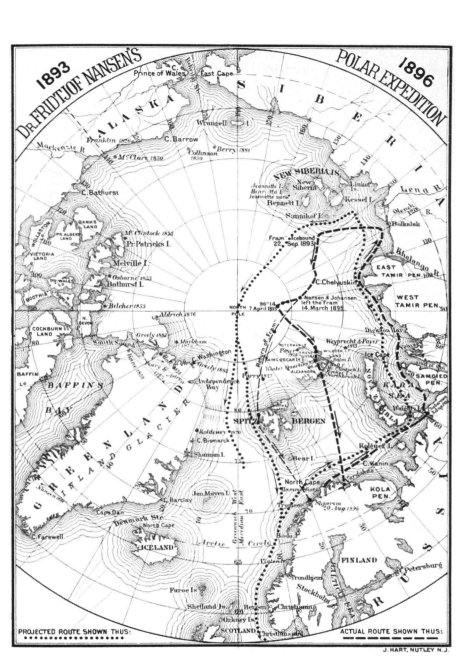

Early twentieth-century map depicting Arctic expeditions. The northernmost points reached by Markham's and Aldrich's expeditions are identified on the map beyond the tip of Ellesmere Island, where the *Alert*'s camp was estalished on Floeberg Beach during 1875–76. Other expeditions, such as those led by Hall, Kane and Greely, are also pinpointed on the map near Smith Sound.

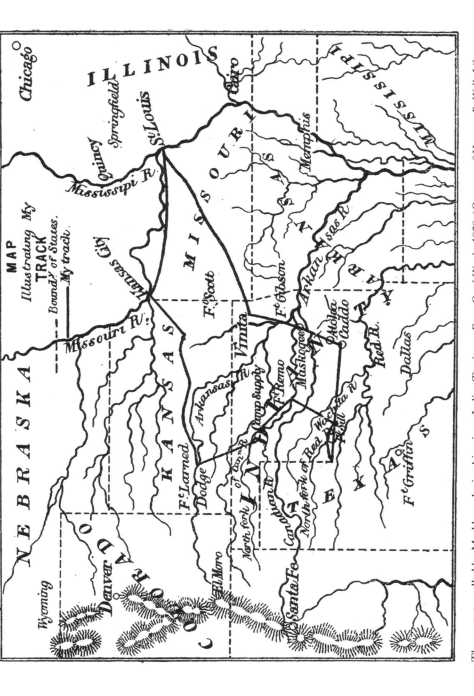

The route travelled by Markham during his trip to Indian Territory. *From Good Words, 1878. (Courtesy of Herman B. Wells Library, Indiana University)*

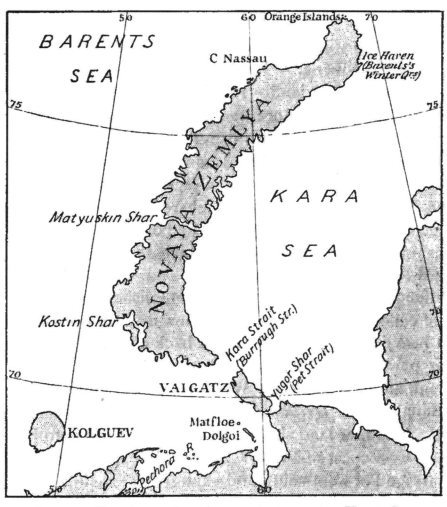

Novaya Zemlya, showing entrances to Kara Sea.

The Arctic Ocean archipelago of Novaya Zemlya. From *Edward Heawood, A History of Geographical Discovery: In the Seventeenth and Eighteenth Centuries*, 1912.

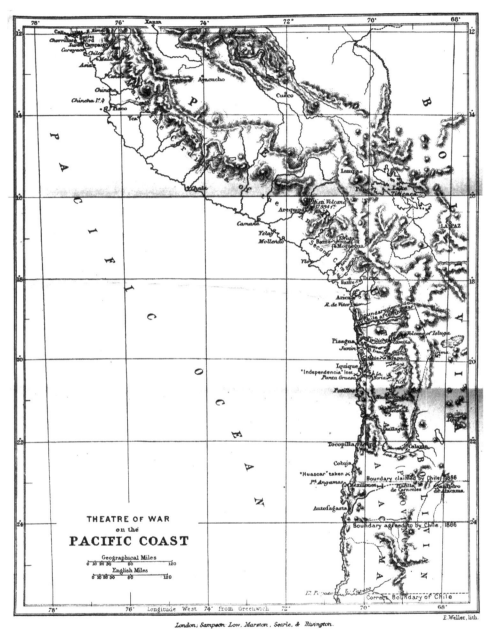

The theatre of war during the War of the Pacific (1879–83). Lima and Callao are located on the northwestern corner of the map. From *Clements Markham, The War Between Peru And Chile 1879–1882*, 1882. (*Courtesy of the Cleveland Public Library*)

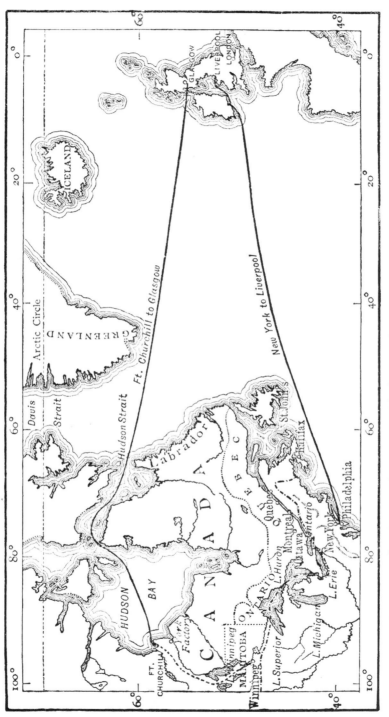

Markham's transatlantic trip to Canada. From *Good Words*, 1888. (*Courtesy of Herman B. Wells Library, Indiana University*)

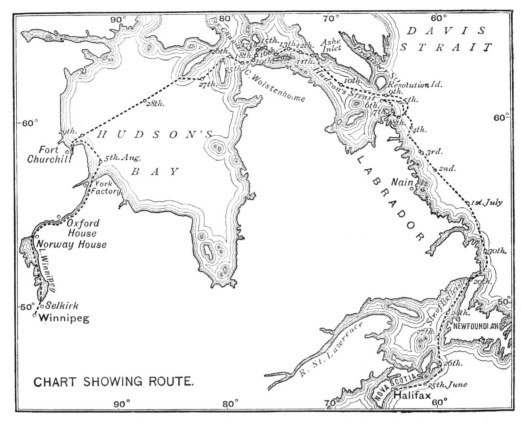

Markham's route from York Factory to Winnipeg. From *Good Words, 1888*. (*Courtesy of Herman B. Wells Library, Indiana University*)

Foreword

By Dr Rodney Atwood

The life of Albert Hastings Markham spanned the great age of the Victorian navy, much less well known than that of Nelson's time. Newspapers today speak glibly of 'gunboat diplomacy', but the senior service gave the Victorian empire unparalleled global reach across the world's oceans, protecting British trade, citizens and interests; suppressing piracy; exploring and charting, extending the knowledge of our globe and aiding navigation. Bluejackets and marines, ashore as Naval Brigades as well as afloat, served in most of Victorian Britain's wars. Markham's adventures read like pages from *Boy's Own* or one of G.A. Henry's adventure stories. Anyone wishing to know of the Victorian navy's breadth of achievement and worldwide duties will read Frank Jastrzembski's biography of Markham with profit. To use an old-fashioned phrase, he was a man of parts, not just an adventurous explorer. He was artistic, with a good standard of penmanship, and he was widely read in history, the travels of Livingstone and the novels of Dickens. He knew Greek. He was a fairly prolific author, and quotes from his books head several of the chapters therein.

But deeds speak louder than words. Always he lived for adventure. Courage, self-discipline and a strong Christian faith marked him out. One of the illustrations shows his perilous climb on a perpendicular wooden ladder up a cliff to a remote monastery, disdaining his own safety. He was in many ways an ideal explorer, pushing back the borders of the unknown. His cousin, the more famous Clements Markham, was an inspiration to him in these endeavours. The home of Clements Markham and his wife at Ecclestone Square in London was filled with memorabilia of Markham expeditions from around the world, among them a statue Albert had carried off during the Taiping Rebellion in China.

Albert Markham's ambition to join the navy and his admiration for his cousin (although the latter had less appetite for the hardships of naval life) shaped his early career. He was soon on the China Station, more important than is usually realised, in action against Chinese pirates and then fighting with the famous 'Chinese' Gordon (later 'Gordon of Khartoum') against the Taiping rebels. He won promotion to acting lieutenant in close-quarter fighting. As a young officer, he had a reputation as a martinet, but cared for his men and saved the life of one of them in a raging gale. Later, he had the sentence of a promising young sailor commuted, realising the man had acted foolishly but out of character.

The war against the slave trade was one of Victorian England's great endeavours. The cruelty of Pacific Ocean 'blackbirders' kidnapping Polynesians for sale was as wicked as that of slavers on the infamous 'middle passage'. Markham's task in the Pacific was complicated, often negotiating with the islanders to avoid misunderstanding, trying to apprehend the murderers of the Bishop of Melanesia, gaining support from missionaries in the fight against the slavers, aware that Australian courts often connived with the criminals.

His greatest service to the navy was as an Arctic explorer. Frank Jastrzembski tells us that the disaster to the Franklin Expedition put a halt for three decades to the Royal Navy's northern expeditions. Markham was one of those who restarted efforts to reach the North Pole, mapping, gaining scientific knowledge with research and observation en route. Beforehand, he had served on a whaling ship in the north to gain experience. The author's well-chosen illustrations as well as his narrative make clear the hardships and challenges on these sledging expeditions after the ships were stopped by pack ice. Temperatures fell to minus 30°F. One march of two hours covered only one mile. The endurance of his men and his qualities of leadership were sternly tested. They failed to reach the North Pole, but planted the Union Jack 400 miles away. Previous accounts have blamed Markham for failing to provide antiscorbutics. Frank Jastrzembski's researches show that he brought what should have been an adequate supply of the standard antiscorbutic provided by the Royal Navy, limes, but unknown to the navy, these provided only half the vitamin C necessary.

Despite many hardships, Markham regarded the Arctic Expedition of 1875–76 as the proudest moment of his life.

A trip to the American West was not in answer to the call of duty, but to satisfy his zest for adventure. His parents and other members of his family had already settled in the Midwest of the United States. On his journey, he was impressed by the fine appearance of the Kiowa and Comanche. He realised from the bleached bones of dead buffalo that this creature, then so numerous, would be brought to the verge of extinction. He kept his revolver and rifle near him when he visited Dodge City, 'a sink of iniquity' full of murderers and criminals. Further adventures followed, in the Barents Sea and a 600-mile canoe trip through the white-water rapids and backwoods of Manitoba, seeking a navigable route.

He enjoyed commanding the Royal Navy's Training Squadron, organised to prepare young officers in seamanship and tactics. Among his trainee crews was the future Captain Robert Falcon Scott, Antarctic explorer.

With so many enterprises and achievements, it is ironic that the last chapter deals with a less creditable moment, the one for which Markham is unfortunately best known. This was the collision of his flagship, the *Camperdown*, with the *Victoria* of Vice Admiral Sir George Tryon, commander of the Mediterranean Fleet. The consequences were disastrous, and shocked a British public that idolised their navy. Frank Jastrzembski's handling of this incident is detailed and even-handed, noting Markham's reluctance to testify to Tryon's culpability. He demonstrates the unhappiness of Markham and his flag captain at their subsequent treatment by the Admiralty. The consequences did have one very happy outcome: the marriage of our hero to a young woman thirty-three years his junior. It was her initiative in writing to the Prince of Wales, the future George V, that secured her husband his last command at The Nore. After forty years in the senior service, he was promoted to the rank of full admiral.

Frank Jastrzembski is a history enthusiast, discovering, researching and writing about largely forgotten wars and heroes of the nineteenth century. *Soldiers of the Queen*, the journal of the Victorian Military Society, features a number of his articles. The Society awarded him its annual medal in 2015. As his CV shows, he has degrees from two universities in Ohio, and was recipient of the Outstanding Graduate Student of the Year Award for 2013–14. His biography of Markham follows an earlier book on another, sometimes neglected Victorian, Valentine Baker, and his heroic rearguard action against the Russians at Tashkessen in 1877.

This book is both an adventure story and an addition to our knowledge of the Victorian navy. I hope that readers will enjoy it as much as I have. It is long overdue as the last biography of Albert Markham was published in 1927. I am delighted to be associated with this book in being invited to write a foreword.

Acknowledgements

It is nearly impossible to recognise every person who has supported me along my journey to complete this book. I have managed to whittle the list down to those whom I could not bear to omit.

For providing me with copies, scans, photos or other valuable information, I would like to thank these individuals and organisations (listed in no specific order): Daniela Schütte González, National Library of Chile; Richard Mammana jun., Project Canterbury; Richard Davie, International Autograph Auctions Ltd. (UK); Patricio Roberto Grene Moller (Chilean translator); Terry Hooker, South and Central American Military Historians Society; Robert B. Stephenson, The Antarctic Circle (New Hampshire); Elaine Herroon, Cleveland Public Library (Ohio); Kostas Chasiotis, Visit Meteora (Greece); Bryan P. Kasik, Library of Virginia; Tom Edsall, The 19th C. Rare Book & Photograph Shop (New York); Savannah Gulick, Archives and Rare Book Library, University of Cincinnati (Ohio); Edwin B. Cheek, Herman B. Wells Library, Indiana University; Bart Lahr, Het Scheepvaartmuseum (Netherlands); Jan Starnes, Dix Noonan Webb Ltd. (UK); Dr Clive Moore, University of Queensland (Australia); Dr Abraham Hauriasi, Anglican Church of Melanesia (Solomon Islands); Bishop Terry Brown, Anglican Church of Melanesia; Jeannie Hounslow, City of Vancouver Archives (Canada); Karen Williams, Clay County Historical Society, Inc. (Texas); Heather Johnson, National Museum of the Royal Navy (UK); Anita Maurice, Roseberys Fine Art Auctioneers (UK); Bernie Lauser, Voyager Press Rare Books and Manuscripts (Canada); Henry Vivian-Neal, Kensal Green Cemetery (UK); Thea Van Veen, National Gallery of Australia; Jodi Duhard, Parks Canada; Tain & District Museum (Scotland); University of Minnesota; The British Library (UK); National Maritime Museum, Greenwich (UK); National Library of New Zealand, Alexander Turnbull Library; and National Library of Australia.

xxvi   *Admiral Albert Hastings Markham*

Thanks to Zsuzsi Hajdu (zsuzsihajduart.com) for her captivating illustrations. I would also like to recognise my commissioning editor, Linne Matthews, for endorsing my second book with Pen & Sword Books and helping me to finally settle on a title. These individuals gave up their precious time to proofread this book: Jonathan Alexander, Rodney Atwood, Amy Marchlen, Jack Perry, Josh Provan, Jarrett Robinson, Joe Teets and Mike Tittensor. I am appreciative of their recommendations for improving the text and for identifying grammatical, spelling and punctuation errors.

Most importantly, I would like to express my gratitude to these individuals for the endless support and inspiration they have given me as a historian, writer and as an individual: my wife, Asha, who besides her devotion, comfort and encouragement, also assisted me with her computer skills; my loving mother, Sherri; my father, Frank, who has continued to fuel my interest in history; my grandmothers, Mary Ann, for her care and tenderness, and Theresa, who has filled my stomach with great Italian food for over three decades; my loyal brother, Joseph, and soon-to-be sister-in-law, Alli. I would not be the man that I am today without their guidance, support and love.

I would also like to take a moment to mention my exceptional friends: Jonathan Alexander, Tom Antloga, Frank Briganti, Cody Burlinski, Nate Cherry, Ian Gough, Tyler Hinshaw, Dan Kriz, Brock Malinowski, Amy Marchlen, Bryan Mullins, Alex Roethel, Chris Sever and Joe Teets. They have accompanied me to many battlefields, historic sites and cemeteries, as well as on other escapades, forging memories that I will forever cherish.

Lastly, I would like to recognise Albert Hastings Markham. It is because of his enthusiasm for writing that I was able to share this tale.

Introduction

ALBERT HASTINGS MARKHAM. This is not a name that most readers would recognise. Nonetheless, this Victorian naval officer lived a fascinating life full of adventure worth investigating. After his death in 1918, *The Globe* claimed that his passing removed from society 'one of the most arresting figures of his time'. This book will explore Markham's adventures to resurrect his name from irrelevance.

Markham's Royal Navy career spanned almost half of the nineteenth century. He first entered the service as a teenage cadet in 1856. Shortly after, he left for the China Station, where he was engaged against Qing soldiers, Taiping rebels and pirates during the Second Opium War and Taiping Rebellion. As a seasoned lieutenant, he assisted with suppressing the blackbirding trade in the South Pacific. He held a number of other important commands until his retirement as an admiral in November 1906. When Kaiser Wilhelm II's legions crossed into Belgium during the summer of 1914, the 72-year-old retired admiral offered to don his uniform once more in the service of his country. The Admiralty politely turned him down. Still, he found a way to serve his country by befriending and hosting officers of the Canadian Expeditionary Force in his home and acting as the treasurer of the Minesweepers' Fund.

Besides serving faithfully in Queen Victoria's navy for five decades, Markham relished visiting remote regions of the world and exploring uncharted lands. He collected fossils, plants and animals, and took detailed notes on his trips. On a trip to Indian Territory in the United States, he hunted buffalo, mingled with Indians on reservations and visited frontier army posts. While in Canada, he surveyed the Hudson Strait and Hudson Bay and canoed Manitoba's hazardous Hayes River. He served as a regular hand on a whaling ship on its voyage to Baffin Bay, fought his way north through the ice-clogged Smith Sound, wintered on the uninhabited northern tip of Ellesmere Island, and voyaged in a

2 Admiral Albert Hastings Markham

chartered Norwegian vessel to explore the archipelago of Novaya Zemlya. 'Geographical exploration is one of the most fascinating pursuits to which a man can devote his energies and his abilities,' Albert declared. 'This fascination is most powerful when investigations are made in those regions which have hitherto been regarded as almost inaccessible – where nature, assisted by the severity of the climate, combines with all her forces to repel the mortal intruders who strive to solve the mysteries of the Pole.' Of all these adventures, his greatest accomplishment was reaching the most northern latitude achieved by man in 1876.

Europe's obsession to reach the North Pole dated back to the late sixteenth century. In 1588, the English explorer John Davis established a new record by travelling within 1,128 miles of the North Pole. Adventurers spent the next 300 years trying to shatter it. Another English explorer, Henry Hudson, sliced Davis's distance in half and reached to within 577 miles of the North Pole in 1607. This record remained unbroken for 165 years until Captain Constantine John Phipps came along in 1773 and passed it by 25 miles. (A member of Phipps's expedition was a 15-year-old midshipman named Horatio Nelson, later the famed vice admiral.) Phipps held the record for five decades until Rear Admiral Sir William Edward Parry trekked on foot to within 435 miles of the North Pole in 1827. In May 1876, Commander Albert Hastings Markham topped Parry's record by 35 miles. Even though his record no longer stood when Lieutenant Lockwood of the Greely Expedition broke it in 1882, Markham was proud of what he and his men were able to accomplish six years earlier; 12 May was a day he continued to cherish and celebrate for the remainder of his life.

An inability to balance work and pleasure caused Albert's cousin Sir Clements Robert Markham to leave the Royal Navy as a young lieutenant, but Albert managed to achieve a balance between his love of travel and exploration and his duty as a Royal Navy officer. It was his idol Nelson who said, 'Duty is the great business of a sea officer; all private considerations must give way to it, however painful it may be.' He took his job seriously and was a stickler for order and discipline. He was a meticulous planner like his counterpart in the army, Field Marshal Sir Garnet Wolseley, and could be demanding of his subordinates. Some of his men resented him for this. But behind the authoritarian demeanor was an officer who generally cared for the well-being of those under his command.

Admiral Sir Sydney Robert Fremantle said it took about three months to gain Markham's confidence, but once someone did, he would remain a lifelong friend. Admiral Sir John Jellicoe, commander of the Grand Fleet during the Battle of Jutland in 1916, proclaimed his friendship was 'indeed worth having'. Markham's colleagues described him as a gentle, unselfish and pleasant man. The letters sent to his wife, Theodora, at the time of his death, are a testament to this affection. 'I was indeed a devoted admirer of Sir Albert,' Admiral Sir Frederick Samuel Inglefield wrote to his widow after Markham's death, 'and have always thought him quite the best officer and finest man that I ever met in the Navy, and his most charming personality and delightful voice will be a vivid remembrance to the end of my days.'

Markham had a gift for penmanship, which he inherited from his great-great-grandfather. He began recording his experiences when he first left England for Hong Kong in 1856. This continued for the rest of his life. His handwriting was neat and legible, and this skill was utilised by his superior officers to transcribe letters, reports and correspondence. His writing progressed to eight books and dozens of articles leading up to his death. The majority of his journals, logs and notes are held by the National Maritime Museum and the British Library. I am grateful for the abundance of written material Markham left behind.

Markham's legacy has been tarnished for his part in the sinking of HMS *Victoria* in 1893. This book will give his account of what happened on that fateful summer day in 1893 and how it emotionally tore at him for years after. After examining his life, it becomes apparent that there is so much more to Admiral Sir Albert Hastings Markham than this one tragic incident. Hopefully, the reader will look at Markham as more than a bungling admiral who ran his ship into another ship. Rather, he was a man who lived a fascinating and adventurous life worthy of study.

A quick note on the names of cities, islands and other geographical features in the text. Whenever I determined it was necessary, especially in the case of Chapter 2, when dealing with China during the Second Opium War and Taiping Rebellion, the modern spelling was included in parentheses next to the nineteenth-century spelling. For example:

Canton (Guangzhou), Ningpo (Ningbo), Fuchow (Fuzhou) and Amoy (Xiamen). But in other cases, such as with mention of the Hudson Bay in Chapter 7, or the Pacific islands Markham visited in Chapter 3, I have adopted the modern spelling.

Chapter 1

A Son of the Ocean

'Well, my boy, you must work the harder for it. Perhaps it is all the better for you.'

Lieutenant William Markham to his son William jun.,
A Memoir of Archbishop Markham, 1719–1807

Albert Hastings Markham could trace his ancestry back to a distinguished line of soldiers, scholars and administrators beginning in the eleventh century. Following the Norman Conquest in 1066, William the Conqueror parcelled out England to his lieutenants. He appointed the Norman baron Roger de Busli as the tenant-in-chief over thirty-nine manors in the county of Nottinghamshire. Busli selected the Saxon chief Claron to manage one of these manors named West Markham. Claron's successors adopted the manor's name, thus establishing the Markham bloodline.

Albert's great-great-grandfather, William Markham (1686–1771), son of Colonel Daniel Markham and Elizabeth Fennell, entered Trinity College at the age of 20 in December 1706. Four years later, as an ensign, he fought with General James Stanhope in Spain. He afterwards received an appointment as Barrack Master in Kinsale, Ireland, with the rank of lieutenant. He married his cousin, Elizabeth, on 25 September 1716, and she gave birth to three sons: William jun. (1719–1807), George (1723–1801), and Enoch (1727–1801). Elizabeth unexpectedly died in 1732, leaving William a widower. He earned only £100 a year while on half-pay and single-handedly raised his children.

William received word that his dying grandfather, Captain Edmund Fennell, planned to leave his inheritance to him. Fennell sent for his grandson when he sensed the end was near. Here was Markham's chance to end his financial troubles for good.

As he prepared to leave for Cappoquin, Ireland, he fell violently ill and had to delay his trip for three weeks. When he was well enough to mount a horse, he rode with his eldest son, William jun., to Fennell's estate. They arrived a few days after the captain had died and learned that he had left his estate to another man in Markham's absence. Markham took the disheartening news as best as he could. He glanced down at his son and uttered, 'Well, my boy, you must work the harder for it. Perhaps it is all the better for you.'

William sen. wanted his oldest son to have the best education England had to offer. Leaving his two youngest boys with family members, he resigned his position at Kinsale and took up residence in a house on London's Vine Street with his 14-year-old son so that he could attend the prestigious Westminster School. To finance his son's education, the retired officer transcribed illegible documents of two solicitors and painted and sold fan mounts on the streets. By June 1733, he collected enough money to enroll William jun. at Westminster.

William jun. excelled as a student during his five years at the institution. In 1738, he was admitted to Christ Church, University of Oxford. His peers considered him to be one of the most promising young scholars of his day. He excelled in Latin and translated versions of Shakespeare's 'Seven Ages of Man' and Virgil's 'Judicium Paridis' (Judgement of Paris) into the ancient Roman language. Fifteen years later, at the age of 34, he replaced the retiring Dr John Nicoll as headmaster of Westminster. In April 1771, he was appointed a chaplain to King George II and an instructor to his sons, the Prince of Wales and the Duke of York. He served as the Archbishop of York, the Church of England's second most senior position, until his death in 1807.

In June 1759, the 40-year-old bachelor married the daughter of an English merchant from Rotterdam, 21-year-old Sarah Goddard (1738–1814). She gave birth to thirteen children – six boys and seven girls – over a period of twenty-three years. One son, John, joined the navy and rose to the rank of admiral. Another son, David, served as a lieutenant colonel in the Twentieth Regiment of Foot and was killed at the age of 28 while leading a charge on a fort at Port-au-Prince, Haiti, in March 1795. William's firstborn son and heir, 21-year-old William Markham III (1760–1815), travelled to India in 1778 to act as an assistant to his friend, Governor General Warren Hastings. He established a reputation as an energetic, bright young man and was appointed Hastings's private secretary two years later.

In 1794, William Markham jun. (III) returned to England and served as the deputy lieutenant for the county of Yorkshire. A year later, he married Elizabeth Bowles (1778–1841), the eldest daughter of the artist Oldfield Bowles. They lived in a stone mansion enclosed by 100 acres called Becca Hall. Together they had eight children. Their second-born son, John (1797–1870), followed his uncle's example and joined the navy at the age of 13. He served on HMS *Northumberland*, the ship tasked with transporting the deposed Emperor Napoleon to the island of St Helena. In 1824, John retired with the rank of captain at the age of 27 due to his failing health and returned to England.

In 1834, at the age of 37, John married 23-year-old Marianne Georgiana Davies Wood (1810–97). He suffered from the same financial troubles as his great-grandfather did due to his early retirement from the service. Four years after the birth of their two sons, John (1835–71) and George (1837–1920), the couple moved to the town of Bagnères-de-Bigorre, France, situated at the foot of the Pyrenees. While living in southern France, Marianne gave birth to four more sons: Frederick (who drowned at the age of 3), Arthur (1840–1919), William (who died in infancy), and Albert (1841–1918). Their youngest son, Albert Hastings Markham, was born on 11 November 1841.

Shortly after Albert's birth, the Markhams relocated for a third time to the island of Guernsey, located off the coast of Normandy. The writer and poet Victor Hugo, who lived on the island as an exile for sixteen years, described it as a 'rock of hospitality and freedom' inhabited by a 'noble small seafaring people'. The Markhams lived in a home with a beautiful view of the island's emerald cliffs and turquoise ocean. The family remained in one location and together for nearly a decade until their oldest, John, departed in 1852 as a student interpreter in the Consular Service.

John sen. thought that one of his sons should follow the family tradition of service in the navy and selected young Albert. The 13-year-old boy would stay with his widowed aunt, Catherine Markham (her husband, and John's brother, the Reverend David Frederick Markham, died in

1853), while preparing for the navy's entrance examination. She could provide her nephew with financial stability and a roof over his head while in London. Perhaps John gave young Albert the same advice William Markham sen. had given to his son before he left the picturesque island of Guernsey for London: 'Well, my boy, you must work the harder for it. Perhaps it is all the better for you.'

Albert arrived at his aunt's home at 4 Onslow Square in South Kensington in the spring of 1855. Life in Aunt Catherine's home was quite different from anything he had experienced before. Local celebrities, like the scientist Vice Admiral Robert FitzRoy, and the novelist William Makepeace Thackeray, who both lived nearby, regularly passed by their window each morning. Albert came from a home made up of all boys, with the exception of his mother. Catherine's three daughters – Selina, Georgina and Gertrude – dominated the household. His aunt had lost two of her three boys at a young age – David William Christian, who died at sea at the age of 18, and Warren, who died as a child – leaving Clements Robert as her only surviving son.

Clements had recently returned from India when Albert arrived at his mother's home. Despite Clements being eleven years his senior, no one person had a more profound impact on Albert. Clements shared his enthusiasm for science, reading, writing, exploration and adventure. He helped to shape the impressionable teenager's identity. Over time, Clements evolved into a mentor, role model and confidant to Albert, who spent his life trying to emulate his older cousin.

It is no wonder Albert looked up to Clements. He had already lived a remarkable life by the age of 25. He had begun his career in the Royal Navy in 1844, as a 15-year-old cadet on HMS *Collingwood*. He spent most of his free time on the ship consuming every book he could get his hands on, especially if it was a historical work or poetry, or written by Shakespeare. He filled his journals with observations about the people he met and the unique places he travelled to. Amicable, easygoing, energetic and studious, he hated the navy's strict rules and regulations, draconic punishments and the constraints it placed on him to do the things he really enjoyed. He would rather sightsee or devour a good book than bother with the mundane duties of a sailor. Early on, it was apparent that the navy was not the right profession for him but he tried to make the best of it.

Clements befriended Lieutenant William Peel, son of Prime Minister Sir Robert Peel and one of the most distinguished naval officers of the Victorian era. Peel earned the Victoria Cross during the Siege of Sevastopol when he picked up a live shell and threw it over a parapet. The distinguished lieutenant suggested to Clements that a good naval officer should be well-read, especially in the subjects of history, geography and poetry, but ultimately had to be willing to devote everything to the navy. Clements was lacking in the latter. He regarded Peel to be 'the perfect model of what a British naval officer ought to be'. He could only aspire to become half the officer Peel was.

While he contemplated resigning his commission, word reached Clements that an expedition was being assembled to track down Rear Admiral Sir John Franklin and his crew, missing since they left to explore the Northwest Passage in 1845. Here was a rare opportunity to go on an adventure to the mysterious, wondrous Arctic. He picked up a copy of Captain William E. Parry's book, *Journals of the First, Second, and Third Voyages for the Discovery of a North-West Passage* (1828), which filled him with an even greater desire to see this uncharted land for himself. His father, the Reverend David F. Markham, pulled all the strings he could to get his son assigned to Captain Horatio Austin's expedition. Clements left on HMS *Assistance* in 1850 and spent a year in the Arctic. Austin's men were unable to locate Franklin and his crew, but the expedition left Clements with a lifelong interest for Arctic exploration.

Facing the reality that he would have to return to his mundane life at sea, Clements resigned his commission and never looked back. That same year, he spent ten months in Peru retrieving cinchona seeds and plants so that they could be harvested in India, a key ingredient in quinine used to treat malaria. History has best remembered him for his more than two decades of service as a secretary for the Royal Geographical Society (RGS) and his commitment to advocating exploration and discovery throughout the world. He continued to study and write about history, exploration and geography, becoming one of the most prolific authors and eminent geographers of the nineteenth century.

Albert understood that if he worked hard enough at his studies and successfully received an appointment as a cadet, it would enable him to travel the world and make discoveries like Clements. Catherine Markham made sure her nephew had the best tutors to prepare him for the naval cadet examination. He first studied with the Reverend William Latimer Neville, an author, Oxford graduate and curate at the Church of the Holy Trinity in Brompton. He then left to study with the Reverend John Benthall in the town of Newport Pagnell. There, Albert befriended Benthall's son, William, an accomplished cricket player for Cambridge University, which likely led to his lifelong interest in the game. Although Albert diligently studied under both Neville and Benthall, he lacked the necessary connections to obtain a cadet nomination.

Albert's chances of obtaining a nomination appeared bleak. He was nearing his fourteenth birthday, which was the cut-off age for admittance as a naval cadet. Was he cursed with his father's bad luck? Aunt Catherine tried to console him as best she could. She encouraged him to rely on his faith to carry him through this most distressing chapter of his young life:

> I need not tell you, my dear boy, how much I feel for your disappointment, as I know how great it will be, but you must try and feel that we do not direct any of the events of this life ourselves. God has not thought it good for you that you should succeed in what you wish, but you may rely upon His goodness … and you may be sure it will not eventually turn out to your disadvantage, though at present you cannot help feeling grieved, having for so many months turned your mind to this profession.

God must have favoured a naval career for Albert Markham after all. He received word that for a short time the Admiralty would be permitting boys who reached the age of 14 to be admitted as cadets. A nomination finally came in from an influential uncle, William Rookes Crompton Stansfield, a Member of Parliament. It is uncertain if Catherine inducing Albert to turn to God for support had an impact on his faith, but he would remain a devout Christian for the rest of his life.

Albert studied at Eastman's Royal Naval Academy to cram as much as he could before taking the examination. He vividly recalled how he felt when all the candidates were summoned to find out if they had passed the test. Thirty boys competed for seventeen spots. If successful, he could have a bright future as a naval officer. If Albert failed, it meant that he would let down everyone that had worked so tirelessly on his behalf and bring shame to his family's name. He could face a similar fate as his brother George, who had planned to enter the army. Since his father could not afford to purchase him a commission, George instead became a farmer. This would never do for Albert.

'It was with a palpitating heart on one fine cold morning in the middle of winter,' Albert remembered, 'that I entered the precincts of that venerable institution to ascertain whether I was fortunate enough to be among the successful candidates who had, the two previous days, been examined touching their qualifications to serve in Her Majesty's Navy.' The insecure youth prepared for the worst, aware that his fate hinged on the result.

The president of the Naval College sat at the end of a long table that seemed to have no end to it as he called out the names of those boys who had passed the examination. Albert grew uneasy when he heard the names of four other boys called. 'I remember so well thinking what happy, lucky fellows they were,' he grudgingly recalled. To his astonishment, the president then called 'Albert Markham'. For a second, he stood still as if there had been some kind of mistake. 'So overpowered was I with surprise and emotion, combined with a certain feeling of pride,' he declared, 'that my name had to be repeated more than once before I could pull myself together and summon sufficient to answer in a very minor key, "Here, sir".' Hardly able to keep his legs from buckling underneath him due to his apprehension, he stepped forward and took the piece of paper from the hands of the president acknowledging that he had met the qualifications required by the Lords Commissioners of the Admiralty.

Albert gushed with enthusiasm upon receiving this sheet of paper. He found it gratifying to think 'that I, a schoolboy of yesterday, was by that same piece of paper raised to the dignity of an office in Her Majesty's Naval Service'. He rushed down to an outfitter's shop and got fitted in his new cadet's uniform. 'Having buckled on my sword,' he explained, 'I swaggered out in full consciousness of my newly acquired dignity to exhibit myself to my schoolfellows.' To celebrate his victory, he marched to the nearest photographer's studio and had a daguerrotype taken for his mother. Those closest to him were equally delighted with his success. Swelling with pride, John Markham wrote to his son, 'Everybody that hears of you pronounces you to have done most nobly in passing such a famous examination.'

The Admiralty granted him fourteen days' leave to visit his family before being assigned to a ship. He did not realise it at that moment, but this would be the last time he would see them for over a decade. His parents had left Guernsey the previous summer, so he joined them in the town of Dinan located in northwestern France. Looking again to escape the creditors, the Markhams purchased a plot of land in the United States and emigrated there in July 1856, leaving behind Albert and his older brother John.

Cadet Markham's first assignment was on Vice Admiral Horatio Nelson's old flagship, HMS *Victory*. He cherished the opportunity to walk the decks of this 'grand old vessel' just as the gallant Nelson had. He strung up his hammock and slept in the same spot where the admiral had died after being pierced in the chest by a ball during the Battle of Trafalgar. He dreamt of becoming an extraordinary admiral like Nelson, universally recognised in England as a brilliant strategist, bold tactician and heroic leader. The Crimean War ended just as Markham entered the service; he would have to wait to see if he possessed the same mettle as Nelson.

On 17 June 1856, after a stint on the *Victory*, Markham was appointed to HMS *Tribune* with orders to report to the Pacific Station, but three weeks later, he was ordered to Plymouth and reassigned to HMS *St Jean d'Acre* under the command of Captain George St Vincent King. The ship was to convey Lord Granville and his staff to the town of Kronstadt on the Russian island of Kotlin so that the diplomat could serve as Queen Victoria's representative during the coronation of Tsar Alexander II.

Markham was devastated. He wanted to see the world and experience adventures like his cousin had, or that he read about, not to be cooped up on a ship catering to the needs of diplomats. He turned to Clements for help. He heard that HMS *Camilla* was leaving for the China Station and pleaded with his cousin to use whatever influence he could muster to get him appointed to the ship before it departed. Clements pulled the necessary strings and his wish was granted.

The raw cadet would spend the next seven years in the hazardous South China Sea, subjected to deadly diseases, an oppressive climate and bloodthirsty enemies, all vying for a chance to end his life.

Chapter 2

Anarchy in the Far East

'Piracy at that time was rampant along the entire sea board of China and hardly a day passed without reports arriving of the energy and ferocity with which the Chinese pursued their cruel and fiendish lawlessness.'

Albert H. Markham, *Reminiscences of My Early Naval Life*,
British Library

Fourteen-year-old Albert Hastings Markham quickly discovered what life in the Royal Navy was like after his ship left for Hong Kong on 25 August 1856. Only five days after departing Portsmouth, Markham watched as a sailor fell from the main topsail, killing him instantly. He took as many potatoes and cans of sardines as he could carry, but unwisely devoured them within ten days. For the remainder of the voyage, he ate rancid salted beef or pork and weevil-infested biscuits. Fresh water ran dangerously low for three weeks, and the captain only permitted the men to drink a pint of brackish water a day to relieve their cracked lips and dry throats. Bathing was not permitted.

Markham was unaccustomed to these types of hardships, having lived comfortably with his Aunt Catherine while in London as he prepared for his naval cadetship. While they were unwelcomed, they undeniably helped to mould him into a seasoned seaman.

The sailors and officers of the *Camilla* were overjoyed when they finally reached the bustling port of Hong Kong on 9 February 1857. 'I shall never forget the relief and pleasure that was felt by all after the weary monotony of the long days at sea,' Markham wrote, 'to find ourselves calmly riding at anchor in the placid waters of the anchorage off the island.' Chinese junks swarmed the *Camilla* the moment it pulled into the harbour. Merchants shoved fresh pineapples, oranges and other appetising fruits in the foreigners' faces; these were luxuries compared to the pitiful rations and thirst they endured during their 156-day voyage from England.

The ship's captain sent Markham ashore to retrieve the canvas mail sacks filled with letters from home. When he returned, his brother John was waiting for him on the *Camilla*. Since leaving Guernsey, John had matured into a courteous and energetic official, serving as the second assistant in the Superintendency at Hong Kong. The brothers exchanged a hearty handshake and embraced for the first time in four years.

John warned his brother of the dangers foreigners faced in this country. He told him about a specific incident that had taken place about a month earlier. A Chinese baker had tried to poison a handful of the European residents living in Victoria by offering them bread laced with arsenic. The baker had administered too much poison, and fortunately, the foreigners vomited it out before it killed any of them. It soon dawned on young Albert that he had arrived in a region of the British Empire immersed in fear, greed, intrigue and death, with the Royal Navy tangled up in it.

The exchange of goods between English and Chinese merchants rapidly increased after the passage of the Charter Act of 1833, which terminated the East India Company's 121-year-old monopoly. The island of Hong Kong – ceded by the ruling Qing dynasty to the English in January 1841 – became the English commercial center of trade, with the town of Victoria as its base. Within four years of this acquisition, Victoria's wooden shacks and dirt roads were replaced by sturdy homes, elegant government buildings and stout streets congested with shopkeepers, tradesmen, merchants, servants, coolies and thieves. Additional access to 'treaty port cities' along the southern coast acquired by the English in consequence of the Opium Wars – including Shanghai, Canton (Guangzhou), Ningpo (Ningbo), Fuchow (Fuzhou) and Amoy (Xiamen) – led to an even greater increase in trade and the exchange of monies between the English and Chinese, making it the second most important colonial possession in the empire next to India.

Exports and imports to and from China became vital to the British Empire's economy by the time Markham arrived in China. The three main exports were opium, cotton and woollens, while tea and silk were the greatest imports. Roughly 50,000–60,000 chests (8,400,000lb) of Bengal and Malwa opium were exported to China in the seven years Markham served in the China Station. From 1857 to 1860, 72 million pounds stirling of tea were imported from China. The English government collected millions of pounds on the tea's import duty. In some years, the revenue covered the expense of the Royal Navy – around 3 to 5 million pounds. So critical to the English economy, these commercial interests in China had to be protected at whatever cost.

English foot soldiers and ships, such as the *Camilla*, were dispatched to China to protect the foreign residents of the port cities and to safeguard the millions of pounds tied up in the China trade. The English resorted to coercion and violence to defend their commercial interests and fought anyone who dared to challenge them. For three decades, the China Station provided young officers who would go on to become senior admirals and generals years later – for instance, Albert Markham, Arthur Wilson, Edward Seymour, Garnet Wolseley, Gerald Graham and Charles George Gordon – with an opportunity to gain experience fighting in a colonial theatre.

As Anglo-Chinese trade mushroomed, piracy made a comeback in the South China Sea. Pirates became one of the Royal Navy's most relentless – and troublesome – enemies in the China Station. 'Piracy at that time was rampant along the entire sea board of China and hardly a day passed without reports arriving of the energy and ferocity with which the Chinese pursued their cruel and fiendish lawlessness,' Markham recalled. The numerous inlets, bays, ravines and small islands along the coast – many never surveyed – provided pirates with a place of refuge and a point to establish strongholds. From these strongholds, pirate junks, camouflaged as peaceful fishing junks, pounced on vulnerable English merchant ships to steal opium or other valuable goods. Once they finished securing their loot, they butchered their captives in cold blood and disappeared.

Qing law sentenced those convicted of piracy to death, usually by beheading. But more commonly, Markham observed, the imperial authorities 'did absolutely nothing for the suppression of this nefarious trade'. They decided that piracy could never be contained, so they often developed a fatalistic attitude towards suppressing it. In many instances, pirate fleets were owned and operated by local mandarins holding high positions in the imperial government, meaning the protection of merchant ships fell on the English.

The *Camilla* shifted between Amoy and Canton during its first twelve months in China. Whenever he had the chance, Markham left the ship to see the attractions on the mainland. He recalled the charm and pleasure he 'derived from a run on shore, and the novelty of seeing strange people with shaven heads and long pig-tails, attired in quaint costumes such as we had seen in picture-books only, or in illustrated stories of travel and adventure'. He hunted birds in rice fields, went for long hikes, dined with officials and merchants living in the cities, visited temples and historic sites, and browsed Chinese shops. He even took up horse racing, winning a couple of competitions while riding his favourite horse, Flash of Lightning.

The *Camilla*'s captain, 31-year-old George Twisleton Colvile, served as a mentor and friend to him during his first couple of years in China. Born in 1826, Colvile entered the Royal Navy as a 'snooty' (midshipman) in the spring of 1840, taking part in the bombardment and capture of St Jean d'Acre, off the coast of Syria, and winning two medals for his service. During the Crimean War, he fought at the Battle of Inkerman as part of the Naval Brigade and commanded a battery at the Siege of Sevastopol. He earned two more medals and the Order of Medjidie for his service in the war. In the summer of 1856, the decorated and esteemed naval officer was appointed as the commander of the *Camilla* before it left for Hong Kong.

Colvile enjoyed Markham's company and treated him warmly. They regularly went for long hikes, hunted fowl and dined together. Colvile allowed Markham on more than one occasion to rest in his cabin when he was sick, even sending food from his own table. The young cadet noted in his journal that the captain helped him purchase a rifle so that he would not have to borrow one when he went hunting. 'The captain told me if I would like to forgo 6 months allowance he would write home for a gun for me,' Markham wrote. 'I thanked him and told him I would.'

Colvile may have been a nurturing and compassionate man, but he also exhibited authoritarian tendencies. The captain did not show his favourite cadet any leniency when it came to breaches of discipline. 'I forgot to take my log into the Captain's cabin,' Markham noted with shame on 26 April, 'so he stopped my leave, the first time I have ever had it stopped in my life.' For Markham, who lived for his rambles on shore, this was frustrating. When Markham had a steward take the misplaced log to Colvile's cabin instead of delivering it himself, Colvile was infuriated; he exiled Markham to an eight-hour shift on deck. (He was not allowed a break, forcing him to miss all his meals.) While he felt that he had been treated unfairly at the time, as he matured, Markham came to understand and appreciate the necessity for maintaining discipline on a Royal Navy ship.

Markham was tasked with a wide variety of duties on the *Camilla*. Most of the time, he acted as a lookout for signals and fetched the mailbags from port. Known for his excellent penmanship, he spent many hours transcribing the ship's logs for the captain of the *Camilla* and for the captains of other English ships. A gifted artist, he sketched the city of Canton and its river for Colvile and filled his journal with beautifully detailed drawings and watercolours. He inherited this artistic talent from his great-great-grandfather. The most unpleasant duty he performed was serving as a witness during the autopsy of a sailor who drank himself to death. 'I am ashamed to say, I was a witness of the whole transaction,' he wrote afterwards.

When not on duty or exploring port cities, Markham followed his cousin Clements's example and devoured every book he could find. He read about forty books over a twenty-four month span. He mainly read history, for example engrossing himself in William Robson's *The Great Sieges of History*, all ten volumes of William N. Medlicott's *A History of England* and Joseph Allen's *Battles of the British Navy*. He also enjoyed biographies and real-life adventure tales, such as Edward Osler's *The Life of Admiral Viscount Exmouth*, John William Kaye's *The Life and Correspondence of Charles, Lord Metcalfe*, George Ryan's *Our Heroes of the Crimea* and David Livingstone's *Livingstone's Travels in South Africa*. He relished fiction too, especially anything written by Charles Dickens, reading *Dombey and Son*, *The Old Curiosity Shop* and *The Life and Adventures of Nicholas Nickleby*. He had not yet acquired an interest for William Shakespeare at this age, but the seventeenth-century writer, playwright and poet would become his favourite author.

Markham also dedicated his free time to studying ancient languages. While the *Camilla* was anchored at Canton, the Reverend John Gray made regular visits to the ship and befriended the young cadet. Gray offered to tutor him in Greek and Latin and he enthusiastically accepted. Under Gray's tutelage, he read the works of Horace and Euclid and translated the New Testament from Greek to English.

Markham had a tough time adapting to the South China Sea's torrid climate and was regularly on the sick list. He suffered from a strange infection of the eyes that left him temporarily blind. 'I have been suffering lately very much from ophthalmia,' Markham wrote in his journal on 27 November. The surgeon noticed him stumbling around and straining his eyes to make out signals. He placed him on the sick list. 'My eyes are very sore and I can neither read or write,' Markham complained. Such an affliction must have tormented him. Luckily, by 5 December, he recovered and regained full sight.

Markham fought his first battle two months after arriving at the China Station. Receiving word that a fleet of two or three dozen pirate junks was terrorising merchant ships, the *Camilla* left Amoy on the night of 18 April. It stuck close to the shoreline as it sailed 100 miles north to avoid being detected.

At dawn on the next day, they spotted the fleet's ships flying the notorious black and blood red pirate flag. Colvile ordered his ship to swoop down on the idle junks and lorchas before they could realise it was an English warship. The *Camilla* rushed the largest one first in the middle of the group. Colvile ordered his gun crews to fire a double shot at the junk's flimsy hull. The pirates returned fire with their jingals (large caliber mounted guns) and matchlocks but did not inflict any damage.

Within thirty minutes, the *Camilla* sank three junks, causing the remainder to panic and flee. A few had been damaged by friendly fire while attempting to attack the *Camilla*. The pirates intentionally ran some of the ships ashore so that their crews could escape by foot, while the others tried to outsail the *Camilla*. Colvile gave the order to send out all the *Camilla*'s boats to board and destroy the fleeing junks.

Lieutenant Henry Hawkes ordered Markham to take six sailors and two marines in a jolly boat to capture one of these damaged junks. 'I felt as proud of my command as any captain of a line of battle ship does in pacing his quarter-deck for the first time,' Markham recalled years after when ordered to take charge of the boat and its crew. 'I assumed an air of the utmost importance, and as much dignity as a boy of fifteen could command, as I jumped into the boat, with my sword in one hand and a pistol in the other, and gave the order to "shove off"!'

The sailors and marines rowed as hard as they could for a mile and a half to catch up to the crippled junk. The boy 'captain' positioned himself at the front of the jolly boat and urged his men on as if he was the legendary Admiral Nelson. 'Although we knew we were going to attack a vessel carrying a crew of some thirty or forty men,' Markham later stated, 'the idea of a repulse or even a check, never entered our heads.'

As soon as the jolly boat jarred up against the junk, nine men, with Markham in the lead, sprung up on its deck with pistols cocked and swords drawn. A moment of dread overcame Markham when he considered the odds they faced, but he was not about to abandon his men or disgrace his family's name by baulking from his duty. The pirates fled as soon as Markham and his men boarded the junk, diving into the water and attempting to swim to shore rather than facing their swords. 'I must acknowledge,' Markham confessed afterwards, 'that it was with no small feeling of relief that I saw our opponents all jumping overboard on the opposite side of the ship as we clambered up over the bulwarks of the enemy.' Most of the pirates were picked out of the water by the other English boats, while the rest drowned.

Markham was overjoyed with the first victory of his brief naval career. A few minutes after its capture, he received a signal from Hawkes ordering him to destroy the junk and to hurry back to the *Camilla*. Not satisfied with merely routing the pirate fleet, Colvile planned to conduct an amphibious assault to obliterate their stronghold on the coast. 'It was with rather a sore heart that I was compelled to superintend the destruction of my first capture,' Markham wrote. 'Setting fire to every part that would speedily ignite, and laying a train of gunpowder to the magazine, we abandoned her to her fate, and she blew up a few minutes after we left her.'

When he returned to the *Camilla*, Markham joined Colvile and fifty sailors embarking to assault the stronghold. The temperature by this point in the day soared to 100°F and not a cloud was in sight to block the sun's punishing rays. Colvile's boats entered a narrow creek and were greeted by the eerie sounds of gongs and tom-tom drums echoing from the pirate base. When the boats reached the makeshift stockade, the pirates unleashed their matchlock and jingal shots at them. Their balls splintered several oars and embedded into the boats' wooden hulls, but incredibly did not harm anyone.

'With a hearty cheer', the sailors jumped into the waist-deep water and waded for the shore. Their ammunition got wet, forcing them to take the stockade at the point of the bayonet. The 500 or so pirates showed little resistance; the engagement lasted only about fifteen minutes. After nine pirates were skewered, the remainder broke and fled into the adjacent hills. Colvile ordered the captured guns spiked and the stockade and houses burned before returning to the *Camilla*. He lost a few men during both the naval and landing operation, while Markham estimated that the pirates lost around 200.

The victors returned to Amoy with forty-eight shackled prisoners and handed them over to the imperial authorities. The local mandarin ordered these 'unfortunate wretches' to be condemned to death by beheading the following day. The doomed men were marched to a field outside the city's walls and placed on their knees in two lines with their hands tied behind their backs. Four men with large knives worked their way down both lines and sliced off each man's head. 'A more revolting and sickening performance can scarcely be conceived,' Markham recalled with disgust after witnessing the slaughter.

For days after, the English officers who watched the executions were still traumatised by what they had seen. Markham declared it 'would have been better to have allowed the poor wretches to drown, then to save their lives in order to be butchered in this cruel and barbarous manner'. Only a 12-year-old boy was spared from execution when Colvile intervened.

During the summer of 1857, Markham underwent a series of tests to earn his midshipman's patch. On the first day, Colvile and Hawkes tested his knowledge on seamanship. On the second day, they tested his fluency in French. This was followed by the boatswain assessing his ability to knot and splice rope. On the last day, the master of the ship, Tom B. Read, evaluated Markham's knowledge of navigation. Satisfied with his overall performance in all these areas, Colvile advanced Markham to midshipman. He was delighted when the captain expressed that he had done very well.

Later that year, on 28 December, an Anglo-French expedition bombarded and occupied Canton after Governor General Ye Mingchen resisted the economic demands of the English, violating the terms agreed upon by his government in the 1842 Treaty of Nanking. The foreign coalition declared that it would 'retain possession of it [Canton] until all questions pending between the Government of China and the Governments of France and Great Britain shall have been satisfactorily adjusted' and placed the city under martial law. After spending eight months on the Min River, the *Camilla* relocated to Canton in early 1858. It would remain there for the next ten months.

The English and French relations with Canton's citizens quickly deteriorated due to these harsh restrictions and the quartering of foreign troops in the city. Relations became so strained that hundreds of former imperial infantrymen disguised as civilians routinely attempted to kidnap or assassinate the *fan-qui* (foreigners). 'We are expecting to be attacked daily by the Chinese,' Markham wrote with alarm on 24 April. Street ambushes became the norm. Markham reported with disgust that '£500 is offered for an officer's head and £100 for a blue jacket's or private's' – the vilified British Consul, Sir Harry Smith Parkes, had a price of £30,000 set on his head.

The months of June and July were especially brutal for the foreigners and Chinese citizens. On 24 June, at around 11.00 am, the sailors and officers of the *Camilla* spotted white clouds of smoke mushrooming into the air from the deck of a French merchant ship. Lieutenant Hawkes left with a party of sailors in a cutter to investigate. To his horror, he found the deck of the French ship soaked with blood and not a soul in sight. The only trace of life he found was a French sailor's pet dog with all its limbs brutally chopped off.

A boat was observed leaving the French ship shortly before their arrival. It must have kidnapped the ship's crew to collect a reward. To protect them against similar attacks, all the merchant ships at that end of the Canton River moved within range of the *Camilla*'s guns.

The French retaliated for this attack. On 30 June, French sailors moved into the city's western suburbs and torched any home in sight. The fire raged for about four hours. Markham, watching from the deck of the *Camilla*, estimated that it destroyed about fifty houses.

The attacks continued to escalate. On 1 July, a party of sailors and marines from HMS *Tribune* and HMS *Actaeon*, under the command of

Captain Robert Jenkins, was ambushed near the Whampoa (Huangpu) District of Canton while returning after a failed raid. Eight men were wounded, including Jenkins. The village where the ambush took place was destroyed, and some of the villagers thought to be involved in the attack were kidnapped. Markham soberly declared that the English sailors then 'blew their brains out on the spot'.

On 3 July, four French sailors belonging to the *Catinat* were assailed by four dozen Chinese. One man was captured. The police discovered his mutilated and headless body dumped in a stream. A joint force of vengeful French and English sailors and marines landed in Canton and murdered fifty Chinese civilians. 'I daresay not one of them associated with the murder,' Markham admitted, sickened by this atrocity.

Eleven days later, fourteen marines were ambushed by a jingal on their way from the Southwest Gate station. The gun had been filled with grapeshot, stones, nails, glass and anything else that could do harm to the men. When it was fired into the group, the flying debris instantly killed one man and wounded eight others. 'With considerable trouble,' recalled Robert Hart, an English customs official in the city, 'the poor fellows got back to their station assisted by some Chinese who were pressed into service.' One man, Corporal Lelson, died, and two men lost limbs. All of Folly Street, half a mile in length, where the attack had taken place, was burned by the English.

While the Chinese and foreigners continued to slaughter each other in Canton, Markham took part in another expedition to eliminate a pirate stronghold. On 20 July, he left with Colvile, Hawkes and a group of light boats destined for the village of Wan-Chu-Ki, about 8 miles up the Canton River. HMS *Amethyst* had been previously attacked by a pirate junk and it was rumored to have belonged to the village. The light boats encountered the junk that had attacked the *Amethyst*, and after a short firefight, they captured it after it ran out of ammunition.

To demonstrate that the English would not tolerate those who abetted pirates, Colvile ordered his boats to bombard the village. His rockets and large guns hammered it for three hours. When the smoke cleared, Markham said that 'we saw nothing but a heap of ruins'. Only two or three homes remained standing. Colvile's sailors landed and razed these buildings. The cadet was getting a taste of total war.

On 7 January 1859, Markham was notified that he had been selected to take part in an expedition to attack the village of Shektsing located 8 miles from Canton. The officer in charge of the English ground forces in China, the untiring Major General Sir Charles Thomas van Straubenzee – nicknamed 'Old Strawberry Jam' by his men – wrote to Lord Elgin, the British High Commissioner to China, asking for his approval to conduct a raid to target 'any town or village in the vicinity of Canton, that was known to have provided arms, men, or munitions of war to be used against us'. The foreign forces occupying Canton had had enough of the daily ambushes. With Elgin's blessing, van Straubenzee planned to strike the village of Shektsing, under the notorious rebel leader Leang-paou-heun, to give 'these pests a sharp blow'.

The following day, those men from the *Camilla* selected to take part in the expedition had an early breakfast and fell in on deck. Each man carried a weapon, twenty rounds of ammunition, a blanket, a water bottle and three days' rations stuffed in their haversacks. Markham added a sword and a revolver to his accoutrements, making for 'a rather heavy load'. He would regret taking these extra items with him.

On 8 January, the men embarked in three boats (a gig, a pinnace and a cutter) in the direction of the village. They were accompanied by a detachment of gunboats as they proceeded upriver. Meanwhile, a land force of 1,000 to 1,500 men – composed of English marines, sappers, miners, artillerymen and French sailors – moved overland from Canton and struck the village. Markham heard the faint roar of artillery coming from the village after travelling about 16 miles on the river. The boats landed about 2 miles further upriver from where the battle was taking place. Markham waded through the water with the ship's colours to a nearby paddy field and waited as the sailors and marines assembled in the area before advancing to the sound of gunfire.

Once Markham and his comrades arrived outside of Shektsing, they spotted the Anglo-French column advancing under the cover of three guns and some rockets. Around 3,000 enemy soldiers and twenty guns held three forts guarding the village. The column encountered stiff resistance while conducting a frontal assault. Swamps, groves of bamboo and fir-clothed knolls to the front of the village slowed the men down and broke up their advancing lines. A single 'picturesque bridge of seven quaint arches' provided the only decent strip of land for the foreigners to advance, and the Chinese defenders concentrated all their fire on it.

Moving at the double-quick, the marines and sailors of the naval column raced along a creek bed and scaled a prominent hill outside the city to outflank the defenders. With a strong enemy force on their front and flank, the defenders lost the will to resist and abandoned the village to the English and French.

The men of the flanking column were spent after having marched the distance of 3 miles over uneven terrain and 'under a broiling sun' in less than half an hour. Markham struggled to reach the top of the hill, weighed down from carrying the colours, his bulky sword and his cumbersome revolver. Moments later he collapsed into the dirt from heat exhaustion. He described feeling 'faint and giddy', and sprawled out on the ground. An hour later, he regained his strength and marched the rest of the way to the captured village, where he spent the night.

Early the next morning, the officers woke their men in preparation for a foray van Straubenzee had ordered to take place that day. Its objective was to destroy any enemy strongholds located in the surrounding region. Markham accompanied this column when it left the village.

The heat became the men's worst enemy as the day dragged on. Their heavy equipment and cotton uniforms exhausted the soldiers, forcing the column to halt throughout the day so they could rest. They finally reached the shade of a bamboo forest six or seven hours later. The senior officers called off the excursion by late afternoon after being unable to locate the enemy. 'Everybody was much disappointed,' Markham recalled after hearing this news, 'as they all expected fighting.' The column retraced its steps and reached Shektsing around 9.00 pm, with a dozen men on stretchers after being 'knocked up by the sun'.

The next day, Markham and seven men of the *Camilla* received orders from van Straubenzee to stay behind to burn the village as the English and French troops embarked to return to Canton. 'We got the place ready for firing,' Markham wrote, 'and at a given signal, we all set fire to the place. It burnt up in a beautiful blaze as the houses were most of wood, with matted roofs.' They made sure Leang-paou-heun's home was 'gutted and burned'. After accomplishing their task, the men assigned to this mission returned to their boats.

Once again, Markham fell victim to heatstroke. 'It was a very warm day,' he noted, 'and after I had been running about by the fire, and marching down in the sun, I got very hot.' Luckily, he made it back to the boats before collapsing. His companions looked after him until they safely reached the *Camilla*.

The senior English officials and officers in Canton felt that the expedition had the desired outcome. Parkes said it helped to subdue the 'so-called patriotic faction' in Canton. 'The affair of Shek-tsing was productive of so salutary an effort upon both the peasantry and the Braves,' *The Cornhill Magazine* declared, 'that it was deemed desirable to conform the impression by military promenades in the neighbourhood of Canton, whereby we should give indisputable evidence of our power – hitherto always denied by the Chinese – to operate by land as well by water.' Rear Admiral Sir Michael Seymour, the Commander-in-Chief of the East Indies and China Station, issued a memo thanking the officers and men for their service in the expedition.

Two days after Seymour's memo was read on the deck of the *Camilla*, Markham began to cram for his intermediate exam. This time the exams were conducted by officers aboard HMS *Hornet*, while Colvile acted as an observer. By 1.30 pm, Markham received word that he had passed the tests. He did not do as well on this examination as on the first, even though he felt confident that he had thoroughly answered all the officers' questions. But he had passed. He promised himself that he would do much better in his next examination.

On 26 February, Colvile summoned Markham to his cabin. The captain broke the news that he had been appointed to temporary command of HMS *Niger*. He would be leaving the *Camilla* for good. He could tell that this news upset the boy and asked him if he would like to be reassigned to the *Niger*. 'Of course,' Markham replied without hesitation. His affection for Colvile had grown over the preceding two years.

Colvile and 17-year-old Markham joined the *Niger* on 3 March. Built in 1848, the steamer weighed an impressive 1,140 tons – this was double the weight of the *Camilla*. It carried thirteen guns and a crew of 180 men. Within weeks of arriving at their new ship, they would be off on another expedition to hunt down pirates.

On 11 March, a raiding party under Colvile's command was dispatched to destroy pirates reported to be active near Macao (Macau). The men detached from the *Niger* for the assignment were dispersed between five boats (a galley, a pinnace and three cutters) and each one placed under the command of an officer. Two 40 horsepower gunboats – HMS *Janus* and HMS *Clown* – towed Colvile's boats west from Hong Kong to Macao. Acting on information received from spies at Macao, Colvile spent the next day tracking down a fleet of pirate junks reported to have been carrying out attacks nearby. Unable to find any enemy junks, Colvile ordered his boats to head to a known pirate stronghold at the village Koolan.

On the morning of 13 March, Colvile's fleet spotted a number of heavily armed junks and rowboats anchored under the protection of the batteries at Koolan. These impressive works, according to Colvile, consisted of 'a water stockade, with a double ditch and high stockade embankment, armed with thirty-six guns, protecting the whole sea face and flanks of Tsoo-Chong [Koolan]'. Colvile sent his boats towards the junks, leaving the *Clown* to provide cover fire on the shore batteries. Once they spotted the advancing English boats, the pirates abandoned their junks and headed for the shore, joining the villagers in their defences. Colvile reported that as they moved closer to the shore, the defenders 'with violent ejaculations and waving white flags, on which the character Hoong-kin-wong (Triad King), was prominent, invited us on'.

Under fire from grapeshot from the pirate batteries, Colvile's boats moved behind a knoll on the left of the stockade so that it could offer them some cover. The pinnace, which Markham was on board, pulled off to provide supporting fire as sixty sailors and marines hit the beach, rushing the pirates' flank. They flooded through a small embrasure next to an eight-gun battery. The Englishmen immediately put their bayonets and the butts of their rifles to work, slashing and clubbing the defenders. 'Paralysed by the vigour' of the English attack, the 500 or so defenders 'retired precipitately' as Colvile's men chased them down for about 2 miles. The pinnace and one of the cutters, originally providing supporting fire, joined in the pursuit.

The sailors and marines destroyed the enemy works and spiked thirty-six guns. Discovering arms and munitions stockpiled in the homes of the village, Colvile directed his men to put the village to the torch. He also ordered eight large junks and eleven smaller boats in the harbour to be destroyed. He predicted that the defenders suffered the loss of 180 casualties during the engagement. Colvile's command did not suffer any casualties. Markham's biographers claimed that a spent shot struck him in the left shoulder during the battle. However, no mention was made of this in Colvile's report or in Markham's journal.

After destroying the pirate base at Koolan, Colvile received intelligence from a local mandarin that seven pirate junks were observed near the village of Lie-wan-moon. Colvile's fleet searched numerous crannies on its way there. In the Bay of Ly-kee, they located and destroyed four pirate junks. In an inlet to the north of Louchow, three more pirate junks were captured and burned.

When he arrived with his boats at the village of Lie-wan-moon, the locals informed Colvile that seven pirate junks had fled up a creek only a few hours before they arrived. The villagers provided the sailors with a graphic account of the barbarities committed by the pirates, which provoked the Englishmen to pursue them. Colvile's fleet, guided by Chinese boatmen of the village, travelled up the winding creek in the direction that the pirates had headed. On the morning of 15 March, they spotted the pirate junks in the distance.

Colvile sent each of his boats to engage the enemy ships. One of the junk's pirates tossed two incendiary stinkpots – filled with gunpowder and sulfur – at the *Janus*, engulfing its extra boats in flames. Markham's boat engaged one of the nine-gun junks for over an hour until it was finally driven ashore, and its crew was captured there by imperial soldiers. Three other pirate junks – a seven-gun, a nine-gun and a twenty-gun – were captured and destroyed. Colvile estimated that at least twenty-one pirates were killed during the engagement. Colvile's victorious fleet returned to Macao that night.

On 19 March, the *Niger* left China for India. The ship was conveying Rear Admiral Seymour, who was to be replaced by Rear Admiral James Hope as the new Commander-in-Chief of the East Indies and China Station. Seymour and his staff disembarked at Point de Galle, located on the island of Ceylon (Sri Lanka). The *Niger* struck a large rock during this voyage, causing considerable damage to its hull and forcing it to spend three weeks in Bombay (Mumbai) on the Indian mainland for repairs.

When its repairs were completed, the *Niger* anchored at Trincomalee on Ceylon and shared the harbour with the thirty-two-gun paddle frigate HMS *Retribution*, under the command of Commodore Harry E. Edgell. Colvile recommended that Markham request to be reassigned to the *Retribution* (Colvile had been ordered to rejoin the *Camilla*) since it would provide him with an opportunity to gain greater experience on a larger ship with a more senior officer. It might also provide him with a better chance for advancement. Even though he regretted leaving Colvile's company, Markham understood how important this move was to his naval career and joined the *Retribution* on 17 June.

Colvile ended up saving Markham's life by making this recommendation. In September 1860, the *Camilla* and all its crew, including Colvile, perished after being caught in a typhoon off the coast of Japan. Markham would have been among this number had he not taken Colvile's advice. Markham never forgot the captain. 'I have always regarded him as one of the best officers I have ever served with,' Markham insisted. '[H]ad he lived, he would without doubt have climbed to the very top of the Naval tree, and have made a great name for himself in the Service to which he was so devoted.'

The *Retribution*'s crew spent most days laying underwater telegraph cables in the Indian Ocean until news arrived from China reporting the repulse of a joint Anglo–French fleet at the Taku Forts. On 25 June 1859, Rear Admiral James Hope and an Anglo–French fleet of eleven gunboats and 1,100 men attempted to muscle their way upriver past the forts after the Qing refused to recognise some of the demands of the 1858 Treaty of Tientsin. A Mongol general named Senggelinqin built three barriers across the mouth of the Peiho (Hai) River to block foreign gunboats from reaching the Qing capital of Peking (Beijing). Hope, in his flagship HMS *Plover*, managed to ram through the first barrier. But as Senggelinqin had anticipated, Hope's ship could not break through the second barrier reinforced with iron chains and cacao fiber. Sixty imperial guns pelted Hope's eleven gunboats chocked in the narrow channel. The Anglo–French fleet could not return fire since the ships were out of range and were at the mercy of the Chinese artillery.

Wounded in the thigh during the fight, Hope abandoned the badly damaged *Plover* and joined HMS *Opossum*. An enemy shell hit the second gunboat and sent an iron chain spiralling through the air, striking Hope in the side and breaking three of his ribs. By the time it was all over, 426 men were dead or wounded, including twenty officers. Hope somehow managed to survive the debacle. Six of his gunboats were sunk or disabled and the Anglo-French fleet's attack repulsed. The losses incurred at the Taku Forts left several vacancies in the China Station and Markham immediately volunteered for service in China after hearing news of this calamity. In May 1860, he departed from India in a P&O mail steamer with forty other replacements for service with Hope on HMS *Chesapeake*.

'An out-and-out Scot', the fiery James Hope was the son of Admiral George Johnstone Hope, a Royal Navy officer who had served with Nelson at Trafalgar. The tall, noble-looking Scotsman followed his father's example and was appointed to the Royal Naval College at Portsmouth in August 1820. He saw service in the West Indies, the Mediterranean and the Crimean War, and by March 1859, Admiral 'Fighting Jimmy' Hope replaced Seymour as Commander-in-Chief of the East Indies and China Station.

Hope saw something special in Markham and appointed him to his personal staff when he arrived at Hong Kong. The admiral utilised his fine penmanship, and in one instance had Markham copy out his private correspondence. This close connection with the influential admiral would pay off.

Markham accompanied Admiral Hope in HMS *Coromandel* when the English and French returned to the Taku Forts in August 1860. This time they were prepared, bringing with them a force of 18,000 men under the command of Lieutenant General Sir Hope Grant. Instead of trying to ram their way up the Peiho River as Hope had tried fourteen months before, Grant advanced on the forts from land. After a two-week campaign, the Anglo-French force captured the forts, killing and wounding 400 imperial soldiers and capturing another 2,000.

After successfully eliminating the forts, the Anglo-French force continued upriver to Tientsin (Tianjin). A delegation and its escort sent to make peace with the Qing were taken hostage after negotiations broke down between the two sides. The foreigners continued their advance to the imperial capital, and after a series of engagements, occupied Peking on 6 October 1860. To revenge several members of the delegation who had died while in captivity, the advancing English and French soldiers sacked the 860-acre Old Summer Palace twelve days later. The soldiers destroyed the most prized pieces of Chinese artwork held in the palace during their three-day rampage.

Captain Charles George Gordon of the Royal Engineers, in a letter to a friend, gave an account of the mayhem:

> We went out, and, after pillaging it, burned the whole place, destroying in a vandal-like manner most valuable property which [could] not be replaced. ... You can scarcely imagine the beauty and magnificence of the places we burnt. It made one's heart sore to burn them. ... It was a scene of utter destruction which passes my description.

The capture and sacking of Peking may have had the desired effect the English wished for, but they would have to contend with an even deadlier adversary in China than the ruling Qing two years later in 1862. 'Affairs are becoming more involved in this part of the world,' *The New York Times* indicated in January. The paper referred to the deteriorating relations between the English and the rebels of the Taiping Heavenly Kingdom. Led by the self-proclaimed messiah Hong Xiuquan – claiming to be the younger brother of Jesus Christ and second son of God – the Taiping rebels fought to overthrow Qing rule. As a result, 20 million Chinese perished during the fourteen-year rebellion.

For the first time since the rebellion began twelve years earlier, the rebels threatened to upset English trade by advancing on their treaty port cities, most notably Shanghai. The Taiping rebels were more concerned with occupying these cities for strategic purposes to cut off the Qing's flow of resources than with the economic damage it did to the English. 'Trade is crushed beneath their tread,' *The New York Times* complained of the Taiping. The English chose to ally themselves with the Qing – the same enemy they had defeated two years before – to oppose this new threat.

Admiral Hope planned to form a 30-mile buffer zone around Shanghai to better defend it against the advancing Taiping rebels. He reasoned that this would utilise fewer soldiers instead of having to man the 4½-

mile wall around the city. It also enabled an English flying column of crack troops to remain in the rear, ready to support outposts manned by imperial soldiers in the event of a Taiping breakthrough. Royal Navy warships would lend support by transporting men and material and by disembarking sailors to fight on land alongside the ground forces.

A month before Hope's 30-mile campaign commenced, Markham passed his examination for sub lieutenant. Hope took notice, and to fill a vacancy aboard HMS *Centaur* on the eve of his campaign against the Taiping rebels, he appointed the 20-year-old to the temporary rank of second lieutenant.

On 21 February 1862, Hope advanced from the protection of Shanghai's walls with a mixed force of English and French sailors, regulars and mercenaries from Frederick T. Ward's Ever-Victorious Army (EVA), supported by the imperial soldiers in the area. Hope's force cleared the Taiping rebels from the zone during March, April and May, and captured and held the strategic towns outside Shanghai until they could be garrisoned by imperial troops.

As Hope's force battled the Taiping rebels around Shanghai, pirates continued to swarm and harass merchant ships. English gunboats were sent to disrupt them, but spies in Ningpo alerted the pirates, allowing them to evade capture. In April, Markham's superior officer on the *Centaur*, Commander John Eglinton Montgomerie, sent him with twenty men, an assistant surgeon and a 12-pounder howitzer disguised in a lorcha named the *Vivid* manned by a Chinese crew, to ambush the pirates. 'Everything being done by night time, and as quietly as possible,' Markham noted in his journal, 'to prevent the spies of the pirates, who are very numerous, from learning anything.' The *Vivid* inconspicuously slipped out of Ningpo's harbour on the night of 2 April and headed south for the Chusan (Zhoushan) Archipelago.

Markham noticed two suspicious junks the next morning at about 11.00 am. He ordered his English sailors from the *Centaur* below deck so that they would not be spotted. Markham, draped in a Chinese fur and resting next to the 12-pounder howitzer hidden under a sail, remained on deck with the Chinese crew. One of the junks suddenly turned and headed in their direction. It then hoisted its red and black flag and the pirates began to beat on their gongs and tom-toms as they prepared to attack the seemingly defenseless ship.

The junk fired its four heavy guns at the *Vivid* from about 100 yards, one shot tearing away the sail directly above Markham's head. He flung off his fur coat, exposing his uniform, and uncovered the howitzer. The sailors rushed up from below deck and unleashed a volley of rifle fire at the pirates. Realising they were now facing Englishmen, the pirates turned the ship around and fled. A direct shot from the howitzer smashed its bow, slowing its retreat.

Markham's Chinese rowers refused to bring the *Vivid* any closer to the pirate junk for fear of being killed in the crossfire. He instead rowed with five sailors in a sampan towards the enemy ship to storm it. When they were within 40 yards of the junk, the pirates opened fire with their small arms, wounding two of Markham's men. The rower operating the steering oar was so frightened he refused to row any closer, forcing Markham to order the sampan back to the *Vivid*. (None of his sailors knew how to operate its steering oar.)

The sailors continued to hurl shells from the 12-pounder howitzer at the damaged junk. Their last round tore away its steering oar, immobilising it. Markham induced the frightened Chinese rowers into manoeurvring the *Vivid* to within 20 yards of the crippled vessel.

The crew of the two ships exchanged small arms fire at this deadly range. The captain of the *Vivid*, a foreigner named Barclay – described by Markham as 'a very nice, quiet, civil man' – fell seriously wounded after a ball hit him in the chest and passed through his body. Two more of Markham's men fell wounded, one shot in the neck and the other in the leg. Markham could see that the pirates had suffered heavy casualties, observing dozens of wounded or dead men spread out on their deck.

As his men prepared to board the enemy junk for a second time, an explosion rocked the *Vivid* and sent wood and metal fragments spiraling through the air. After a three-and-a-half-hour engagement, the pirates fired the magazine rather than face surrender. 'We had to shove off to get clear of the fragments which were falling down in all directions,' Markham recalled as the *Vivid* raced to escape the tumbling debris.

The *Vivid* picked up thirteen pirates among the wreckage. Markham ordered these prisoners to be shackled. Two bled out on the deck. The

Vivid returned with its prisoners to Ningpo, where they were tried, but only two out of the eleven men were found guilty of piracy. Most confessed to being fishermen pressed into service under the threat of death. The local mandarin ordered the two found guilty to be beheaded.

Markham received praise from his superiors for his successful operation at the Chusan Archipelago. 'The captain was very much pleased at what I had done,' Markham proudly declared. The Lords Commissioners of the Admiralty acted on Hope's recommendation and promoted him to lieutenant and commended the 'gallant young lieutenant's pluck and resource'. The letter of promotion, sent by Secretary of the Admiralty Clarence Page, was read in the presence of the *Centaur*'s crew:

> Referring to Sir James Hope's letter of the 19th of April last No. 153, reporting the gallant conduct of Mr Albert H. Markham acting Lieutenant of H.M. Ship *Centaur* in capturing a Pirate with a Party under his command, detached from the ship. I am commanded by my Lords Commissioners of the Admiralty to acquaint you that their Lordships have been pleased to promote Mr Markham to the rank of Acting Lieutenant in Her Majesty's Fleet, with seniority from the 3rd of April last, and he will be confirmed provided he shall pass the several examinations on his arrival in England, according to the Regulations.
>
> The Commission is enclosed herewith.

During the summer of 1862, the *Centaur* transported troops from one port city to another threatened by the Taiping rebels. Around this time, Markham befriended the 29-year-old engineer officer Charles George Gordon, who gave the disturbing account of the sack of Old Summer Palace, and who later commanded the EVA following the death of its leader, the American Frederick T. Ward, in September 1862. Markham praised Gordon for transforming the EVA into a disciplined fighting force, proclaiming that he 'showed the world what he could with Chinese soldiers when properly organised and disciplined and efficiently led'. Both Markham and Gordon were devout Christians and Gordon was a good friend of Albert's brother, John, then serving as the Vice Consul at Shanghai. Ten years after they first met, Markham wrote to Gordon asking him if he could borrow some notes and journals lent to him by John so that he could write a history of the Taiping Rebellion. Writing from Constantinople, Gordon agreed to send the materials and requested three copies of Markham's forthcoming book. For whatever reason, Markham never did publish the book.

Most of the *Centaur*'s crew came down with dysentery during the fall of 1862 and the ship travelled to Japan hoping that a change of climate would provide some relief. Japan's borders had only been open to foreigners for eight years when Markham arrived with the *Centaur* in September. Some Japanese saw the economic advantages of cooperating with the foreigners, while others feared their encroachment. Foreigners residing in port cities lived in constant fear of being attacked by dissidents who opposed them being there at all.

On 14 September 1862, around 4.00 pm, Markham, in temporary command of the *Centaur* in the absence of Montgomerie, received word from First Secretary at the British Legation at Edo, Abel Gower, that a group of samurai had attacked a party of English travellers composed of Charles Lennox Richardson, William Marshall, Woodthorpe C. Clarke and Marshall's sister-in-law, Margaret Borrodaile, on their way to visit a Japanese temple at Kawasaki. Richardson was rumored to have been killed. 'I knew him very well in Shanghai,' Markham wrote of Richardson in his journal. Markham likely met Richardson when the Qing authorities hired him to transport 9,000 imperial soldiers from Nankin (Nanjing) to Shanghai for the price of £7 a head during the Taiping Rebellion. 'He was a fine fellow, and had just made his fortune in China and was making a visit to Japan before he returned to England.' Gower asked Markham to land his sailors to recover the Englishman's body. He immediately left with twenty men, unsure of what he would discover.

About halfway to Kawasaki, Richardson and his party collided with Prince Shimazu Hisamitsu's caravan on the Tōkaidō Road. Failing to move off the road for the prince was considered a grave insult. A burly samurai named Narahara Yonezaemon stepped forward after the foreigners had been repeatedly told to turn back. Markham stated that as the foreigners finally turned their horses around, 'the man above mentioned drew his sword and rushed at Mr. Richardson who was the last of the party giving him a mortal blow, by cutting him along the left side, exposing his intestines.'

Yonezaemon continued his frenzied attack after slashing Richardson. He swung his sword at Borrodaile's head but missed, taking off a chunk of her hair. He hit Richardson again with his third strike, nearly severing his arm as he frantically tried to shield himself from the blow. Clarke and Marshall were also wounded by other samurai from the party but escaped to the American consul at Kanagawa. Borrodaile became separated from the two men, but she managed to flee to Yokohama. Richardson retreated a short distance but collapsed along a riverbank where a samurai delivered the final blow that ended his life.

Markham's detachment met the English *Chargé d'Affaires*, Lieutenant Colonel Edward St John Neale, once they landed and cautiously advanced down the Tōkaidō Road in the direction of where the attack took place. They met some Frenchmen on the road who had already retrieved Richardson's body. Markham recalled in vivid detail the appearance of his friend's mutilated corpse. 'Poor Richardson's body when discovered was a frightful spectacle,' he declared, 'between 20 and 30 wounds, his head was nearly severed from his body, and his bowels were protruding, and a spear wound in his left breast; all mortal wounds.'

Neale and Rear Admiral Augustus Leopold Kuper, who succeeded Admiral Hope as the Commander-in-Chief of the East Indies and China Station, decided against retaliatory action for the attack. Neale argued that if the Satsuma were attacked, or if Prince Hisamitsu was taken a prisoner, the samurai would react by attacking the foreign settlements. They did not have the manpower to defend every foreign citizen living on the Japanese mainland. Kuper argued that their advantage lay in the guns and armour of their ships; landing a naval detachment to face the samurai would put them at a severe numerical disadvantage. Instead, Neale demanded that the Satsuma put Richardson's killers on trial and pay an indemnity of £25,000 to the families of the victims.

Markham and other naval officers were not satisfied with anything short of an all-out assault on the Satsuma. 'We all expected that we should have "a go in" at them,' he complained, 'and our men were all in readiness to land, but Colonel Neale would not allow anything to be done much to the disgust of everyone.' The next day, at 4.00 pm, sailors from each ship watched bitterly as Richardson's remains were interred in Yokohama.

Yokohama's foreign population got on with their lives as best they could after the murder of Richardson until Neale notified them of an attack rumoured to take place on 25 June 1863. He advised all foreigners to evacuate the city as the days drew closer to the date of the attack. Markham was familiar with living in this kind of terror, having spent the bloody summer of 1858 in Canton and prepared for the worst.

The English sailors were on alert but had little to do since the shops and businesses were shut down, so they organised a cricket game on the day of the projected attack. Michael Galbraith, a historian of Japan's first cricket match, suggests that the real motive for scheduling this match was to have plenty of men and guns on the shore when the attack came. The officers stationed in Yokohama challenged the officers on the ships anchored in the harbour. Markham was one of the players recruited to play on this hastily assembled team.

The two teams – Yokohama and The Fleet – met on a grassy field near Yokohama's Foreign Settlement. The players carried revolvers and armed guards patrolled the area as the two teams battled. 'It is, I suppose,' Markham later recalled, 'the only match on record in which the players had to be armed.' Fortunately, no attack came and the game went on unhindered. Despite Yokohama being captained by the 23-year-old James Campbell Fraser – a skilled cricketer – The Fleet was victorious. Markham teased Fraser years after about the 'jolly good licking' his team gave to the Yokohama.

The officers who wanted Richardson revenged ended up getting their wish after all. Neale grew impatient when the Prince of Satsuma refused to reply to the English demand for reparations and requested that Admiral Kuper proceed to Kagoshima and use whatever means necessary 'to awaken the Prince of Satsuma to a sense of the serious nature of the determinations which have brought Her Majesty's squadron to this anchorage'. On 15 August, Kuper's seven ships proceeded to Kagoshima and bombarded the Satsuma stronghold for two days. Meanwhile, Markham remained behind with the *Centaur* to protect the foreign citizens in Yokohama, missing the action. Kuper's ships destroyed all eighty-one guns of the Satsuma shore batteries, the Prince of Satsuma's palace and most of Kagoshima, killing and wounding 1,400 people.

The Satsuma paid the indemnity in December, but no trial was held to prosecute Richardson's murderers.

In February 1864, the *Centaur* was at the end of its commission and left the China Station to be paid off, and arrived in England four months later. Markham had left Portsmouth as a naïve, teenage cadet seven years before, and returned as a 22-year-old veteran lieutenant with the silver China Medal hanging from his chest. Under the tutelage of two able mentors, Colvile and Hope, Markham had matured into a resourceful naval officer. He came to realise that war was a messy business but a necessary evil to protect the British Empire's global interests. But unlike his cousin Clements, who was out of the navy by the age of 21, Albert found a sailor's life tough but rewarding. He chose to stick with it.

Chapter 3

The Martyrs of Nukapu

Why should we mourn their glorious fate,
Or weep that they have won their crown?
There is a glory far too great—
Too glad for tears their bright renown!

Nobly they fought and gained the prize—
The martyr's radiant diadem;
What need for tears or bitter cries,
While smiles in Heaven are circling them?
A section from William H.H. Yarrington's poem
'Patteson, Atkin, Stephen, Martyrs, 1871'

Upon his return to England in the summer of 1864, Markham successfully passed the examination for lieutenant at the Royal Naval College. Four months later, he was assigned to the Mediterranean Station's flagship, HMS *Victoria*, and spent three years on it. This assignment allowed him the opportunity to explore port cities and make excursions to historic and archeological sites in Spain, Italy and Greece. When his service on the *Victoria* ended in the summer of 1867, he was granted leave and decided to travel to the United States to visit his parents and brothers.

The same year that Albert left for China, the Markhams had departed France to escape their financial troubles and arrived in the United States. When they reached Black River Falls, Wisconsin, George Markham went ahead with two other men to settle on 300 acres in the wilderness. They built a log cabin before winter set in, but freezing temperatures and starvation nearly killed the men. Due to George's heroic efforts – he travelled between Black River Falls and the cabin with a sled numerous times to retrieve supplies – the men survived the winter. Arthur joined his older brother later that season, and by the spring of 1857, John and Marianne arrived from Black River Falls to establish their new life.

Albert reached New York City on 25 September 1867. He arrived at the village of Trempealeau a few days later, relieved that he would be at his parents' farm within the hour. He asked a local to point him in the right direction. The man told him that he had another 26 miles to go. The Markhams lived in the county by that name, not the village. Albert left his luggage behind, took only a carpet bag with him, and began to hike north. He walked about 12 miles until he waved down a man in a wagon and paid the driver four dollars to take him the rest of the way to his parents' home.

He was pleased with what he found. George and Arthur managed a prosperous farm, raising horses and cattle, harvesting grain and vegetables, and planting a large orchard. George, who originally wanted to pursue a career in the army, married an American woman, had a son and became a respected farmer in the community. To replace the rickety cabin erected during the winter of 1856–57, the family constructed a beautiful four-story, octagon-shaped home they christened 'Ronceval'. It became known within the local community as Markham Castle. Albert cherished the twenty-four days he spent at the farm before heading back to England. It would be the last time he would see his father, who passed away in October 1870 at the age of 73.

On 7 January 1868, Markham was assigned to HMS *Blanche* destined for the Australia Station. The *Blanche* – weighing 1,286 tons and 350 horsepower – was under the command of his former commander on the *Centaur* while in China, Captain John E. Montgomerie. A journalist who visited the *Blanche* around the time Markham joined it described the ship as a hideous looking vessel:

> The *Blanche* presents a somewhat awkward and bizarre appearance, particularly in the form of her stern, which, instead of being flat or round, as in all the ships we see in these waters, is angular and clumsy-looking. Her bow, also is a projecting one, and altogether, she looks more like one of the curiously shaped vessels, with which the woodcuts in the *Illustrated London News* made us so familiar during the time of the American War, than a British ship.

What the *Blanche* lacked in appearance, it made up for in its speed and firepower. It made its voyage from the Cape of Good Hope to Australia in a mere thirty days. Its impressive armament consisted of two 6½-ton Woolwich guns, four 64-pounder shunt guns, a 12-pounder Armstrong gun and two 24-pounder Hale's rockets. The men also had an armory at their disposal of breech-loading Snider and Enfield rifles, cutlasses, boarding axes and pikes to face any adversary that might challenge English supremacy in the Pacific Ocean.

During the summer of 1868, the charismatic Māori leader Te Kooti Rikirangi formed a band of guerrilla fighters and delivered several defeats to local militia, volunteer and armed constabulary units at Paparatu, Te Koneke and Ruakituri. Meanwhile, Riwha Tītokowaru waged his own guerrilla war against the New Zealand Colonial Government. Fearful of attacks on English settlements and ports along the New Zealand coast, the government called on Royal Navy warships to ensure the protection of life and property against the Māori guerilla fighters. This plea for aid led to the *Blanche* being dispatched to New Zealand.

Even though the Royal Navy warships did not see any action, the New Zealand Colonial Secretary William Gisborne praised the effect their presence had on the settlements. 'It discourages the rebel Natives and gives courage to the loyal Natives,' Gisborne declared. '[I]t has been also a very reassuring effect upon the settlers, who naturally feel, when they see the British flag flying on one of these vessels, that they have, besides themselves, a mighty power to protect and to support them.' The Civil Commissioner of Tauranga, New Zealand, Henry T. Clarke, singled out the *Blanche* and one of its sister ships for the 'moral support and lively interest they have taken in this district' and their ability to restore confidence among the settlement's European population.

In August, the *Blanche* left New Zealand and steamed to the Solomon Islands following an attack by natives on the crew of the *Marion Rennie*. Arriving at the islands, Montgomerie ordered a blank shot fired at some natives gathered on a beach to demonstrate his firepower. On 11 September, the *Blanche* attacked a native village located on Rendova Island. A party of sixty sailors and marines landed and razed the village. The press reported that 'three or four chiefs' were killed during the engagement, while one sailor, George Eastough, was killed either from friendly fire or from an accidental discharge of his rifle.

During his service on the *Blanche*, Markham earned a reputation among some of the ship's subordinate officers for being a martinet. Unlike his cousin, who loathed the navy's discipline, Albert embraced it. Order and discipline were crucial for the Royal Navy to maintain its efficiency throughout the isolated posts of the British Empire. One disgruntled junior officer on the *Blanche*, Sub Lieutenant Charles James Norcock, criticised Markham's 'exceedingly disagreeable manner' and branded him as 'a man who has prevented our whole commission from being, what it might have been, a happy one and who has on many occasions made things very miserable'.

Despite the stern reputation he gained among some of his comrades on the *Blanche*, Markham genuinely cared for the men under his command. On two separate occasions, he intervened to save the lives of his sailors. In the first incident, he rescued a young sailor who had accidentally fallen overboard. He saved another man's life when a raging gale carried away the ship's jib boom, knocking the sailor into the water. Markham secured a boat, called for volunteers, and braved the storm to retrieve the man before he drowned.

On 12 October 1871, Markham was appointed as the temporary commander of HMS *Rosario* to replace Captain George Palmer. The *Rosario*, a wooden sloop-of-war about half the size (673 tons) and speed (150-horsepower) of the *Blanche*, carried three revolving guns – one 6½-ton Woolwich and two 42-pounder breech-loading Armstrong guns. It comprised of a crew of 145 men, a portion of whom were survivors of the HMS *Megaera* wreck.

Commodore Frederick Stirling, the Senior Naval Officer on the Australia Station, assigned Markham on a special mission to investigate alleged cases of kidnapping committed against natives living in the South Pacific. Markham whipped his men into shape over the next few weeks by ordering them to perform regular drills such as clearing away for action, organising landing parties and shifting sails and spars. The *Rosario*'s greatest flaw was its speed, and Markham tried to alter its trim hoping to make it quicker so that it could more easily overtake smaller and faster ships that might try to evade capture.

Between 1863 and 1904, roughly 60,000 natives from the New Hebrides (Vanuatu) and the Solomon Islands were brought to Australia to work as labourers on plantations. The American Civil War led to a drastic increase in the price of raw cotton due to the Union blockade of the cotton-producing Confederate States of America, leading Queensland and Fiji planters to establish their own cotton plantations to profit from the global shortage. Plantation owners turned to cheap labour from the South Pacific islands to perform the work.

An Australian merchant and plantation owner named Robert 'Bobbie' Towns was the first to recruit natives to work on his cotton plantation. Born in 1794, Towns carried convicts to Australia and settled in Sydney in 1842, married into an influential family, and founded Robert Towns & Company, a successful business managing whale, seal and merchant ships. Towns was one of the first to take up cotton farming in Australia, dedicating 2,000 acres of his land to cultivating it. With an inadequate workforce available on the mainland, Towns employed the natives of the South Pacific to handle all the necessary weeding, cleaning and picking of cotton on his plantation.

Towns may have been a shrewd businessman, but he was unsure of how to go about hiring the natives. He turned to a New Hebrides trader, Henry Ross Lewin, who was familiar with the customs and languages of the South Pacific islanders. The illiterate Lewin had served in the Royal Navy in China during the First Opium War, but was either kicked out or had deserted and wandered to Australia to find work. Towns, with Lewin's help, eventually recruited and employed an army of 260 labourers on his plantation, which led to him harvesting 183,630 pounds of cotton. Other plantation owners followed Towns's example, recruiting hard-working and inexpensive native labourers. These islanders remained a staple in Australia's economy for the next four decades.

Men like Lewin made a business out of acting as middlemen between labourers and plantation owners. They were dubbed 'blackbirders' and the trade 'blackbirding.' Some of these men turned to immoral methods to make an easy profit and fill labour quotas. The worst offenders found it far easier to kidnap the natives, resorting to deceit and coercion rather than lawful means to acquire them. Blackbirders tricked natives to come aboard their ships under the guise of wanting to trade, disguised themselves as peaceful missionaries, ran down native canoes and bought prisoners from local chiefs in exchange for severed heads or muskets to secure their labour quotas. Most plantation owners cared little for how the labourers got to their plantations as long as able-bodied workers continued to arrive.

The crimes committed by blackbirders did not go unnoticed throughout the rest of the empire. Tales of the atrocities committed against natives stirred humanitarian organisations such as the Anti-Slavery and Aborigines' Protection Society in England. Christian missionaries of the New Hebrides Mission claimed blackbirding was a 'modified form of slavery'. They were horrified with this practice since slavery had been officially abolished throughout the empire over three decades earlier. Eight missionaries presented a petition to the governor of Queensland condemning the trade and requesting a formal investigation into these wicked activities.

The Polynesian Labourers Act, passed by the Queensland legislature in 1868, closely monitored the activities of the ships engaged in blackbirding and placed restrictions on the trade. The act made it mandatory for the ship's captain carrying labourers to be able to furnish a list of its native passengers, provide a certificate that each native had agreed to work, present an official licence verifying he was permitted to partake in the trade, show that the natives had proper amenities and space, and prove that the natives would be returned to their homes at the termination of their employment.

At Queen Victoria's urging, Parliament passed a bill outlawing the kidnapping of natives in the South Pacific. The Lord Chancellor read her plea to both Houses of Parliament on 6 February 1872:

The Slave Trade, and practices scarcely to be distinguished from Slaves Trading, still pursued in more than one quarter of the world, continue to attract the attention of my Government. In the South Sea Islands, the name of the British Empire is even now dishonoured by the connexion of some of my subjects with these nefarious practices; and in one of them the murder of an exemplary Prelate has cast fresh light upon some of their baleful consequences. A Bill will be presented to you for the purpose of facilitating the trial of offences of this class in Australasia; and endeavours will be made to increase, in other forms, the means of counteraction.

Even with the restrictions put in place due to the public outcry, blackbirding still continued. The Royal Navy lacked the manpower in the Australia Station to patrol every sector of the South Pacific to enforce these laws. It was not easy either to distinguish between law-abiding ships and those breaking the law without making a thorough investigation of a ship and its papers. Wealthy plantation owners in government positions used their influence to circumnavigate these laws and gain favourable court rulings for blackbirders employed by them. Even worse, charges could be made against Royal Navy officers for stopping or detaining ships. Unfavourable court rulings made it hard to find officers eager and willing to crack down on blackbirders.

Commodore Stirling inspected the *Rosario* on 16 October, four days after appointing Markham to temporary command. A few days later he sent Markham detailed sailing orders for his mission. He tasked Markham with boarding and inspecting all the ships he encountered flying the Union Jack to determine if they were deporting natives to Queensland or Fiji. If they were, he was to make sure the ships were acting in accordance with the law. 'Although it is the desire of the British Government to prevent any irregularities connected with the so-called labour traffic in those islands,' Stirling cautioned Markham, 'you are in all your proceedings to act in accordance with the law.' If time permitted, he also wanted Markham to visit the New Hebrides and Santa Cruz Islands to communicate with 'every missionary, planter, or other person from whom information can be obtained relative to the murder of British subjects which have recently taken place there, and to the alleged kidnapping of natives which is supposed to have led to these acts'. Markham was to return to Sydney with a detailed report on blackbirding and the murders committed against ships manned by white crews.

Stirling gave Markham vague instructions for dealing with the native islanders. 'As a rule,' he explained, 'the display of arms should be avoided where the natives are known to be friendly, and where their suspicion would be aroused by such display; but commanding officers must be guided by their judgment on this point.' Stirling further indicated that 'at places where the inhabitants are of an unfriendly or doubtful character, sufficient force should always be at hand to prevent any hostile attempt on the part of the natives'.

Markham was uneasy about his new assignment and his ability to fulfill Stirling's orders. 'On leisurely reading over my instructions, I felt that I had a most difficult and responsible duty to perform,' he noted, 'knowing, as I did, that the labour traffic was closely associated with the cotton-planting interest of the colonies, and that the vessels engaged in the so-called labour trade, were owned, more or less, by large and influential houses in Sydney, Melbourne, Brisbane, and Auckland.'

While eager to stamp out the trade, he knew he could face the threat of prosecution in a court of law if he did not proceed with caution:

> I was also aware that hitherto the Commanders of the men-of-war had not been supported by the Colonial Law Courts, in their endeavours to put a stop to the nefarious practice of stealing natives from the different islands by means of vessels owned, commanded, and manned by white men; and that, on two glaring occasions, when slavers were seized and sent to Sydney for adjudication, they were acquitted, and their captors were themselves condemned in heavy damages for detention and injury done to those vessels. With these facts before me, I felt that I might, and probably should, involve myself in some difficulty, in the event of my seizing or detaining any vessel which it might be my lot to detect in the perpetration of illegal acts.

One of these glaring occasions of injustice he was referring to was when the *Blanche* confiscated the blackbirding ship *Challenge* for illegally transporting natives in June 1871. The 50-ton *Challenge* kidnapped six natives from the Torres Islands, located south of the Solomon Islands, and in an attempt to escape, the natives jumped overboard 7 miles from land and drowned. On the same cruise, two more natives were kidnapped from the island of Vanua Lava. The *Blanche* stopped and boarded the ship, and learning of these crimes, Captain Montgomerie ordered a lieutenant and some of his sailors to confiscate the *Challenge* until the ship reached Sydney. Despite the damning evidence against the *Challenge*'s crew, they were acquitted when put on trial for their crimes. Even more disheartening, a bill for £900 was sent to Montgomerie by the *Challenge*'s owner for damages sustained during its detainment.

Markham made three important decisions before he left Sydney on 18 October 1872. First, even though he detested the 'lawless and unscrupulous ruffians who infest the beautiful South Sea Islands', he decided that unless he caught blackbirders in the act of kidnapping or murdering natives, he would release them with only a stern warning since it was unlikely that they would face any charges in an Australian courtroom. Second, he planned to adopt a 'more conciliatory policy' than his colleagues had taken towards Chinese civilians during the Second Opium War or that he had witnessed while serving on the *Blanche* when dealing with natives accused of committing crimes against whites. 'I determined to do all in my power to shield and protect the Islanders,' Markham declared, 'and where I had occasion to visit them with punishment, to do so, in as mild and lenient a form, as was consistent with the circumstances of the offence.' Last, he intended to 'mete out impartial justice to white and black alike'.

Twelve days after leaving Sydney, the *Rosario* made its first stop at Norfolk Island. Markham wanted to ask Bishop John Patteson, the head of the Melanesian Mission, about the recent murders in the region before continuing on his cruise. Chief Magistrate Daggett and a son of the Reverend George H. Nobbs boarded the ship and told Markham that Bishop Patteson had been murdered the month before. Anxious to learn more, Markham travelled to the headquarters of the Melanesian Mission located on the northwest end of the island. There he met the Reverend Robert H. Codrington, who had replaced Patteson, and his companions. The missionaries provided him with the disturbing details he desired.

The 44-year-old Bishop John Coleridge Patteson had worked tirelessly to win over and convert the natives of the South Pacific before his untimely death. The son of a judge and an Oxford graduate, Patteson was recruited by Bishop George Selwyn while serving as a young curate in Devon. In the early days of his missionary work among the islands, Patteson went barefoot and wore only a shirt, trousers and top hat. He respected the natives' customs and way of life, allowing him to earn their trust and admiration. Captain George Palmer, who observed Patteson in action, declared that he 'was the *beau ideal* of what a missionary should be – loving, humble, devoted, and intellectual. … You might go a long way before you saw a face in which nobleness and sweetness were so intimately blended.'

On 20 September 1871, Patteson arrived at the island of Nukapu for a routine visit in his missionary ship, the *Southern Cross*. The natives usually received him with enthusiasm, but this time they seemed reluctant to row out to greet him. He knew that something was off. 'We had better lower the boat, and go to them,' Patteson said to his comrades. At 11.00 am, a small boat with Patteson and four men inside – the Reverend Joseph 'Joe' Atkin, and three Mota converts, Stephen Taroniaro, John Nonomo and James Minipa – headed towards the four waiting canoes.

The natives in the canoes insisted that Patteson come ashore, but the tide was too low for his small boat to clear the reef skirting the island. Patteson instead climbed into one of their canoes. Two more canoes carrying the chiefs Moto and Taula trailed behind as the canoe with Patteson in it headed for the shore. Before leaving, the bishop told his comrades that he would wave a white handkerchief as a signal when he was ready to return.

As the canoe carrying Patteson paddled out of sight, another native canoe came up to the missionary boat waiting behind for the bishop's return. The men inside the canoe asked the white men to trade, but they directed them to go to the *Southern Cross* for that. Noticing an extra oar inside the boat, the natives insisted that the missionaries trade it to them, but they abruptly declined. Atkin and the others were relieved when the canoe left them alone and finally paddled away. Atkin recalled that suddenly, 'a man stood up in one [of the canoes], with a bow in his hand, and called out, "Do you want this?" or something to that effect – picked up an arrow, and fired at us.' The men in the other canoes followed this man's lead and began to shower the missionary boat with arrows.

Three of the four men in Patteson's boat were wounded before managing to row back to the *Southern Cross*. Nonomo was struck in the shoulder, while six arrows pierced Taroniaro in the upper body. Minipa managed to avoid being wounded by ducking down in the boat just at the right moment. When they reached the missionary ship, Atkin, wounded in the shoulder, called out, 'We are all hurt.'

Atkin revealed that Patteson was still on the island and in grave danger. Atkin, despite being wounded, joined the other crew members heading out in a boat to rescue the bishop. The rescue party waited until the tide rose so that they could row over the reef and reach the shore. As they closed in on land, two native canoes headed in their direction. The canoes halted halfway between them and the island; one continued to drift towards them while the other hung back. At first, it did not appear as if anybody was directing it. When it came close enough for them to see inside, they discovered Patteson's body wrapped in a rug and stripped of his clothing, with the right side of his skull shattered. Atkin attested that this act of violence was peculiar for the islanders:

> The Bishop had frequently visited this island, and always found the people friendly and well-behaved. Last year we landed, and our boat lay on the beach about an hour, while the Bishop was with the people in the village. Until this year the canoes used to meet us three or four miles from the island, and the people to clamber on board the vessel without the least fear.

He attributed this shift in their attitude to blackbirders:

> The only account to be given of this change of feeling – one that is unfortunately justified by what we have seen and heard wherever we go – is, that a vessel has been here, and committed an outrage, perhaps killed some of them, and that they had resolved to take the life of the first white man who fell into their power.

A surgeon treated Atkin and the other wounded men after they returned with the bishop's remains to the *Southern Cross*. Five arrows were extracted from Taroniaro's body, but the sixth penetrated too close to his lungs to be safely removed. The day after the attack, Atkin, wrote to his mother:

> Stephen is in great pain at times to-night; one of the arrows seems to have entered his lungs, and it is broken in, too deep to be got out. John is wounded in the right shoulder, I in the left. We are

both maimed for the time, but, if it were not for the fear of poison, the wounds would not be worth noticing. I do not expect any bad consequences, but they are possible. What would make me cling to life more than anything else is the thought of you at home; but, if it be God's will that I am to die, I know He will enable you to bear it, and bring good for you out of it.

The next day, Atkin again wrote his mother with promising news: 'We are all doing well. Stephen keeps up his strength, sleeps well, and has no long attacks of pain. We have had good breezes yesterday and today – very welcome it is, but the motion makes writing too much labour.'

Four days later, Atkin and Taroniaro were dead after infections set in. Both died in agony within hours of each other. Before he passed away, Taroniaro received Holy Communion from Atkin. 'His sufferings for two days were dreadful,' the captain of the *Southern Cross* wrote of the reverend. '[I]t was heartrending to see him.' The Reverend Charles H. Brooke described his final hours:

> Mr. Atkin became suddenly worse on the 26th, and spent a night of acute pain; the whole nervous system was being jerked and strained to pieces. Almost leaping from his berth upon the floor, in his intolerable agony, he cried, 'Good-bye!' and lay convulsed upon a mattress on the floor. About seven o'clock in the morning of the 27th I asked him would he have a little sal volatile. 'No!' 'A little brandy?' 'No!' 'Did he want anything?' 'To die!' These were his last words, and, after another hour's acute suffering, he passed away.

Brooke read the burial service in both Mota and English as the bodies of the three martyrs – Patteson, Atkin and Taroniaro – were committed to the sea. 'Thus perished, by the hands of those of whom he was labouring with untiring energy,' Markham afterwards wrote of Patteson, '[T]hat good and unselfish man, who had given up home, friends, and eventually his own life, in his endeavours to add to the flock of which he was a good and faithful shepherd.'

Patteson had not died in vain. People began to attribute his murder as an act of retaliation for the misdeeds committed by blackbirders. 'It is a terrible price to pay,' Brooke wrote, 'but the Bishop's death will at last open people's eyes to the state of exasperation these natives are now in, owing to the violence practised against them by these labour-seekers.' Only days before Patteson's arrival at Nukapu, five natives were kidnapped from the island by a blackbirding ship. There has been some debate over whether Patteson's murder was an act of retaliation for these kidnappings, but in 1871, Patteson's martyrdom provided a rallying cry to end blackbirding once and for all.

Markham planned to visit the island of Nukapu to investigate Patteson's murder after hearing the account of his death. Before he left, the missionaries made him promise that he would not harm the natives responsible for his slaying. The Reverend Codrington claimed that Patteson said that in the event of his death, he did not want revenge taken out on those responsible, and asked Markham to abide by his wish. Rather, the missionaries urged Markham to focus his attention on stamping out the 'iniquitous trade' they believed to be the reason for the bishop's death. They handed him a letter signed by all present condemning the use of force. Markham agreed to respect their wishes.

The *Rosario* left Norfolk and steamed to the Pitcairn Islands. There they encountered the descendants of John Adams and Ned Young from the famed eighteenth-century HMS *Bounty* mutiny. Markham found these men to be 'fine strapping young fellows', while he described the young ladies as 'modest and pleasing in appearance'. They told him of a recent series of murders committed by a blackbirding ship in the area. The blackbirders had purposely dropped one of their boats on top of a native canoe, crushing it, and forcing its occupants to abandon ship. They were then lassoed and their heads chopped off. A local chief exchanged some younger men fit for labour on a plantation for the decapitated heads.

The *Rosario* next proceeded to investigate the southernmost island of the New Hebrides Islands, Ambrym, on 11 November. Around 3.00 pm, they spotted a suspicious schooner, later identified as the *Marion Rennie*. It attempted to elude the *Rosario*, so Markham ordered his ship to chase it down. The *Rosario* managed to overtake it. Markham sent Navigating Lieutenant Benjamin Jackson aboard, where he discovered twenty-three natives stowed below deck, destined for a Fiji plantation. After the ship's captain provided Jackson with a licence signed by the Consul of Fiji and a certificate of registry, he concluded that everything appeared legitimate. He reported his findings to Markham, who ordered it to be released.

The next day, while at anchor at the island of Efate, the *Rosario* discovered five more suspicious ships. Jackson searched each one and found native labourers on all of them but the captains presented the appropriate paperwork required of the Polynesian Labourers Act, so the ships were left alone. While inspecting these ships, Markham encountered Ross Lewin, the most notorious man-stealer in the region. He had set up a large corn and cotton plantation on the island of Tanna, where he constructed a base surrounded by 4-foot-thick coral block walls guarded by his loyal native bodyguard. As much as he would have liked to have arrested Lewin, Markham had no authority to do so. Without providing much detail about this encounter, Markham briefly mentioned that the *Rosario*'s officers treated him 'with what our cousins across the Atlantic would call "scant ceremony"'.

While at Efate, Markham learned of an attack that had taken place on the schooner *Fanny* four months before. The *Fanny* had arrived at the island of Nguna on 9 July to return six native labourers who had ended their term of service and planned to replace them with six new recruits. The villagers attacked the *Fanny*'s crew rather than allow them to leave with any more of their people. For two days, the captain and his mate defended the ship. The mate died of wounds received, but the captain was rescued by the *Strathnavar* ten days later and reported the incident to the authorities.

Markham met with the Reverends Peter Milne and William Watt of the New Hebrides Mission when he arrived at Nguna. The clerics identified which villages were involved in the attack. On the morning of 14 November, Markham left with seven officers and thirty-seven sailors in three small boats and headed towards the closest village. The boats halted a few miles short of the village and Markham sent a messenger ahead to request an audience with its chief. He did not receive a reply, and after a short time advanced with twenty men into the village, which he found abandoned.

Markham and two officers were inspecting the huts when suddenly, several musket shots rang out from the woods. They could also distinctly hear the sound of men blowing into conch shells calling to rally more troops for a fight. Markham ordered the rest of his men up from the boats. He gave strict orders not to return fire, hoping that it would demonstrate to the natives that he came in peace and had no intention of fighting them. Still, they continued to fire on his men, so he ordered half of the village burned and his command to fall back. He sent a second messenger to find the chief with a promise to meet him unarmed at a place of his choice to further demonstrate his peaceful intentions.

After two hours went by with no reply, Markham advanced on the village for the second time and destroyed the other half of it along with several canoes. His men marched 2 miles along the coast in the direction of the second village identified by Milne and Watt. The whole time, his men were under sporadic gunfire from the natives, but they suffered no casualties. The sailors reached the other village and destroyed it too before returning to the *Rosario* that evening. Markham asked Milne to contact the chief after they left to tell him that had he met him and gave a reasonable defence for attacking the *Fanny*'s crew, and had the natives not fired on his sailors, he would have only inflicted a fine, instead of destroying the village and canoes. At around 1.30 pm the following day, before leaving Nguna, the *Rosario* stopped at the southeastern part of the island and fired a warning shell in the direction of some natives gathered on the beach to demonstrate their firepower and the futility of challenging the might of the British Empire.

On the morning of 17 November, the *Rosario* encountered a 256-ton brig flying the English colours along the southern coast of Malekula. Lieutenant Jackson boarded it, where he discovered seventy-six natives from the Solomon and Banks Islands destined for plantations on Fiji. He questioned the natives to determine if they had been kidnapped, and one of them held up three fingers and said something along the lines of 'three yam', which he interpreted as meaning that he had signed up for three years of service. Jackson reported to Markham that everything seemed in order with the *Carl*'s papers and its passengers and it was released.

Markham and Jackson could not have known it at the time, but only two months before, the *Carl*'s crew had committed one of the most appalling crimes in the history of blackbirding. The *Carl* had kidnapped roughly 100 natives from several New Hebrides Islands over the preceding weeks to sell them for the price of £3 a head. On 13 September, the captives fashioned spears out of the legs of their wooden bunks and planned to overtake the crew. For eight hours, Captain Joseph Armstrong's crew fired through the hatches at the natives 'huddled together like herrings in a barrel' as they fought to escape from the lower deck. The ship's owner, Dr James Patrick Murray – described as 'a monster in human shape' by Markham – was said to have been casually singing *Marching through Georgia* as he continued to load and fire his weapon through the night. By next morning, half the natives were dead and the remainder surrendered.

After enjoying a cup of coffee and glancing through his prayer book, Murray ordered the bodies of the dead dumped overboard. He handpicked sixteen of the most desperately wounded men – those unlikely to make a quick recovery and deemed worthless to a plantation owner – and had their hands and legs bound. He then ordered them to be pushed overboard. The crew whitewashed the ship and continued its journey as if the killing spree never happened. The natives questioned by Jackson were survivors from the massacre. The crew had coerced them into not speaking about the incident and had them rehearse holding up three fingers to satisfy any inquisitive naval officers that may question them.

When the *Rosario* next arrived at the western edge of the island of Aniwa, Markham observed several natives on shore waving branches in the air and holding up coconuts, branches of taro and bananas indicating that they wanted to trade. In need of some fresh provisions, Markham signaled to them his desire to trade. They boarded the *Rosario* and exchanged yams, taros, bananas, coconuts and breadfruit for calico, clay pipes and tobacco. The ship's visitors asked to see a demonstration of the Armstrong gun, so Markham ordered a shell fired at an elevation of 4,000 yards. At dawn the next day, Markham landed with a few officers and met the white-haired chief named Pelegatonga, whom he described as 'a wretched looking old imbecile, apparently suffering leprosy or some cutaneous disease', but as someone who 'seemed to entertain great respect and vernation'. Markham and his comrades returned to the *Rosario* that evening after being entertained by the chief, steaming westwards from Aniwa towards Nukapu.

On 29 November, the *Rosario* reached the heavily wooded, 2-mile-long island of Nukapu. A party of natives on the western shore waved branches above their heads gesturing peace. Several large sailing canoes then appeared and paddled towards the *Rosario*. Markham dispatched Jackson in a gig to meet the canoes. Before departing, Markham stressed to him that on 'no account' was he to open fire on the natives if they appeared to be hostile. Jackson's gig was unable to clear the 1½-mile coral reef that nearly enclosed the island due to the low tide, forcing it to return to the *Rosario*.

Markham ordered his ship to the northern end of the island, hoping to bypass the reef at its lowest point. Jackson held two white handkerchiefs in the air as he approached the shore dotted with natives. When within 100 yards, the natives suddenly unleashed a hail of arrows from their bows. Abiding by Markham's orders, Jackson turned back without firing a shot and returned to the *Rosario*. After a short while, Markham ordered Jackson to go back out again, hoping that the natives would realise that he came in peace. For a second time, the gig was met by arrows, and Jackson withdrew.

Markham chose to punish the natives for their hostility by burning their village just as he had done at Nguna. This effort would be more challenging since he would have to make an amphibious assault and drive off the natives before falling on the village. At 2.00 pm, he ordered three shells fired from his Woolwich and Armstrong guns in the direction of the canoes, hoping to frighten them off. The *Rosario*'s gunners then fired six shots in the direction of the village. This caused most of the natives to disperse into the undergrowth and woods or to seek shelter behind a 4-foot stone wall previously constructed to defend their village. The most courageous men chose to stand their ground during the bombardment, even shooting arrows in the direction of the *Rosario* and taunting their enemy.

At 3.30 pm, the tide rose enough for two cutters and two gigs loaded with sailors to clear the reef. One arrow bounced off Markham's pith helmet, while he was in the lead gig. When the boats reached the shore, the sailors hopped out and into the knee-deep water and stormed the village. After driving the natives back and clearing the village, the sailors ignited the bamboo and coconut leaf roofs of the huts and destroyed several canoes before returning to the ship.

Markham assumed that the natives suffered some losses during the brief engagement, but he had no way of knowing how many. He suffered two casualties, both the men hit by arrows during the landing – James Bryan in the left groin and left side of his chest, and Corporal William Marcus, his orderly, in the left arm. Corporal Marcus lingered for nearly a month until an infection killed him. 'He was a fine brave young soldier,' Markham lamented. '[H]ad he lived he would have been an ornament in his profession.'

The *Rosario* left Nukapu without gathering any information related to Patterson's murder and arrived sixteen days later at the island of Espiritu Santo. There Markham met the Reverend J. Goodwill of the New Hebrides Mission. Goodwill informed him that the crew of a blackbirding ship, the *Wild Duck*, had not been seen in at least a year. The next morning, Markham, Goodwill, two native interpreters and a detachment of sailors proceeded in boats along the west coast of the island to the village where the ship was last known to have visited. Markham ordered the men to remain behind in the boats while he advanced ahead with Goodwill, two officers and the two interpreters.

The men found the village deserted. The chief, with red paint smeared on his face and in his hair, and accompanied by a few men armed with clubs and tomahawks, reluctantly appeared from the bush. After being questioned by Markham about the *Wild Duck*, the chief admitted that they had murdered its crew for attempting to kidnap some of his villagers. They hid because they feared that the white men had come to seek revenge. Markham assured the chief that he did not intend to do them any harm, and asked him to point out the men's graves. To his horror, the chief told him that they had been eaten after being killed.

After consulting Goodwill, Markham decided to impose a fine of twenty-five pigs on the village. He told the chief that if they were unable to pay the fine, his village would be destroyed. After about an hour, the chief returned with only four pigs and the natives scattered in fear. After a couple hours of being unable to convince them to come back to the village, Markham ordered his men up from the boats and they set fire to the village and three large canoes. Before departing, he explained to the chief that next time they should take blackbirders prisoner and notify the missionaries of their crimes instead of retaliating. He hoped the punishment inflicted upon the villagers would rapidly spread along the coast so that it would prevent similar incidents from taking place.

Two days later, the *Rosario* stopped and investigated another blackbirding ship, the *Helen*. Jackson reported that the schooner was not cleared from its last port, had no licence to carry the seventeen natives it was transporting and could not present a log or record of its voyage. Markham boarded the ship and informed its captain, Kenneth McKenzie, that he felt justified in seizing his ship and sending him and his crew to Sydney to face trial. But the lack of faith he had in the Australian courts, and the acquittal of other blackbirding ships with even more damning evidence than this, caused Markham to allow the ship to continue on its voyage with its native cargo. He forced McKenzie to sign a written statement admitting to 'the illegality of his proceedings', which he could use in a court of law against him.

On 27 December, the *Rosario* reached the southwest end of the island of Aurora. Its crew noticed natives on the beach signaling that they wished to trade. Markham ordered the ship's paymaster, Shuldham S.C. Hill, to go ashore and acquire vegetables or fruit to replenish the *Rosario*'s stores. The sailors' salty diet lacking fruit or vegetables, combined with the unbearable heat – the ship was 95°F at times at the coolest spot on deck – left many of the crew ill. They desperately needed fresh provisions.

The *Rosario* remained less than a mile and a half from the shore as Hill negotiated with eight natives for provisions. He was offering beads in exchange for some coconuts when one of the natives pulled out his club and struck him in the back of the head. Before they scattered, Hill's assailant took another swing at him while he lay helpless on the ground to make sure that he had finished him off.

Markham ordered a shell fired at the perpetrators and sent a party of sailors to pursue them. The sailors were unable to locate them but burned their village. Markham also ordered the huts of a neighboring village burned, hoping that 'the inhabitants, in revenge of the loss of their houses, would themselves punish the scoundrel that had behaved so treacherously'. He attributed the attack to a young man trying to make a name for himself. Fortunately, Hill was still breathing when the sailors reached him and regained consciousness as he was being carried back to the *Rosario*. He had a large gash on his forehead and one above his right ear from the attack but made a full recovery.

The *Rosario* returned to the island of Nguna six weeks after their first visit. Markham again met Milne, walking with him to the charred remains of the village that they had burned. He met the village's chief, Marewatta, who admitted that the natives had murdered the *Fanny*'s crew after his wife was kidnapped by the blackbirding schooner *Donald McLean*. The chief described the girl as being albino. Markham saw this as an opportunity to make amends with the villagers. As a goodwill gesture, Markham agreed to visit the island of Tanna, where she was believed to have been taken.

When the *Rosario* reached Tanna, Markham, accompanied by Lieutenant Francis W. Sanders, rowed in a boat to a village located about 8 miles north of Port Resolution. There he interrogated two Englishmen living in the village, Bill Easterbrook and James Cooper. Both had worked on the *Donald McLean*. 'I found "Bill" to be a very stupid and thickheaded specimen of the genus homo,' Markham declared, 'from whom it was almost impossible to obtain any clear and truthful evidence concerning the practice of the labour vessels.' Easterbrook did confess to helping to steal Marewatta's wife from Nguna but refused to tell Markham where to find her.

By a stroke of luck, Markham spotted a pair of white feet sticking out from under a doorway of one of the huts while exploring the village. Using Easterbrook as his translator, he told the girl, named Lepolow, that he had come to take her home. On 9 January 1872, the *Rosario* delivered the young albino girl to Chief Marewatta. In a show of gratitude, the villagers showered the *Rosario*'s crew with as many yams and pigs as they could fit on the ship.

After a sixteen-week voyage, the *Rosario* was nearly out of provisions and Markham decided to conclude his cruise. He inspected all the ships he encountered flying the Union Jack and thoroughly investigated all the reported attacks on Englishmen. The *Rosario* arrived at port in Sydney on 8 February.

Markham presented his report to Stirling on the deportation of natives two days after his return. He had searched a total of sixteen ships transporting natives to plantations. Despite only encountering a few ships acting illegally, he saw the negative impact blackbirders were having among the islands. It led to the mistrust of whites and caused the natives to retaliate by attacking Australian ships and their crews. Besides being detrimental to the relationship with the natives, Markham found the trade to be immoral, concluding that it 'amounts to downright slavery, and in many cases, where blood is shed in a most wanton manner, to murder'. Something had to be done to thwart it. Markham advised Stirling how he thought best to accomplish this:

> The only way in which I see to put a check, for I believe it almost impossible to put a decided stop to this traffic, as it has now assumed such gigantic proportions, is by men-of-war repeatedly visiting the different islands, and for them to be empowered to seize all such ships as are unlawfully kidnapping the islanders, or are in any way infringing the rules laid down in the 'Merchant Shipping Act', and to bring to justice such men as Mr. Ross Lewin, who is openly cruising about in a whale boat, without flag of license, procuring labour for his own plantation in Tauna [Tanna].

While he severely criticised blackbirders in his report, Markham could have never fathomed that he would be condemned by the public just as the man-stealers he spent nearly four months trying to deter. Although he tried to remain as neutral as possible when dealing with the natives he encountered at the different islands, his conduct at Nguna and Nukapu came under fire in the press. It even attracted the attention of some Members of Parliament. He was not being criticised for burning the two villages at Nguna, but rather for indiscriminately firing his guns at the natives on the shore the day after. He gained greater censure for his actions at Nukapu, when he was accused of having gone there to revenge the murder of Bishop Patteson. The press portrayed him as a vengeful and murderous bully unsuited to handle the sensitive assignment he was tasked. The Australian paper *Mercury* even went so far as to claim that his name 'will henceforth be associated by Englishmen with all that is injudicious and reprehensible'.

It did not help his cause when the clergymen of the Melanesian Mission declared that they did not approve of his decision to go to Nukapu without an interpreter, which at the time, was unavailable. 'So soon as the services of an interpreter were unavailable,' the Reverend

Charles H. Brooke professed, 'the question we asked ourselves was this, "What good can they [the *Rosario* and its crew] do there? The enterprise is fraught with peril."' He believed that Markham was naïve to think that peaceful attempts to communicate with the natives at Nukapu would be reciprocated. He then asked, 'how could it be expected that these "bloodthirsty cannibals, etc., etc." could understand the friendly intentions of this huge thunderer? A flag of truce would probably have the same effect on them as a red rag has on an enraged bull.'

Although the missionaries did not approve of Markham going to Nukapu, they were convinced that he had not gone there bent on revenge. Brooke insisted that Markham 'left us without in the least degree contemplating vengeance on these natives'. Rather, he departed Norfolk with 'the very opposite idea of gaining their confidence and eliciting information from them'. Only after pacific overtures had failed did he assault the island. 'Nothing would grieve us more,' Brooke declared, 'than to think that Commander Markham, whose short visit here attached us all to him, should in any way, suffer wrongfully, as he does most assuredly when accused of having committed an act of retaliation for the murder of Bishop Patteson, than which nothing was farther from his intention.'

While there was some debate among the missionaries whether Markham should have gone to Nukapu in the first place, he received unanimous support from them for his conduct at Nguna. In August, a correspondent in *The Colonial Church Chronicle, and Missionary Journal*, using the pen name 'G.T.', praised Markham's 'zeal, tempered with moderation', stating that 'he united firmness with conciliation, and carefully avoided collisions with them [the natives], whenever it was possible'. At Nguna, Markham claimed he used 'rare forbearance' by not allowing his men to return fire. The next day, Markham ordered a shell fired in the direction of natives gathered on Nguna's shore, 'carefully avoiding all chance of doing the people any injury', only intending to demonstrate 'the range of the guns and the power of a man-of-war'.

On 25 June, Secretary John Kay, Convener and Secretary of the Foreign Mission Committee of the Reformed Presbyterian Church in Scotland, sent a statement to Parliament declaring that the committee unanimously concluded that the course taken by Markham at Nguna 'was upon the whole judicious, and that it will have the effect of repressing violence on the part of the natives of that island'. They asked 'that accusations which the Committee believed to be groundless may not be held over the head of a meritorious officer, who has, as they conceive, carried out the work entrusted to him with energy and discretion'.

Discrepancies in Markham's letter and despatches involving both incidents were another matter for contention. The Admiralty, incensed with the negative attention of Markham's cruise, ordered an inquiry to investigate if he had inflicted casualties on the natives at both islands. Vernon Lushington, Secretary to the Lord Commissioners of the Admiralty, wrote to Markham on 22 June scolding him for the 'embarrassing character' and the 'remarkable difference' between his earlier and later accounts of the events at Nguna and Nukapu. 'In these letters,' Lushington wrote, 'are passages which differ very considerably from accounts given in his despatches.' Markham wrote back asking the Lords Commissioners to clarify what discrepancies they were referring to. 'My Lords cannot but feel surprise,' Lushington replied, asking how he was '"unable to guess what particular points the charge of having uttered discrepancies refer" [Markham's quote from his original letter]'.

Lushington expanded on these points in his reply. In his despatch of the 25 November 1871, regarding the firing at the natives at Nguna on 15 November, Markham stated:

> I steamed close along the Island of Nguna and seeing a party of natives assembled near to one of the villages which we have destroyed on the previous day I threw a few shot and shell amongst them for the purpose of dispersing them as I had been led to believe that the natives were inclined to ridicule the power of a man of war, having been repeatedly threatened by the presence of one without having actually come into contact with one.

By 16 February 1872, Markham refined his original statement:

> With reference to paragraph 2 of my letter of 25 November 1871, I beg to state that the shot and shell discharged at the Island of Nguna was fired over the land for the purpose of frightening the natives, and

showing our power, and was fired in a contrary direction from their village. I am certain that no casualties occurred on that occasion.

He amended his response for a third time three months later:

> The reason I fired shot and shell at the Island of Nguna on the following day, was to show the natives that in an extreme case, it was in the power of a man of war to throw destructive missiles amongst them; but the missionary resident on the Island had taken the precaution of warning the natives of my intentions and therefore no harm was done of my second visit. The Chiefs assured me that was the case (I take this opportunity of explaining, that the word amongst in my original letter should have been over).

The Lords Commissioners also found noticeable contradictions in Markham's despatches and letters related to his attack on Nukapu on 29 November 1871. From his despatch of 12 February 1872, after having landed his men and burned the natives' village, Markham reported, 'Their loss would be difficult to ascertain though I fancy it must have been severe.' His letter of 16 May downplayed the natives' losses, stating that 'with reference to the last paragraph of your letter that in my letter of the 12 February 1872 I did not state that the loss among the natives must have been severe – my words here as follows. Their loss would be difficult to ascertain though.' He concluded this letter by stating that 'in all probability no loss of life was inflicted on these Islanders'.

The Lords organised a board of inquiry made up of Commodore Stirling and three other senior naval officers from the Australia Station to investigate these inconsistencies by interviewing the *Rosario*'s officers. Stirling, who headed the inquiry, had mixed feelings with how Markham acted at both islands. In a letter to the Admiralty dated 27 February 1872, he commended Markham for 'some of the steps he has taken' on his cruise and praised 'the diligence with which he carried out my instructions'. While he found Markham's decision to burn the village at Nguna for the murder of the *Fanny*'s crew 'proper', he admitted that 'I do not agree with him in regard to the firing at a body of natives'. He did not approve either of him attacking Nukapu, but understood Markham 'did not intend to attack the Nukapu Islands [*sic*] in retaliation for the Bishop's murder, and would not have fired upon them if they not had first fired upon him'.

The *Rosario*'s officers provided their testimonies to the board of inquiry on 3 September. Each man was asked if Markham had ordered the ship's guns fired at or near the natives at Nguna and if they appeared to have suffered any losses. Lieutenant Francis W. Sanders affirmed that Markham used rocks and trees located at about 1,000 yards off as targets, not the three or four natives in sight, and confirmed that all the projectiles struck these targets. He believed none of the natives could have been killed or wounded since they dispersed as soon as the shots were fired. Sub Lieutenant Archibald O. Hill corroborated Sanders's testimony. The Captain of the Guns (his name was omitted) declared that he received direction to fire 'at conspicuous objects on the shore'. He believed that no natives were targeted or hit by the shells. He wanted it noted in his testimony that the sailors 'were repeatedly fired upon without returning it' after burning the native village the previous day. When they visited the island two months later, he said 'no mention was made of any one having been killed or wounded'.

The officers also testified on the likelihood of native losses at Nukapu. Lieutenant Sanders stated that there was one specific instance when a shell burst over the native canoes, in which he said there was 'a probability of a loss of life', but then declared that 'no one was observed to fall'. Sub-lieutenant George Wilson, who was on the bridge of the ship, saw the same shell burst over the canoes, causing the natives to abandon them, but did not observe any casualties. Bombardier James Gliddon (Second Captain of the Guns), Midshipman James T. Daly, Boatswain Thomas Baskerville and Surgeon James L. Whitney gave similar accounts that the shell burst well over the canoes and the natives did not suffer any loss of life. Sub Lieutenant Hill, in charge of the landing boats, did not think any losses were inflicted during the bombardment and was the only officer who admitted that some natives 'must have been struck by the rifle fire' during the landing, but said he did not see any fall.

The testimonies were forwarded to Commodore Stirling at Sydney. After reviewing the statements, the board sent their final report to the Admiralty. The officers concluded that Markham did not give the proper order to ensure that none of the natives were killed or wounded at Nguna, but, more importantly, he did not purposely target them. The Captain of the Guns, who received the order to fire, was directed to aim his shots at trees and rocks, not the natives gathered on the beach. They scattered as soon as they heard the thunder of the *Rosario*'s guns. There was no way of knowing if the shell that burst over the canoes at Nukapu caused any casualties, but from what the board gathered from the officers' testimonies it concluded that 'the balance of evidence is against their having been injured'. They could not confirm either if any natives had been killed or wounded by rifle fire during the landing. None of the officers could be sure, and only one expressed concern that some natives may have been hit by the sailors' rifle fire.

Stirling added a few remarks to the board's report before forwarding it to the Admiralty. He expressed that after hearing the evidence 'that there was no party of natives in sight to fire at, and that no loss of life occurred at Nguna: I withdraw the expression of disapproval'. Even though he retracted his previous disapproval, he again stressed that 'it does not appear proper cautions were taken to ensure that no loss of life could occur when firing at the trees, rocks, etc.'. As for Nukapu, he said that Markham had 'acted within the spirit of orders' by going to the island but 'that it would have been better if he had waited for instructions' after hearing the report of Bishop Patteson's murder. Markham should have also refrained from sending Lieutenant Jackson's boat out again to communicate with the natives after being received in 'a hostile manner' on the first instance.

Lushington wrote to Markham on 20 November, forwarding him a copy of Stirling's report and the Admiralty's ruling:

> My Lords are glad to accept the conclusion of the Court of Inquiry, and of Commodore Stirling that probably no loss of life was inflicted on the natives of Nguna when shot and shell were fired by your order in passing that Island on the 15 of November last, and they also accept the view that probably the natives of Nukapu did not suffer in the encounter which took place on the 29 November.

While they praised him for acting with 'spirit', the Lords Commissioners scolded Markham for the inconsistent statements in his original reports and for not giving clearer directions to ensure that the natives at both places were not harmed. He had acted carelessly on both occasions. Lushington finished the letter by acknowledging that 'My Lords … have now the pleasure of approving generally of your proceedings in a service which their Lordships are well aware was one of more than usual difficulty'. Markham had dodged a bullet and escaped with his naval career intact. Still, the criticism he received troubled him enough to publish a book in 1873 titled *The Cruise of the "Rosario" Amongst the New Hebrides and Santa Cruz Islands, Exposing the Recent Atrocities Connected with the Kidnapping of Natives in the South Seas* giving an account of his cruise.

Markham could have avoided the embarrassment of an inquiry had he been mindful of the words he used in his letters and despatches and had he acted more cautiously. He should have given clearer directions to his men not to direct fire on the natives at Nguna, or avoided firing on them at all. The missionaries at Norfolk warned him to wait for an interpreter before heading to Nukapu but he imprudently decided to go anyway. He also unwisely proceeded to the island without alerting Stirling of Patteson's murder and waiting for his orders. His conduct at Nukapu made him appear to others as being obstinate and pugnacious.

In Markham's defence, he was following Stirling's vague orders for dealing with hostile natives and was acting in a manner he judged to be the most appropriate. To say that he intended to butcher the natives at Nguna or Nukapu, and had gone to the latter island to revenge Patteson, is an unfounded claim, especially after considering his overall effort to treat the natives fairly and to win their favour. He loathed blackbirders and saw them as a cancer in the region, and was sympathetic towards the islanders. He reasoned that it would have been 'unwise and injudicious' for him to have departed Nukapu once he was attacked without inflicting some kind of punishment for their contempt for the English flag. 'I feel confident that the punishment which was inflicted upon the islanders for the murderous and treacherous attack made on the boats of the "Rosario",' Markham declared, 'will have a most beneficial effect.'

Instead of having a beneficial effect on Nukapu, the assault kept white travellers away from the island for a decade. In 1885, an iron cross was erected there to commemorate Patteson's memory. One hundred and forty-seven years later, the natives of Nukapu are still haunted by these events. A formal reconciliation has been set for 2021 – on the 150th anniversary of Patteson's death – between the islanders and Bishop Patteson's relatives. Hopefully, this ceremony will close an unfortunate chapter in Pacific history.

Markham never returned to the Australia Station after being paid off at the end of his commission. Despite the negativity his conduct at Nguna and Nukapu generated, he was promoted to the rank of commander not long after. By the end of 1872, he came under the Arctic spell, as many other naval officers before him, and wholeheartedly devoted himself to the study of it. His efforts during the next four years would be focused on penetrating this uncharted and mysterious realm to bring greater glory to England.

Chapter 4

The Chosen Band

'It was, indeed, a proud moment for us as we witnessed this unmistakable demonstration, and felt that we, a small but chosen band, had been selected to carry out a national enterprise of such importance.'

Albert H. Markham, *The Great Frozen Sea*

Roughly 100,000 men, women and children passed over the decks of HMS *Alert* and HMS *Discovery* in the weeks before they departed from Portsmouth for the North Pole. Among the thrilled visitors were two of Queen Victoria's sons, the Prince of Wales and the Duke of Edinburgh, and the exiled Emperor Napoleon III's widow, Empress Eugénie, with her 19-year-old son, the Prince Imperial. Nearly everybody in England longed to see the ships that would shatter all the previous records set by explorers in the Arctic.

On 29 May 1875, the Lord Commissioners of the Admiralty – Right Honourble G. Ward Hunt, Lord Gilford, Sir Alexander Milne, Sir Massey Lopes and Vernon Lushington – arrived at Portsmouth. At 10.00 am, Admiral Sir George Elliot and Rear Admiral Sir Francis Leopold McClintock escorted the Lords to Captain George Nares's flagship, the *Alert*. The party was met by Captain Nares and his officers at the *Alert*'s gangway. Each of the ship's officers was introduced and the names of each sailor called out from the muster list. The Lords inspected every inch of the ship, accompanied by McClintock, Nares and his second-in-command, Albert Markham.

Pleased with his tour, Hunt stepped forward and gave the expedition his blessing, which was printed by the *Morning Post*:

Captain Nares … Your country is watching this expedition with great interest, and indeed I have never knew its interest so excited by any similar expedition. Whatever your success may be, and to what extent you may be successful, none of us, of course, can foretell. I am sure that you will all faithfully do whatever brave and prudent men can accomplish. I wish you God speed in your enterprise, and a prosperous and happy return to old England.

An hour before the ships departed, Nares received a telegram from Queen Victoria from her estate at Balmoral Castle. 'I earnestly wish you and your gallant companions every success,' she wrote, 'and trust you may accomplish the important duty you have so bravely undertaken.' Three packages arrived with her note, addressed to the three senior officers of the expedition – George S. Nares, Albert H. Markham and Henry F. Stephenson – containing various pictures, including her portrait. The officers hung the portraits of the queen in their cabins next to the ones they had already received from the Prince and Princess of Wales and Empress Eugénie. They served as a reminder of the importance and enormity of the task ahead.

By 4.00 pm, well-wishers crammed Portsmouth's waterfront and pier to catch a glimpse of the ships one last time. 'Thousands of excursionists arrived in Portsmouth in the course of the morning, there being the double attraction of the departure of the Arctic Expedition and a grand review of the troops at Southsea Common,' the *Reading Mercury* recalled. '[A]fter the review had taken place, every available spot which afforded a view of the *Alert* and the *Discovery* was filled by spectators.' A band dressed in scarlet lined the dock and played the Scottish tune *Auld Lang Syne* as the two ships steamed away. Thousands cheered and wished them 'Godspeeds'. The ships managed to navigate through the dozens of boats cluttering the harbour to wish them a final farewell. 'The water was literally covered for three miles out with one great flotilla of steamers, yachts, and every description of sailing and rowing boats,' the *Morning Post* observed.

For Markham, this was the greatest moment of his life. 'It was indeed a proud moment for us as we witnessed this unmistakable demonstration,' he indicated, 'and felt that we, a small but chosen band, had been selected to carry out a national enterprise of such importance.' Everyone involved, from the captain down to the cook, knew that they were part of something monumental. If they reached the North Pole it would be one of the greatest achievements in the history of exploration. 'I would not exchange [it] for any other appointment and double the pay,' Dr Edward L. Moss, the assistant surgeon on the *Alert*, wrote to his mother. 'Everyone on the *Alert* is of one mind. I think we have the prospect of working well together and "with God's help we will do our best".'

The government had not sponsored an Arctic exploration in the previous three decades owing to one of the worst naval tragedies in English history. In May 1845, Rear Admiral Sir John Franklin's crew of 129 men on two ships, HMS *Terror* and HMS *Erebus*, left England for the Northwest Passage and were never seen or heard from again. Their disappearance stimulated a decade-long quest by the government to find out what could have possibly happened to Franklin and his sailors.

The government finally called off the search after twelve years. Fifteen Royal Navy expeditions and many more privately funded expeditions were sent out and had little success besides locating a few relics related to Franklin and his men. These expeditions racked up huge bills, costing the government over £600,000. Besides the massive expenditure, these voyages jeopardised the lives of the men assigned to the ships by exposing them to disease and the dangers associated with Arctic travel. While they were unsuccessful in finding out what exactly had happened to Franklin and his men, the search expeditions did have one benefit: they led to huge strides in geographical and scientific discoveries. However, the Franklin disaster was a bitter pill for the government to swallow and they ultimately terminated funding for any Arctic expeditions for the foreseeable future.

The yearning to explore and conquer the Arctic lived on through Royal Navy officers, scientists and members of the Royal Geographical Society. Clements Markham and Admiral Sherard Osborn emerged as the movement's leaders and called for a renewal of the government's support of Arctic exploration in the years leading up to 1875. They spent this period lecturing and publishing papers on the benefits of Arctic exploration and the probability of an expedition's success.

Both men reasoned that a renewal of Arctic exploration would help to shape the character of Royal Navy officers. No major wars had taken place in a decade – the Crimean War was the most recent – and they saw this lull as harmful to the spirit of officers. Osborn argued that Arctic exploration would help to wake the Royal Navy 'from the sloth of routine and save it from the canker of prolonged peace'. Sir Rutherford Alcock, a diplomat in China and Japan, and President of the Royal Geographical Society (1876–78), declared that the same kind of heroism and courage found on the battlefield also existed on Arctic expeditions:

> We are, perhaps, too much in the habit of associating the word 'hero' or 'heroism' with the battlefield, the storm, and the fight that takes place either between bodies of men on shore or ships at sea, but I think very few will have through this bare narrative, unfilled up as it is, of the hairbreadth escapes, of the constant perils, of the marvellous adventures that these ships and the sledge parties have incurred, without feeling that it is a great mistake to limit the heroism to the mere carrying of a flag through storm and peril to victory.

These perilous encounters and hardships were just what Royal Navy officers needed to reinvigorate their spirits.

Rekindling Arctic exploration would reclaim the stature England once held in the field. The Swedes, Norwegians, Germans, Austro-Hungarians and Americans conducted their own Arctic expeditions in the years after English exploration waned, encroaching on English achievements in the field of exploration and overshadowing the exploits of their past explorers. By the 1870s, the United States had made substantial gains in the field. In 1853, an impulsive physician from a well-to-do Pennsylvania family, Elisha Kane, led an expedition up Smith Sound – the passage between Greenland and Ellesmere Island – along the western coast of Greenland. Eighteen years later, Charles F. Hall, a Cincinnati, Ohio, newspaper editor and blacksmith, followed Kane's lead and planted the Star-Spangled Banner at the latitude of 82° 16′ N, coming close to breaking Rear Admiral Sir William Edward Parry's 1827 record (82° 45′ N) of an explorer to reach the most northern latitude.

This rapid American encroachment left some in England unnerved and the leaders of the Arctic movement called for action. Osborn said that England needed to regain its 'rightful place once more in the van[guard] of Arctic discovery'. Sir Henry C. Rawlinson, a retired major general, Member of Parliament and President of the Royal Geographical Society

(1871–72 and 1874–75), expressed his regret that his country had slipped behind the Americans. 'England should do something more than look on and applaud, while others work,' he demanded. '[T]he time for urging renewal of these enterprises, which form so proud a page in our history, has now arrived.'

Although the Americans had success in the field, the English leaders of the Arctic movement maintained that their efforts had been largely bungled and these mistakes prohibited them from accomplishing even greater achievements. They attributed this to the Americans' poor preparation, inexperienced leadership, inadequate equipment and provisions, and lack of discipline among their crews. Osborn declared that the American expeditions were 'equipped by private persons without proper means, and without the advantage of naval discipline' and claimed that 'none of the brave Americans who have attempted to explore Smith Sound have even been sailors'. All these factors frustrated the Americans from obtaining greater success, maybe even reaching the Holy Grail of the Arctic: the North Pole. An English expedition made up of professional sailors led by resourceful naval officers would easily surpass the recent American achievements.

Osborn stressed that the deaths suffered during the Franklin expedition should not dissuade the government from sending out other expeditions. What had happened to Franklin's crew was an aberration. The proportion of deaths from climate and disease in the Arctic did not compare to the average death rate of sailors stationed in any other part of the empire. Osborn explained:

> In ten expeditions engaged in the search for Sir John Franklin, out of 1,878 men the percentage of death was only 1 in 7. This is lower than on any other naval station, and proves that the risk from climate and accidents which is run during an Arctic Government Expedition is not greater than that which the 'Challenger' will incur during her cruise round the world.

He guaranteed that the proper precautions would be taken on an Arctic expedition to protect the sailors from past mistakes and remove any chance of fatalities. Crews would set up supply depots to prevent starvation and numerous cairns would be constructed to mark their route. Fresh game would be hunted and lime juice added to the the sailors' diets so that scurvy outbreaks never materialised. Other advances in hygiene, such as making sure that the ships were properly ventilated and maintaining the physical and psychological well-being of sailors, would also contribute to ensuring the crew's vigour. Osborn promised that with these 'modern appliances, and by working in the light of former experience, there is no undue risk in Arctic service, provided that the expedition is under naval discipline and Government control'.

Despite the ardent campaign to obtain government sponsorship, the members of the Arctic Committee, appointed by the Council of the Royal Geographical Society to spearhead the Arctic movement, struggled to convince the English government to finance an expedition without hard evidence ensuring its success. The Arctic Committee needed to send an intelligent, inquisitive and daring naval officer to the Arctic to corroborate that an expedition would be safe, prove worthwhile and promise success. In 1872, Albert Markham eagerly offered his service for this assignment. He became fascinated with the Arctic after Clements Markham, Admiral Sherard Osborn and Commodore James G. Goodenough encouraged him to learn all that there was to know about this mysterious region. His connections to these men and study of the subject paid off, as he was selected to undertake this special mission.

Markham took leave from the navy in the summer of 1873 and accompanied a whaling ship, the *Arctic*, on its voyage to the icy Canadian waters of Baffin Bay and the Gulf of Boothia. The whaling ship did not have a licence to carry passengers, so Markham signed on as a regular crew member, relinquishing his naval rank and any luxuries that may have come with it. He served as a second mate, earning one shilling a month – less than the three teenagers serving on the ship – but received one penny for every ton of oil and one farthing for every ton of whalebone he helped to bring back. He planned to study whaling, take notes on the region's geography, and most importantly, observe the steamer's ability to navigate in the ice.

Markham specifically arranged to join the *Arctic* because of its commander's reputation for 'dash and enterprise'. William Adams was a well-respected captain and Markham felt confident that he would be willing to test the ship's mettle in the Arctic zone. The *Arctic*, a steamship of 439 tons with a 70-horsepower engine, was fortified with timber and iron to allow for it to easily crush through heavy ice. The ship's crew – described by Markham as 'a fine sturdy set of fellows' – was made up of fifty-five Englishmen, Norwegians and Scotsmen. When the *Arctic* left Dundee, Scotland, on 3 May, this would be its seventh trip to Baffin Bay.

While he praised the experience of the captain and his crew, Markham found the organisation and cleanliness on the *Arctic* absent. Its upper deck was always slimy, wet and cluttered with equipment. He wrote with disgust:

> Words cannot describe the filthy state of the whale-ship. The whole of the quarter-deck is covered with coal and whalebone; sawdust is sprinkled everywhere to prevent the men slipping in the slimy matter with which the deck is coated, and this, combined with the grease and coal dust, clogs and sticks to the soles of our boots, rendering it quite impossible to avoid bringing it down into the cabin.

When one of the boats returned from hunting whales, it was smeared with so much blood that he thought that it was painted red. He would never allow one of his ships to sink into such a foul condition, but he would have to tolerate it for the time being.

For most of the voyage to Baffin Bay and the Gulf of Boothia, Markham dedicated his time to note-taking, using his scientific instruments to record data, observing the condition of the ice, hunting wildlife and collecting botanical and geological specimens. He corrected several geographical inaccuracies on his maps and named an unrecorded cape after Admiral Osborn. He collected seventeen different types of Arctic plants. This was only a sliver of what could be achieved if a government-funded expedition was sent to the region for a period of one or two years instead of one summer.

Markham took part in the dangerous and gruesome work of hunting whales when called upon by the captain. When a crewman injured his foot, Markham took his place on a whaleboat and watched in horror as a whale came under fire from the boat's harpoons and three rockets and was brutally butchered. He took the place of David 'Davy' Deuchars, another injured steerer, on a second whale hunt. He pulled the boat alongside a whale pierced by three harpoons as it spewed blood from its blowhole and flailed about in the water. He failed to steer the boat out of the way before the distressed whale's fluke came crashing down, throwing Markham and another man into the freezing water. Weighed down by their heavy boots and jackets, the two men struggled to stay afloat until they were rescued by a nearby boat. If the whale's fluke had been a foot nearer, Markham would have been crushed to death.

Two months into their voyage, the *Arctic* encountered a fellow whaling ship, the *Ravenscraig*, off Admiralty Inlet (Nunavut), which carried survivors from ill-fated American ship USS *Polaris*. Fourteen crewmembers in two boats had been picked up by the *Ravenscraig* near the entrance of Smith Sound on 23 June. Dr Emil Bessels, Captain Hubbard C. Chester (the ship's first mate), Chief Engineer Emil Schumann and four other survivors from the *Polaris* came aboard the *Arctic* to clear some room on the crowded *Ravenscraig*. Markham viewed their arrival as a 'god-send' and relished the chance to question them on the conditions in Smith Sound. Bessels and the others told the English officer that they experienced little snowfall during the winter, that the temperature had been mild and there was an abundance of fresh musk ox along the coast. They claimed that they had encountered 'a very insignificant stream of ice', but their captain, Charles Francis Hall, had ordered them to halt their advance after his sailing master, Captain Sidney O. Budington, had advised him to turn back. Bessels was of the opinion that Smith Sound was the best, if not the only route, that an expedition could reach the North Pole.

From what he gathered from the survivors, Markham attributed Hall's mismanagement and lack of experience as the reason for the expedition's misfortune. 'He was thus in no sense a seaman, but rather an enthusiastic leader, depending on others to navigate his vessel and to render his discoveries useful,' Markham declared of the amateur explorer. The former blacksmith did a poor job selecting his crew, which Markham said consisted of an 'ill-assorted company, without zeal for discovery, without discipline or control, and in which every man considered himself as good as his neighbour'. Hall bickered with his junior officers, which created tension within his command. The American captain died under mysterious circumstances – he was rumored to have been poisoned – in November 1871, leaving Captain Budington in command, who ran the ship aground on Greenland. Even under pitiful leadership, the American expedition still progressed 250 miles up Smith Sound in these favourable weather conditions. This was encouraging news to Markham.

The *Arctic* returned to Dundee in the middle of September. During their four-month voyage, the crew slaughtered twenty-eight whales – furnishing 265 tons of oil and 14 tons of whalebone. They killed nineteen narwhals, twenty seals and twelve bears, and captured one bear cub, which they afterwards donated to the Clifton Zoological Gardens. But for Markham, the information he had gathered was far more significant than the fruitful haul made during the whaling cruise.

A year after he returned to England, Markham published *A Whaling Cruise to Baffin's Bay and the Gulf of Boothia, and an Account of the Rescue of the Crew of the "Polaris"*, supporting the Arctic Committee's argument that a well-organised English Arctic expedition under strong leadership would face little risk and promise many rewards. From the information he gathered from the survivors of the *Polaris*, Markham concluded that Ellesmere Island would offer the best prospect of setting up a winter base, making discoveries and providing a safe retreat for a crew should its ship become trapped in the ice. He witnessed how steam power had revolutionised Arctic exploration and how whaling steamers regularly reached high Arctic latitudes with ease. In the foreword of Markham's book, Osborn acknowledged that it had taken seamen of past generations 'years of toil and hardship' to reach these high latitudes, but now they 'were seen and visited by Commander Markham in a summer's holiday'.

Markham urged that an expedition should be dispatched to the Arctic without delay to take advantage of the ideal travelling conditions in Smith Sound. The ice would be weak, allowing a steamer to easily bore through it and make significant progress. 'Everything points to the ensuing year,' he concluded, 'as being the season for Arctic exploration.' A second mild winter like Hall's expedition experienced would guarantee that an English expedition would attain a higher latitude than any of their predecessors, perhaps even reach the North Pole. 'With a stout ship, and a well-organised and an efficiently conducted expedition,' Markham declared, 'there is no reason why that hitherto unapproachable spot, the North Pole, should not be reached in a couple of seasons.'

The leaders of the movement could lecture and publish books and articles promoting an Arctic expedition, but Albert Markham's cruise provided them with hard evidence to support these claims. 'The information brought home by Commander Markham,' Osborn reasoned, 'proves how right the Royal Geological Society has been in recommending Smith Sound as the route on which a Polar expedition should be sent, and shows at the same time how large a measure of success may be anticipated, as well as the comparative immunity from risk of life.' *The Spectator* concluded that if 'the gentlemen who are so perseveringly bent on an Arctic expedition' could win the government's support, Markham's book 'will prove most valuable' to their cause.

Markham's voyage and his subsequent book prompted the leaders of the Arctic movement to draft a memorandum proposing an expedition. They had a 'very satisfactory interview' when they presented the memorandum to Prime Minister Benjamin Disraeli on 1 August. They reasoned that with good discipline, careful planning, proper organisation, strong leadership, the advances in steam power and ideal weather conditions, the probability of a government-funded expedition ending in failure was nil. Disraeli, who had assumed power from William Gladstone six months earlier, saw an Arctic expedition as an opportunity to advance the glory of the empire, unlike his predecessor. On 17 November, in a letter addressed to the Royal Geographical Society, Disraeli announced that the government would pledge their support of an expedition for the first time in almost two decades:

> I have the honour to inform you that, having carefully weighed the reasons set forth in support of such an expedition, the scientific advantages to be derived from it, its chances of success, as well as the importance of encouraging that spirit of maritime enterprise which has ever distinguished the English people, Her Majesty's Government have determined to lose no time in organising a suitable expedition.

He agreed to grant them £100,000 to fund the enterprise. Osborn was indebted to Albert, afterwards admitting to Clements 'that the crowning arguments which turned the scale were derived from the voyage of Commander Markham to Baffin's Bay'.

Sadly, Osborn died of a heart attack on 6 May before he even had a chance to see English ships leave for the Arctic. 'The loss of its truest and wisest friend,' Clements Markham declared of the expedition's most vehement advocate, 'is a calamity to the Arctic Expedition.' The admiral left a lasting impression on Albert Markham, who later dedicated his book *The Great Frozen Sea: A Personal Narrative of the Voyage of the "Alert" During the Arctic Expedition of 1875-6* published three years after Osborn's death, to his memory. 'To the memory of Rear-Admiral Sherard Osborn, C.B.,' Markham wrote, 'who, while he lived, was the moving spirit in securing the despatch of the Arctic Expedition, and whose past deeds in the same field reflected a bright ray of hopeful light on those who strive to emulate his example whilst following in his footsteps ...' Osborn's premature passing luckily did not hinder the expedition in any significant way since preparations were already well under way at the time of his death.

Fifty-three-year-old Captain George Strong Nares was hand-picked to lead the expedition. Born in 1831, Nares joined the Royal Navy at the age of 14. Like Sherard Osborn and Clements Markham, he had distinguished himself in one of the Franklin search expeditions as a young officer. Best known for his scientific work, he surveyed and explored the ocean while commanding HMS *Challenger* during its voyage from December 1872 to December 1874. He was a level-headed, serious and brave officer. His obituary published in *The Geographical Journal* described his most admirable qualities in greater detail:

> He was in fact, himself a plain man in modesty, in quiet reserved nature and lack of fluency in speech, but he was essentially a man of action, of clear thought and quick decision, indefatigable, and unsparing of himself when work had to be done. His superiors deemed him a man of sound sense and good judgment, and those who served under him loved him for his equal temper, patience, and thoughtfulness, believed in him, and trusted him in all things.

Captain Nares received a memo from the Lords Commissioners announcing his selection and objective:

Sir, Her Majesty's Government having determined that an expedition of Arctic exploration and discovery should be undertaken, My Lords Commissioners of the Admiralty have been pleased to select you for the command of the said expedition, the scope and primary object of which should be to obtain the highest northern latitude, and, if possible, to reach the North Pole, and from winter quarters to explore the adjacent coasts within the reach of travelling parties, the limits of ship navigation being confined within about the meridian of 20° and 90° west longitude.

The men selected for the expedition were the finest sailors that could be found in the Royal Navy. Thousands applied for service but only 150 made the final cut. The average age of the sailors who took part in the expedition was 27 years old, while the average age of the officers was 32 years old. Each man had to undergo a rigorous examination of his age, height, character, constitution and temperament – the Admiralty favoured men 'of happy and genial disposition' to those who appeared to be 'morose and taciturn'. Some applicants were turned away for minor defects such as bad teeth – no man with bad teeth can eat a frozen biscuit – or old wounds. Each man was asked if he could sing, dance, play an instrument, or how he could contribute to the general cheerfulness of his comrades – critical for an expedition that would spend at least two or three years in the Arctic.

The final roster of the officers and staff of the *Alert* included Captain George S. Nares, Commander Albert H. Markham, Lieutenants Pelham Aldrich, Alfred A.C. Parr, George A. Giffard, William H. May, Sub Lieutenant George Le Clerc Egerton, Dr Thomas Colan, Dr Edward L. Moss, the Reverend Charles E. Hodson, Captain Henry Wemyss Feilden (naturalist), James Wootton (engineer) and George White (engineer). The officers and staff on the smaller *Discovery* included Captain Henry F. Stephenson, who had served with distinction in Pearl's Naval Brigade during the Indian Mutiny and commanded a gunboat during the Fenian raids in Canada, Lieutenants Wyatt Rawson, Lewis A. Beaumont, Robert H. Archer, Reginald B. Fulford, Sub Lieutenant Crawford J.M. Conybeare and the Reverend Henry W. Pullen. Markham brought along his 4-year-old black retriever, Nellie, who was raised on HMS *Sultan*.

The Lords Commissioners also granted Clements Markham special permission to accompany his cousin's ship as far as Greenland's Disko Island.

Most of the officers selected were familiar with one another from previous years of service together. Lieutenant Pelham Aldrich had served with Captain George Nares on the *Challenger*. Commander Albert H. Markham, Lieutenant Alfred A.C. Parr and Lieutenant William H. May had served on the *Victoria* in the Mediterranean Station a decade before. Lieutenant Lewis A. Beaumont had also served with Markham on the *Blanche* in the Australia Station. The familiarity of working together would have to make up for what the officers lacked in Arctic experience.

Nares, Markham and the six ice quartermasters Markham recruited in Dundee were the only men who had been to the Arctic before. Each ice quartermaster had spent fifteen years or more at sea, including 29-year-old Davy Deuchars, who had served alongside Markham on the *Arctic* during his whaling cruise in 1873. The rest of the sailors depended on the knowledge Nares and Markham gained from their past Arctic voyages to direct the expedition.

Of the two ships assigned to the expedition, the *Alert* was the more impressive vessel. The seventeen-gun sloop weighed 1,045 tons and had already seen three tours of service at foreign stations before being selected as the expedition's lead ship. The *Discovery*, a Dundee whaling ship originally known as the *Bloodhound* employed off the coast of Newfoundland, was purchased by the government for the expedition and pressed into service. The Lords Commissioners decided to change the *Bloodhound*'s name to something more appropriate for a ship slated to take part in the greatest Arctic expedition in England's history.

Under the supervision of the Admiral Superintendent of Portsmouth Dockyard, the renowned sledge explorer Sir Francis Leopold McClintock, both ships were converted to better handle the severe conditions they would face in the Arctic. The *Alert* was fitted with a 430-horsepower engine manufactured by Messrs Hawthorne of Newcastle, originally produced for HMS *Cygnet*. The ships were strengthened by affixing a thick 'doubling' of timber, defective beams replaced with sturdier beams, and extra iron brackets added to the ships' frames. The sterns and bows were covered with an inch-thick planting of wrought iron. Thick felting sheets called 'fearnought' were fastened on the interior lining of the planking of the ships to provide extra insulation for the winters to come.

Each ship was supplied with items to keep the sailors engaged and entertained to help them pass the time during the delays, long stretches of idleness and around-the-clock darkness they would face during the winter months. 'It is a very important point in an Arctic expedition to keep the men constantly employed and interested,' Markham warned, 'otherwise they would, more especially when their onward progress was checked, be subject to gloomy moods and fits of despondency.' The ships were provided with theatre costumes, a piano (on the *Alert*), an organ (on the *Discovery*), books, games, a magic lantern with slides, pictures, ice skates and a football. An anonymous warrant officer, having endured a number of Arctic winters himself, sent a small case with four bottles of punch and some old books and periodicals addressed to 'my friends on the *Alert*'. These items may have seemed insignificant at the time, but they would be a blessing in the months ahead.

Besides transporting their crews, the ships were crammed with provisions, equipment and coal. Blocks of preserved coal supplied from the Crown Preserved Coal Company of Liverpool, weighing anywhere from 28lb to 56lb each, were stockpiled in the bunkers. The *Alert* carried 5 tons of wine, 10 tons of bread, 85 tons of beef, pork, bacon, coffee, sugar, flour and preserved meats and 10 tons of pursers' stores. The *Discovery* carried half the amount of wine as the *Alert*, 9 tons of bread, and 78 tons of beef, flour, sugar, bacon, pork, coffee and preserved meats. Both ships were stockpiled with enough supplies to last for two to three years in the Arctic.

To the alarm of the authorities in Portsmouth, the ships began to sag in the water even before they were fully loaded with all the necessary supplies. It would be too dangerous for the ships to make the voyage across the Atlantic Ocean weighed down by the provisions. The Lords Commissioners purchased the *Valourous*, an old paddle-wheel sloop, to carry a portion of the ships' supplies and equipment. The *Valourous* would accompany the *Alert* and *Discovery* to the west coast of Greenland to replenish what the two ships had used while crossing the Atlantic. The old sloop, not fit to make the trip to the Arctic, would return to England after completing its mission.

The ships finally departed from Portsmouth in May. The voyage across the Atlantic to Greenland was slow and uncomfortable. The bad weather caused the ships to incessantly pitch for most of the voyage. 'Everything wet and uncomfortable,' Markham complained in his journal on 14 June. 'All the fouls [fowls] drowned.' During one of the rougher days, Markham's dog was thrown from the top of the companion ladder, severely bruising herself. Clements Markham, who slept in a storage room, had a 'nasty fall', leaving him battered and bruised. Albert sarcastically wrote that he was 'Getting use to this sort of life'.

Despite the poor weather and rough voyage, the men's morale remained high. On 2 July, Albert invited Clements, Dr Thomas Colan, Lieutenant William H. May, Lieutenant George A. Giffard and Sub Lietenant George Le Clerc Egerton for dinner in his cabin. They dined on mince pies, chicken soup, sardines and biscuits, and drank champagne and dry sherry. There was 'plenty of singing after'.

Two days later, the ships crossed the Arctic Circle. To celebrate reaching this northern latitude, Captain Nares ordered a supply of Samuel Allsopp's chestnut brown Arctic Ale to be tapped and served out to all hands on deck. (The 11 per cent ABV beer was specifically brewed for the expedition since it would not freeze easily.)

On 6 July, the ships reached Godhavn (Qeqertarsuaq), located on the island of Disko. The town had been established as a whaling base by the Danish government during the eighteenth century. Nares purchased fifty-five dogs from the Danish officials and hired three dog handlers, the Dane Nels Petersen, and two Eskimos, a man named Frederick and Hans Hendrick (previously employed by both Elisha Kane and Charles Francis Hall). After provisions from the *Valorous* were offloaded, the ship began its voyage back to England, joined by Clements Markham. 'He has been a most pleasant and instructive companion to us,' Dr Moss wrote. '[W]e all regret the necessity of his leaving us.'

The *Alert* and *Discovery* proceeded north along the western coast of Greenland in the direction of Smith Sound. Markham landed with a party of sailors and erected the first of many cairns and filled it with letters for loved ones back home. He left a letter for his cousin, which was published in the papers. 'We are all naturally much elated at our success so far, and quite count upon reaching 85° without any serious check,' Markham proclaimed in the letter. 'In a week's time we ought to be on "the Threshold of the Unknown Region", when our real work will commence; hitherto it has all been child's play.'

While the crews of both ships anticipated some obstacles the further they ventured north, the ice at the entrance of Smith Sound ended up being thicker and harder to break through than anyone had predicted. The pack ice – large chunks of drifting ice driven together into a continuous mass – was so thick that the men were able to walk between the *Alert* and the *Discovery*. The ships could only inch forward or wait for an opportunity to move through a lead (an open water passage through the pack ice). Their crews had to be cautious in these conditions to ensure that they did not collide with the many drifting floebergs, or massive pieces of sea ice. Markham somberly noted that the impenetrable wall was 'blocking up all passage to the North', far from the conditions that the *Polaris*'s crew had encountered two summers before. So much for easy travelling, mild weather and rotting ice.

Captain Nares lived in the *Alert*'s crow's nest as he guided his ships towards leads and tried to dodge the oncoming floebergs. He rarely came on deck, even to eat. 'Patience, combined with caution and perseverance, is an indispensable qualification,' Markham stated when describing the necessary traits of an Arctic explorer. He required a 'quick determination and an ever-ready eye' and 'must be prepared, when occasion offers, to make a bold dash'. Luckily, Nares possessed an even blend of these attributes and safely navigated his ships through these hazardous conditions.

Both ships reached the protection of an inlet near Cape Hawks on 4 August, where the crews spent about a week to get some much-needed rest. Markham described the scenery along the coast as being gorgeous. 'Such a scene, with all its surroundings,' he wrote, 'could scarcely be equalled in beauty, certainly not surpassed, even in sunny Italy.' Six days later, a football game was held between the crews of the two ships. Afterwards, Markham harpooned a walrus, and steaks were served that night among the *Alert*'s crew. All hands were put to work with saws and pickaxes when Nares decided to leave the inlet and resume the advance, cutting and chipping away at the ice encasing the two ships and blasting away the floebergs blocking their exit with gunpowder.

By 16 August, their progress was completely checked by the ice, so Nares and Markham rowed out to Cape Fraser to search for a lead. What Markham saw he described as a 'cheerless sight': icefields as far as he could see blocked the ships' route. The ice was too thick to cut through with saws or chisel away at with pickaxes. The ships would have to bore through it and hope for the best. They made little progress during the first three weeks since entering Smith Sound, advancing at a rate of less than a mile a day. At that rate, they would never reach the North Pole before winter set in.

Despite the obstacles they encountered, they also came across some unpredictable breaks. They discovered a decent lead around Cape Fraser, allowing them to squeeze through some decaying ice for a short while. When the ships met another wall of ice, they patiently waited for Mother Nature to offer them an opening. On 21 August, Nares spotted open water and headed straight for it, but his ships were unsuccessful since rapid-moving ice clogged their path and reduced their speed before the lead was sealed off. And just like that, their opportunity vanished. They returned to their anchorage and waited for another opportunity. Locating another lead, the ships steamed towards it, this time successfully boring through some weak ice and emerging into what Markham described as 'a magnificent' lead. This agonising process continued each passing day the further the ships advanced north.

At a place called Lady Franklin Bay, some of the men observed a large herd of musk ox roaming along the shore. Markham and a party of sailors landed and made a 'grand haul', bringing back 2,000lb of fresh meat to be dried out on deck and stored for the subsequent months. Confident that fresh meat was abundant in this location, Nares ordered the *Discovery* to set up its winter quarters. The *Discovery*'s camp would serve as a secondary base in case the *Alert* suffered a disaster as it continued to push ahead. Saying their farewells and exchanging cheers with the *Discovery*'s crew, the *Alert* pressed on towards the North Pole.

By 30 August, she was fenced in by floebergs ranging in size from 80 to 100 feet, while below, the men could hear the eerie sound of the ice squeezing her hull. Markham admitted that the sound was 'anything but pleasing to listen to'. The thought of being shipwrecked was not far from his mind. Despite the increasing obstacles, the *Alert* 'bored, rammed, and jammed' its way through the pack inch by inch. On 1 September, the ship reached a greater northern latitude than achieved by their predecessors. At noon, the ship's colours were hoisted and the men celebrated their accomplishment. Markham declared that this feat was 'a red-letter day in the annals of naval enterprise, and indeed English history'.

Hidden behind the men's gratification was a sense of disappointment. Reaching the North Pole this late in the year would be impossible, even suicidal. The temperature had dropped to -24°F, the coldest the men had experienced since entering the Arctic Circle. Winter was fast approaching. The ice was far too thick for them to continue on.

Nares called off the advance and decided to set up their winter camp, not willing to risk the lives of his men to gain a few more feet. The captain settled on the northeastern tip of Ellesmere Island – dubbed Floeberg Beach – as the location for the *Alert*'s winter camp. 'It is difficult to imagine a more desolate position to pass a winter than the one in which we were placed,' Markham wrote of the site Nares chose for their camp. Beyond the sounds of breaking floebergs and gusts of wind, he described it as a 'solemn, and motionless' wasteland.

Nares planned to use Floeberg Beach as a base to send teams out to explore the region and to gather scientific data. On 11 September, the first man-hauling sledge parties departed to begin depositing provisions, equipment and boats at depots in preparation for the spring and summer sledging expeditions. All the men assigned to these sledges, regardless of rank, wore the same outfits – sealskin suits, wool guernseys, caps and mooseskin boots pulled up to their knees – and carried identical equipment. Leather could not be used in the Arctic since it hardened like stone as soon as it was exposed to the freezing conditions. The sealskin suits stank, but they were effective at shielding the men from the frigid temperatures and frostbite.

Captain Nares was the only man on the expedition who had previous sledging experience. He warned his crews before leaving England, 'that if they could imagine the hardest work they had ever performed in their lives, intensified to the utmost degree, it would only be as child's play in comparison with the work they would be called upon to perform whilst sledging'. Despite not having hauled a sledge in nearly two decades, Markham stated that the men profited 'to a very great extent by the knowledge and experience of Captain Nares'. The men also relied heavily on the advice given to them before they left Portsmouth by master sledge traveller Rear Admiral McClintock, who had not hauled a sledge since the 1850s.

Nares placed Markham in charge of two sledges made up of eighteen men under the command of Lieutenant Parr and Sub Lieutenant Egerton. After only four days away from the ship, Markham's men returned exhausted, battered and afflicted with snow blindness. Nothing could have prepared them for the suffering that they endured: their shoulders ached and legs felt like rubber; hunger gnawed at their guts; and freezing gusts of wind, unbearable as they already were, caused pointed bits of ice to leave painful gashes on their faces. Markham's party crawled back to camp in early September with two men, Daniel Harley and John Shirley, bundled on the sledges after collapsing from fatigue.

Ten days after his return, Nares sent Markham out for a second trip to establish a depot as far north as he could reach. On the morning of 25 September, Markham, Parr and Lieutenant May left with twenty-one men and three sledges loaded with 1,500lb of pemmican and bacon to last for twenty days. Only 1 mile out, Parr's sledge fell through the ice and began to slide into a pool of water. The men from the other sledges rushed over and grabbed hold of the sledge before it was completely submerged, and after a fifteen-minute struggle, managed to pull it back to solid ground. Everything on the sledge was soaked, so Parr returned to camp and restocked it with dry equipment before rejoining his comrades. Another 3 miles out, the same thing happened to Markham's sledge, saturating some of its gear and provisions and increasing its overall weight. But instead of wasting more precious time by returning to retrieve dry equipment and rations, Markham pushed on.

On the third day away from the *Alert*'s camp, Markham's party encountered a 2-mile-wide field of ice ridges. His men had to unload their equipment and provisions and carry each item over the ridge one piece at a time. It started to snow and continued for the next ten days, causing it to accumulate each ensuing hour and forcing the men to dig a path so that they could drag the sledges.

By 4 October, half of their provisions remained so Markham halted their advance to establish the expedition's northernmost depot. His men offloaded 870lb of pemmican and 240lb of bacon at a place they christened Cape Joseph Henry. On their return journey, they passed over a range of snowy hills – appropriately dubbed 'Frostbite Range'. Here they frequently sunk into crevices concealed by snow, causing their feet to become drenched and frostbitten. The only way to restore circulation in their frostbitten limbs was by rubbing the infected area and dressing it with glycerine ointment and lint. One of May's big toes became so badly frostbitten that it had to be amputated. As the days became shorter, indicating the approach of winter, and the temperature dropped, the sledges raced to get back to the *Alert*'s camp.

Markham's men were in poor shape when they finally returned to base. More than half were placed on the sick list and some of them had to have frostbitten toes amputated. Nares allowed them to rest for a few days and ordered an extra ration of musk ox meat added to their meals to help restore their health. 'The pleasure of a warm bath and the enjoyment of brushing one's hair are beyond all description,' Markham declared after being away for twenty days from the ship.

He felt that the experience they gained immensely benefitted the men, despite their suffering and a few losing toes. 'From the autumn travelling,' Markham stated, 'we derived much useful experience, which materially assisted us in our operations whilst organising and equipping the sledges for the spring campaign.'

When the remainder of his sledge teams returned to camp, Nares ordered that the *Alert* be winterised for the forthcoming season. Awnings made of the same material used to cover wagons were stretched over the upper deck of the ship to shield it from the wind and snow. On 11 October, the sun vanished for the season. Lanterns were strung up on deck to light the ship. Hanging ropes were tied together to avoid the sound of them banging against the spars, a tormenting noise the men nicknamed the 'devil's tattoo'. Snow was packed on the upper deck to insulate the inside of the ship. A 4-foot-high snow wall was constructed 6 feet from the ship and snow was packed in between the area to further insulate the inside of it.

The crew unloaded the ship's provisions on shore and constructed 'halls' out of the wooden casks and cases. 'Everyone [is] seized with a mania for building new houses,' Markham declared. '[Q]uite a settlement [is] springing upon shore. Large enough almost to be denominated, in America, a city.' The supply of salted beef was stored in 'Deptford Hall'. Another hall built to store the powder was named 'Woolwich Hall'. To store the sails, ropes, sledge gear and other random articles of equipment, the crew built 'Markham Hall' and named it in honour of the expedition's second-in-command. 'It was altogether a very grand edifice,' Markham proudly wrote of the structure, 'and we were, and I think with some reason, very proud at the result of our architectural skill.'

Observatory halls were constructed and connected to the ship by a 120-foot snow trench to store the scientific instruments and collect data. Markham and Lieutenant Giffard patiently watched, adjusted and jotted down the instrument's measurements in the magnetic observatory. The officers generally put in nine hours a day, regardless of the weather or temperature outside. On more than one occasion, Markham and Giffard became imprisoned by snowdrifts that obstructed the observatory's door, forcing them to crack the framework to break free. After heavy snowfalls, they had to cut a path through the trench to reach the observatory hall to begin the day's work. By no means experts in the handling of these sophisticated instruments, Markham and Giffard sometimes spent days taking observations, only to find out that their recordings were useless because the equipment had not been properly set.

Nares and his officers went to great lengths to look after the crew's physical and psychological well-being during the winter months. Some of the negative side effects of wintering in the darkness, lingering in high latitudes and dwelling in cramped quarters for long periods, described by Dr Lawrence A. Palinkas and Dr Peter Suedfeld in their 2008 study on the psychological effects of past expeditions to the Arctic, include fatigue, headaches, boredom, reduced motivation, intellectual inertia, gastrointestinal problems, rheumatic aches, sleep deprivation, diminished alertness, interpersonal tension and conflict, anxiety and irritability – all symptoms that can be detrimental, or even deadly, to an Arctic expedition. Even in 1875, the officers of the *Alert* were aware of some of the adverse effects of long-term exposure in the Arctic and took precautions to make sure that the men were protected.

The officers maintained a healthy diet among the crew to help prevent sickness and ensured that the men remained physically fit. One pound of fresh meat (musk ox or sheep) was given to each man twice every two weeks. Lime juice, mixed with sugar and water, was also issued and swallowed in the presence of an officer to prevent scurvy. Nares ordered each man to spend at least two hours a day outside the *Alert* to get a sufficient amount of exercise. Most of the sailors were assigned to work outside the ship for at least five hours a day anyway. A half-mile path was cut along the ship, marked at every 2 or 3 yards by a small heap of empty tins placed there by Dr Colan, so that the men could stretch their legs or get away from their comrades for a short while by pacing the track. Taking Nellie, or accompanied by a fellow officer, Markham made it a habit to walk the track almost daily, beginning in December. Unable to stay cooped up indoors for long periods, he also went on long 'rambles' of 5 or more miles, regardless of the temperature outside – even when it dropped to -61°F.

Keeping the men mentally engaged was equally as important as keeping them healthy and physically fit. Classes were held in the evening each day from November to February on the lower deck. Each 'class' sat at a different mess table. The ship's officers taught courses on reading, writing, history, arithmetic and navigation. Markham taught writing, dictation and reading. The four men who could not read or write, known as the 'cripples' – only two of them were English, while the other two, Petersen, the Danish dog handler and interpreter, and the cook, a native of Gibraltar, Duminick – were taught English by Dr Colan.

To ward off melancholy, special programmes were held every Thursday, dubbed the 'Thursday Pops'. These programmes consisted of plays, magic lantern exhibitions, lectures, readings, songs and music. Sub Lieutenant Egerton and the sailors with the best voices sang during some of the programmes. Lectures were given by Captain Nares, Commander Markham, Captain Feilden, Dr Moss, Engineer White and Lieutenant May on such diverse topics as astronomy, magnetism, steam power, geology, paraselene, the Spanish Armada, Arctic plants, hydrostatics and sledging. Feilden used magic lantern slides with his lecture on geology.

The most popular lecture was Nares's account of his past sledging experiences.

Plays performed by the 'Royal Arctic Theatre' were the most anticipated form of entertainment during these winter months. Lieutenant Giffard and Robert Symons operated the ship's printing press and issued programmes the Wednesday before each event. 'Much effort was put into the costumes,' Markham wrote, 'and the men spent much time rehearsing in their cramped cabins.' He acted in some of these plays, such as the last dramatic of the season, a burlesque written by the Reverend Pullen titled *The Little Vulgar Boy*. His character was listed on the programme as 'Mr. Brown, an old buffer, slightly green'.

Birthdays and holidays helped to further break the monotony. Two elaborate bills of fare were printed for the dinner held on Trafalgar Day (21 October). Lieutenant Aldrich sketched the *Alert*'s winter camp and a scene from the Battle of Trafalgar, adding the motto 'England expects every man to do his duty!' to the menus. To celebrate the memory of his favourite naval hero, Markham distributed a ration of beer to his men that evening. On 5 November, an effigy representing Guy Fawkes was stuffed with squibs and its face smeared with tar. The men dragged the dummy on a sledge around the ship as they played the *Rogue's March* on the drum and fife before taking it to a neighboring hummock and lighting it on fire to observe Guy Fawkes Day.

They held nothing back for the Christmas celebration. Markham described the lower deck as being 'very pretty and tastefully decorated'. Duminick fixed musk ox and mutton for the feast. Dinner was followed by singing and dancing until 10.30 pm. Afterwards, the men opened up gifts and read Christmas cards made by the ladies of Queenstown. To make it appear as if they had actually been delivered in the mail, a postage stamp was attached to each envelope. For a time, each man momentarily forgot that he was confined to a frozen prison over 1,000 miles away from his loved ones.

On New Year's Eve, Markham wrote the longest journal entry of the year. He praised what the expedition had accomplished so far and what could still be gained, but regretted their failure to reach the North Pole:

So passes the year 1875 – that it has been eventful, no one can gainsay – the British flag has been carried, both afloat and onshore (not forgetting the ice) to a higher northern latitude than has been attained by civilised man. It is perhaps disappointing to think, that so far as the Pole is concerned, our future labours will be unsuccessful, but we have a glorious future before us, the exploration of unknown regions where mortal foot, so far as we know, has never trodden, but in which valuable observations in the interest of science in general, will be made and important results accrue – and then – return to those who will be anxiously expecting us and hope for our return. We cannot regard the past year as one thrown away, a victory has already been achieved, and we all are ready and anxious to follow it up and gather fresh laurels ...

Since the expedition failed to reach the North Pole in 1875, Nares would instead turn his efforts in the spring and summer of 1876 to collecting scientific data and specimens and mapping Ellesmere Island's interior and coastline. The *Alert* may not have been able to reach the North Pole by ship, but Nares planned to send a sledge team on foot to come as close as possible to it. But these plans would have to be put on hold until the weather conditions improved and the sun resurfaced, liberating the *Alert*'s crew from the bone-chilling temperatures and enduring darkness.

Chapter 5

Into the Arctic Unknown

As we call to mind that joyous sight
On an April morning cold and bright,
When a chosen band stepped boldly forth
To the unknown west and the unknown north;
And we from our haven could only pray—
'God send them strength for each weary day!'

Stanzas from a poem composed by the
Reverend Henry W. Pullen of HMS Alert

The year 1876 started off terribly for the English sailors trapped on Floeberg Beach. The temperature averaged a record low of -70.52°F during the first four days of March. On 4 March, it fell to -74°F, the lowest temperature the men experienced since their arrival. Markham, who continued to go out on his daily walks despite these awfully low temperatures, had one of his big toes frostbitten but fortunately he was able to save it. Whisky and rum froze and chloroform turned into a jellylike substance. The men struggled to catch their breath and suffered from malaise. It was unlike anything that they had faced before.

They had not seen sunlight in months, something they had always taken for granted before coming to this desolate region. On 28 February, Markham recalled the crew's disappointment when the sun failed to reappear as expected:

A general holiday, a day of excitement, (it doesn't take much to interest us now) and a sad disappointment. All hands went to welcome the return of the 'Prodigal Sun', but it would not be welcomed ... the Captain and myself took a long walk to the S.W. [southwest], between 10 and 12 miles, in the hope of seeing the sun but like the rest were disappointed.

On 3 March, some of the men detected the sun's rays peeking over the snowy mounds to the south. Three days later, sunlight completely enveloped the *Alert*'s deck for the first time in 142 days. Within days of the sun's return, the men started to regain the color in their ashen faces and their eyes began to adjust.

Most importantly, the sun revitalised the *Alert*'s crew and they began preparations for the spring/summer sledge expeditions. Three teams would be sent out in April: two from the *Alert*'s camp, and one from the *Discovery*'s camp. Lieutenant Aldrich and his sledge team would explore the west coast of Ellesmere Island. Lieutenant Beaumont, from the *Discovery*'s camp, would take a sledge team to explore Greenland. Commander Markham and Lieutenant Parr would take their sledge team north with orders 'to attain the highest north latitude possible; and to ascertain the possibility of a more fully equipped expedition reaching the North Pole'.

Of the two teams leaving the *Alert*'s camp, Markham's men would be at the greatest risk since they would be trekking over the polar pack and travelling the furthest distance. Nares feared they might be cut off or drowned if the ice began to melt before their return. If Markham experienced any shift in the pack, Nares wanted him to immediately head for land to avoid risking a disaster. The captain was also aware of the difficulty of moving over this rugged landscape, recalling that William E. Parry's team averaged about 3 miles a day when travelling over similar ground in 1827. 'The journey on which you are about to engage is therefore a far more arduous one than arctic journeys usually are,' Nares warned his second-in-command. 'The heavy nature of the ice across which you have to travel has hitherto baffled all attempts made to cross it, and the formidable obstacles it presents at present, while stationary, must be considerably increased once it is in motion.'

The sixteen men assigned to Markham were divided between two sledge teams as listed below. (Clements Markham provided the biographical information about each crewmember.)

Markham's Command

'Marco Polo' Sledge Team
Commander Albert H. Markham (34 years old)
Thomas Joliffe (A native of Portsea, 32 years old, married with one
   child)

Daniel Harley (Born at Madras, India, 26 years old, married, received a medal for his service in General Garnet Wolseley's Ashanti Expedition, 1873–74)

Thomas H. Simpson (A native of Kent, 24 years old)

William Ferbrache (A native of Jersey, 23 years old)

Thomas Rawlings (A native of Portsmouth, 32 years old, married with one child, a former shipmate of Markham's on the *Blanche*)

John R. Radmore (A native of Faversham, 32 years old, married)

John Shirley (A native of Landport, 34 years old, married with four children)

Alfred B. Pearce (A native of Surrey, 26 years old)

'Victoria' Sledge Team

Lieutenant Alfred A.C. Parr (27 years old, Markham's second-in-command)

John Hawkins (A native of Bristol, 33 years old, married with four children)

Reuben Francombe (A native of Oxfordshire, 25 years old, married)

George Winstone (A native of Gloucestershire, 29 years old)

Edward Lawrence (A native of London, 25 years old)

John Pearson (A native of Hastings, 25 years old)

William Maskell (A native of Essex, 22 years old)

George Porter (A native of Birmingham, 26 years old)

Markham tried to achieve a flawless distribution of weight and supplies on his sledges. 'The question of weight is one requiring the closest attention,' he explained. He knew that Parry had failed to go further because his men were overburdened with equipment and lacked the necessary provisions to last very long away from their base. Everything from cooking utensils, pemmican and bacon rations, medicine, clothing and camp equipment that needed to last for at least two months had to fit on these sledges. Taking too much of one thing or not enough of another could lead to failure or a catastrophe. Markham had the sledges packed, rearranged, weighed and reweighed to ensure that his men would not be overexerted by carrying too much weight, while also making sure that they would not starve.

Abiding by Nares's warning about advancing over the frozen pack, Markham loaded two 20-foot boats on his sledges. 'It was, therefore, not only a measure of prudence, but one of absolute necessity,' Markham stated, 'that the party destined to travel over this frozen ocean, should be provided with the means of safety to themselves, if a disruption should take place at an earlier period than was anticipated.' The boats would be used to ferry the men, equipment and provisions from one block of ice to the next in the event that the pack started to melt. The downside to taking the boats was the extra weight they added to the sledges and place they took of other essential supplies.

Markham did what he could to prepare his men to face snow blindness. This debilitating affliction caused painful burning to the eyes and temporary loss of sight. He allowed his men to paint the backs of their jackets with brightly coloured animals and crests and mottos to help relieve the strain on their eyes from the featureless white wasteland. They also painted the hulls of the two boats with roses, shamrocks, thistles and the Royal Arms. 'The design of these devices or crests were left entirely to the artistic imaginations of the men,' Markham declared. To prevent exposure to the sun's ultraviolet rays, the men wore goggles made of tortoiseshell. He only permitted his men to remove the goggles when they were safely inside their tents for the night.

Markham looked for ways to improve his equipment. He tested the cooking instruments to see how long it took to fix a meal after setting up camp and the fuel they expended. One of his men, John Shirley, fashioned his own device that he proposed could cook faster than the old one Markham had planned to take. Markham was enthusiastic to test Shirley's instrument. However, after multiple trials, he found the timing of Shirley's device off and too unpredictable. 'I have come to the conclusion that we gain little or nothing on the older ones,' Markham wrote of Shirley's design. Despite this result, he refused to give up trying to find a better solution. '[W]e must see what we can do by the way of improving them.'

None of the sledge expeditions took with them the dogs Nares had purchased in Greenland. The officers were not impressed with how they had performed the previous autumn. The dogs struggled to pull the sledges through the snow when it was more than 12 inches deep, and if the sledge received the slightest check, the dogs would lie down until the obstacle was removed or the sledge was carried over by its crew. Markham said the dogs were 'invaluable' for short trips but 'it is almost impossible to use them for long journeys'.

The dogs suffered from a mysterious rabies-like disease that made them a liability. The illness caused them to undergo five-minute seizures, roll on their sides, foam at their mouths and urinate in a 'spasmodic manner'. After this debilitating attack ended, the dogs would run around in a frenzied state, sometimes charging off into a blizzard never to be seen again or rushing into the water only to drown. Dr Colan spent a considerable amount of time investigating these strange attacks but was unable to find a remedy. The sledge officers could not risk the dogs slowing down their progress, so they chose instead to rely on men, rather than dogs, to pull their sledges.

Markham routinely drilled his outfit in the weeks preceding their departure to boost their speed and efficiency. He took the *Marco Polo* and *Victoria* out on short 1 or 2-mile practice runs, on a long 7-mile trip and sent them on another occasion to deliver provisions to the *Discovery*'s depot at Cape Rawson. Markham did all of this to build each team's stamina, get them accustomed to travelling in their gear and using their equipment, and to better acquaint them with working together. He noted with satisfaction in his journal after a day's hard work: 'A good day ... for the "Boys"'. The men also frequently practised setting up camp, to make certain they could instinctively assemble and dismantle it at a moment's notice. Markham refused to risk failure or a disaster because his men were unprepared.

On 8 March, Sub Lieutenant Egerton, Lieutenant Rawson and the Dane Petersen prepared to take another sledge, the *Clements Markham*, pulled by nine dogs, 70 miles to communicate with the *Discovery*'s camp for the first time since they had last made contact. What transpired was not exactly encouraging for Aldrich's and Markham's own sledge expeditions. The dog sledge's departure was postponed for four days since the temperature suddenly dropped to -58°F. It returned only three days after leaving because it was hindered by brutal winds, immense snowdrifts and frostbite. On the sledge lay the 38-year-old Petersen, frostbitten and quivering in pain. Markham described him to be 'utterly prostrate and helpless'. Dr Colan had no choice but to amputate both of Petersen's feet; two months later, he was dead.

On 3 April at 11.00 am, Markham's and Aldrich's men stood to attention for inspection before heading out on their expeditions. A total of fifty-five men bundled in snowsuits lined up next to seven sledges to receive the blessing of the Reverend Pullen. He led the men in prayer, and they joined him in singing the hymn *Praise God, from whom all blessings flow*. On the preceding Sunday, Pullen gave a sermon comparing the challenges they would face to the march of the Israelites to the Promised Land. For most, it would be the greatest challenge of their lives.

Each leader had a unique silk standard attached to his sledge. Markham's had the lion of St Mark embroidered on it. He had a motto from William Shakespeare's play *Macbeth* engraved on the standard's staff: 'I dare do all that may become a man; Who dares do more is none.' It was a fitting saying to embody his willingness to do anything within his power to carry out his mission.

The sledge teams had orders from Nares to proceed together until they reached Cape Joseph Henry, 40 miles northwest of the *Alert*'s camp. This was the last depot both teams would encounter before heading off into the Arctic unknown. From there, they would split up, Markham continuing north and Aldrich turning west. Support sledges – the *Bulldog*, *Alexandra*, *Bloodhound* and *Poppie* – would accompany them to the depot to transport extra provisions so that Markham's and Aldrich's teams would limit the use of their own provisions. The extra hands from the support sledges would also help Markham's and Aldrich's men scale the barrier of floebergs aligned along the coast.

Nares and the remaining officers of the *Alert* wished the sledge crews good luck and Godspeeds as they disappeared over the horizon. Progress from the start was slow since the snow was deep and soft, making dragging the sledges tedious and exhausting. The men were forced to 'double-bank' – pulling one sledge ahead a short distance, then returning to repeat the process with each sledge in succession. This laborious process meant that for every 1 mile they advanced, they actually trekked 5 miles. The Arctic's unforgiving climate and terrain have a way of crushing the spirit of even the most resilient man.

Only five hours after leaving the *Alert*'s camp, the men began to complain of cramping, stiffness in their legs and thirst. It was nearly impossible to keep the water in their tin bottles from freezing. Even though they were surrounded by ice and snow, Markham prohibited his men from eating it since it would lead to frostbite on their lips and faces. They could only take a drink when they stopped to eat and were able to boil the snow. They might as well have been stranded in the Sahara Desert. Markham halted early that evening at 5.30 pm, the sledge teams having completed 6 miles that day, hoping this would give them a chance to rest and recuperate in preparation for the hard work ahead over the ensuing weeks.

For an entire week, the sledge crews worked eight to ten hours a day in temperatures well below $-30°$F. They could not tear or bite through their bacon rations, so they had to defrost them in a pannikin of warm tea, which turned them into an unappetising soup. Any of their cloth articles, such as sleeping bags or tent robes, became stiff as a sheet of metal and had to be thawed. Some of the men started to suffer from frostbite. One of the supply sledges, the *Bloodhound*, had to turn back when a man fell seriously ill. Despite the efforts to prevent it, Markham and Parr suffered from snow blindness, and Dr Moss, who commanded the *Bulldog*, had to assist Markham with guiding the sledges through the fields of hummocks (broken ice that has been forced upwards by pressure, giving it the appearance of a hill or series of hills).

Still, day by day, the sledge teams pressed on until they reached the depot housing the provisions left the previous autumn at Cape Joseph Henry on 10 April. The support sledges replenished Markham's and Aldrich's provisions before turning around and heading back to the *Alert*'s camp. This brought the total weight being transported by Markham's sledges to 6,080lb – *Marco Polo* (2,728lb), *Victoria* (1,626lb) and a third support sledge he added to his ranks (1,726lb). Having regained his eyesight, Markham climbed to the top of a 650-foot hill to get a look at what his men faced ahead. 'The prospect was anything but cheering,' he admitted. 'To the northward was an irregular sea of ice, composed of small floes [flat pieces of sea ice] and large hummocks. Our anticipations of slow travelling and heavy work seem about to be realised.'

The next day, Aldrich's men moved west, while Markham's men continued north. If the rate of progress was anything like what it had taken them to reach Cape Joseph Henry, it was doubtful that Markham's men would make it very far north. 'It became only too evident, even before we bade farewell to the supporting sledges that our hopes of attaining a very high latitude would not be realised,' Markham declared. Although he had reservations about his chances of success, he would lead his men as far north as was humanly possible.

As he had predicted, the hummocks were heavier and larger than anything they had experienced on land. The ice and snow on the polar pack looked as if the sea's whitecaps and swells had suddenly been frozen in place, forcing the men to drag hundreds of pounds of supplies and provisions over and around these irregular hummocks. 'A journey through, and over, hummocks is the most unsatisfactory kind of travelling that can possibly be imagined,' Markham later grumbled. Despite the difficulties, morale remained high among the sledge crews. 'The men are all well and cheerful,' Markham declared, even though 'we are all suffering from cracked skin, the combined action of sun and frost, our lips, cheeks, and noses being especially very sore, our faces resembling raw beef-steaks.'

Markham sent Parr and a team of six men ahead to cut a path through the hummocks so that the sledges could be dragged more easily. The work took skill rather than brute strength. Like a first-rate engineer, Parr directed his roadmakers. Markham recalled watching Parr, ahead of the sledges, working like a 'slave with pickaxe and shovel'. The 27-year-old lieutenant was the type of man who led by example and did not baulk from sharing in the hardships of his men. Markham could not have found a better man among the *Alert*'s officers to serve as his second-in-command on this expedition.

Only three days after leaving Cape Joseph Henry, one of Markham's men, John Shirley, began to complain of throbbing ankles and knees. His swollen limbs were treated with turpentine liniment. Unable to walk any further, he was bundled up in a sleeping bag and tent robes and placed on the *Marco Polo*. George Porter, a marine artilleryman with the *Victoria*, began to complain of stiffness in his knees. Within days, Porter had to be relieved from the drag ropes and hobbled along behind the sledges. Markham supposed that a break from dragging the sledges would allow Shirley and Porter to recover their strength.

On 15 April, Markham's sledges halted when a blinding snowstorm made it impossible for them to see even a few yards ahead. Some of the men suffered from frostbitten faces. They spent all of the next day, Easter Sunday, confined to their tents. 'For forty hours,' Markham wrote, 'I did not have the slightest feeling in my feet and would not really declare that I was in possession of those useful members – as for sleep, under the circumstances, that was quite out of the question.' Crammed on top of each other, the men tried to ease their misery by drinking grog and giving three cheers in honour of Captain Nares's birthday and the first anniversary of the *Alert* being commissioned for the expedition. The cheering led to a shouting match between the two tents to see who could yell louder. Markham encouraged anything that would keep up the men's spirits during this period of misery. 'We all unanimously came to the conclusion,' he declared, 'that it was the most wretched and miserable Easter Sunday that any one of us had ever passed.'

A few days later, Markham decided to abandon one of his boats since it was drastically slowing down their progress. The loss of Shirley and Porter on the drag ropes – combined with their added weight on the sledges – made hauling the sledges even more burdensome. Besides his bad leg, Porter complained of pain in his stomach, weakness in his arms and faintness, and he occasionally spat up blood. A third man, Alfred Pearce, had to be relieved from the drag ropes, suffering from the same symptoms as Shirley and Porter. A fourth man, John Hawkins, also began to suffer from swollen ankles but stayed on the drag ropes. Fortunately, Shirley improved enough to walk for a while with the support of a staff instead of having to ride on the sledge. Pearce also recovered enough to resume his place alongside his comrades. During the evenings, Markham treated the invalids by rubbing their limbs in glycerine ointment and wrapping them in bandages.

The men continued to advance through the maze of ice at the rate of about 7 miles a day. Markham described the landscape surrounding them as a 'cold, desolate and inhospitable looking scene'. He further added, 'Everything of the same uniform colour, nothing to relieve the eye, nothing but one sombrous, uneven, and irregular sea of snow and ice.' Some of the hummocks they encountered were 25 feet high, and it was nearly impossible for the men to tell if they were going uphill or downhill. When they found themselves on top of one of these hummocks, they had to lower the sledges about 7 feet down to the bottom. The *Marco Polo* capsized with Porter strapped to it, but he was not injured. The handles of their shovels broke off from overuse. The sledge crews were so exhausted that they fell asleep at their posts if they halted for even a few moments.

By 2 May, Markham began to fear that his men may be suffering from scurvy. This was alarming since each man had undergone a final medical examination days before they had left the *Alert*'s camp. Fresh meat had been added to the men's rations and doses of lime juice given to them to prevent it. Still, Markham's men began to show the trademark symptoms: Shirley's knees and Hawkins's ankles began to turn 'a livid purplish hue'; Porter complained of general weakness, giddiness and stomach cramps; Francombe's calves were now swollen and he could hardly walk; and Pearce could 'only just bobble along' with his tender ankles. Markham privately expressed these fears in his journal:

> Invalids <u>not</u> improving … I am inclined to think they have all three a touch of scurvy although we have not been led to suppose that there is the slightest chance of our being attacked with this disease indeed we have came away without even having medical instructions written out, by our careful + thoughtful doctor, for our guidance should we be so attacked; so improbable was the idea. Our strength is diminishing rapidly. I would not have cared so much if they had only remained well for another fortnight, as our time for turning back is drawing nigh. … We are certainly experiencing what I never expected or anticipated. I felt firmly convinced that as we advanced northwards and away from the land, we should find larger and more level floes and less snow. Whereas the reverse is the case!

Markham shared this unsettling news with Parr, but hid it from his other men, fearing the effect it would have on their morale. He administered lime juice instead of grog to those most severely afflicted, telling them it was a 'better blood purifier' to conceal the real reason, which was to treat scurvy. One of the glass bottles of lime juice cracked and spilled out when Markham put it too close to the heating apparatus, forcing him to thaw the last couple of bottles by placing them between his legs in his sleeping bag at night. 'I only wish I had more of this excellent antiscorbutic,' he admitted. 'We have only a couple of bottles on each sledge, but it was extremely fortunate that we thought of carrying any.'

The condition of the sledge crews continued to worsen with each passing day. Porter and Francombe rode on the sledges while Pearce, Hawkins and Shirley staggered behind them. By 6 May, Hawkins joined Porter and Francombe on one of the sledges. Some of the other men started to complain of stiff and aching legs and suffered from discolouration on the inside part of their thighs and behind their knees. Markham's party was fortunate if it moved 1 mile a day.

After nearly forty days of being away from the *Alert*'s camp, Markham realised his men could go no further. On 10 May, he expressed this regret in his journal:

> Reluctantly, very reluctantly I have, after very serious consideration and due consultation with Parr arrived at the conclusion that this must be our Most Northern Camp. I feel mean and small! Now totally different are the realisation of my hopes of a year ago! To be the leader of such a glorious expedition, with the ball apparently at my feet asking only to be rolled on, and yet to experience such a total failure. God knows that our want of success cannot be attributed either to a lack of energy or performance. I am satisfied in my own mind, no matter what the world may say, that the quotation on my staff has been fully carried out.

In the same entry, he explained in greater detail why he halted the advance:

> My reason for not advancing further northwards are manifold – in the first place another man George Winstone, one of Parr's crew, is complaining of his legs + is only just able to drag, thus with five totally prostrate and four more, out of my small band of 15, exhibiting decided symptoms of the same complaint, it would be folly, nay sheer madness, on my part to attempt pushing on, for if they were to break down altogether I should hardly be able to move at all. The day after tomorrow I shall be 40 days out, and only have 31

days' provisions left, and I fully anticipate it will take me as long to return as it did to come out, for having to carry 5 men is equivalent to an extra weight of 2,000lbs! This is the weight of 5 men to carry + the loss of power in dragging of the same number. Prudence and discretion, however much I am desirous of advancing, unite in saying return. ... It is a bitter ending to all our aspirations! Although we have accomplished so little, I must do my brave companions the justice to say, that no men under the existing circumstances could have done more.

The men set up camp to get some rest and gather scientific data before turning back. Markham ordered the healthy men to cut a hole through 64 inches of ice so that he could calculate the depth of the ocean floor and its temperature with a Casella thermometer. He lowered a bread bag filled with crumbs of pemmican and stewpan scraps into the hole to collect small crustaceans and foraminifera. He dumped these specimens into a glass bottle to undergo microscopic examination when they returned to the *Alert*'s camp. He also tried to capture an Arctic cod to provide the sickest men with fresh meat but was unsuccessful.

On 12 May, Markham headed north with ten men to plant the Union Jack exactly 400 miles from the North Pole. George Porter, John Shirley, Reuben Francombe, John Hawkins, Alfred Pearce and George Winstone were too sick to move so they stayed behind. The eleven men still able to make the trek – Albert H. Markham, Alfred A.C. Parr, Thomas Rawlings, Edward Lawrence, John Radmore, Thomas Joliffe, Thomas H. Simpson, Daniel Harley, William Ferbrache, William Maskell and John Pearson – spent two hours hiking through snowdrifts to travel just 1 mile. Before noon, they reached 83°, 20' 26" N, exactly 399½ miles from the North Pole. No other men had made it this far north in the history of Arctic exploration. The news was met by three cheers, with an extra one added for Captain Nares. Markham ordered the Union Jack unfurled and the little band huddled around it and sang the *Union Jack of England*, the *Grand Palæocrystic Sledging Chorus* and *God Save the Queen*. After this short-lived ceremony, they packed up the colours and returned to camp.

They continued the celebration into the night. The invalids even joined in. Each man took a swig from a magnum of whisky supplied by the Dean of Dundee before leaving England. After finishing their dinner of hare stew, they puffed on cigars given to them by Lieutenant May and sang. For a time, 'All seemed happy, cheerful, and contented,' Markham later wrote. This cheerfulness would dissolve over the next two weeks.

The men's strength diminished drastically each subsequent day on their trip back to the *Alert*'s camp. All of them suffered from aching limbs, insomnia and a reduced appetite. The little lime juice that remained was used up. By now, most of the men had the suspicion that they were being afflicted by what they dared not call by name, but dubbed the 'John Henry mange'. Some of them even began to eat tea leaves hoping that this would ward off the scurvy. This failed to have any effect.

If the men's worsening health was not bad enough, Markham noticed large cracks in the ice. This was an indication of Nares's greatest fear: a melting pack. On 31 May, one of the sledges broke through the rotten ice but the men managed to pull it back on solid ground before the supplies were lost and the invalids resting on it drowned. Markham ordered the second boat, their grog, ammunition and 170lb of pemmican abandoned to lighten their load so they could make better time. They were now in a race to reach land before their bodies gave in or the decaying ice swallowed them up.

By the end of July, Markham, Parr, Radmore and Maskell were the only men fit enough to work the drag ropes. 'We are a perfect band of cripples,' Markham avowed. They had trouble locating the road that Parr's team had carved out only weeks before. They searched for any sign of tobacco ash, tin pots or other equipment that may have fallen off the sledges. Finally, they completely lost track of it, and began the gruelling process of carving out a new path.

Thankfully, on 5 June, they reached land after being on the pack for two months. When they reached the depot at Cape Joseph Henry, they discovered the bodies of three hares and a letter from Nares stating that his party had left them there only a day before. Markham had missed them by a matter of hours.

Realising that it would take at least three more weeks to reach the ship at the rate they were moving, Parr volunteered to hike 40 miles back to camp to get help. Markham reluctantly consented to the dangerous mission since he had no other choice. 'He [Parr] is the only one of our

1. Ships anchored at Macao. From Matthew C. Perry and Francis L. Hawks, *Narrative of the Expedition of an American Squadron to the China Seas and Japan, performed in the years 1852, 1853, and 1854, under the Command of Commodore M.C. Perry, United States Navy by the Order of the Government of the United States, Compiled from the original notes and journals of the Commodore Perry and his officers, at his request and under his supervision*, 1856. (*Courtesy of the Library of Congress*)

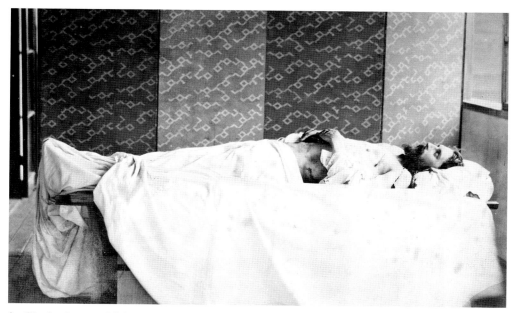

2. Charles Lennox Richardson's body after his murder. (*Courtesy of Het Scheepvaartmuseum*)

3. Rear Admiral Sir James Hope (1808–81). From William Laird Clowes, *The Royal Navy: A History from the Earliest Times to the Death of Queen Victoria*, 1903.

4. Sir Clements Robert Markham (1830–1916) at 25 years old. From Albert Hastings Markham, *The Life of Sir Clements R. Markham, KCB, FRS*, 1917.

5. The Fleet defeated Yokohama in Japan's first cricket match. Markham is seated second from the left. From Geoffrey Rawson, *Life of Admiral Sir Harry Rawson*, 1914. (*Courtesy of the Alexander Turnbull Library, Wellington, NZ*)

6. Markham as a young lieutenant. He was said to have recommended the design that would become the national flag of New Zealand while serving in the Australia Station. It was officially adopted in 1902. Helen Lambert, portraits of Lieutenant Frederic A. Sargeant, Lieutenant Albert H. Markham, and unknown naval officer, 1868–70. Albumen silver photograph, pen and ink, 27.9 x 23.5 cm. (*Courtesy of the National Gallery of Australia, Canberra*)

7. Bishop John Coleridge Patteson (1827–71). From E.S. Armstrong, *The History of the Melanesian Mission*, 1900.

8. HMS *Blanche*. From Halton Stirling Lecky, *The King's Ships Together With the Important Historical Episodes Connected with the Successive Ships of the Same Name from Remote Times, and a List of Names and Services of Some Ancient War Vessels*, 1913.

9. Native labourers on an Australian plantation. From Albert Hastings Markham, *The Cruise of the 'Rosario' Amongst the New Hebrides and Santa Cruz Islands, Exposing the Recent Atrocities Connected with the Kidnapping of Natives in the South Seas*, 1873. (*Courtesy of the Cleveland Public Library*)

10. HMS *Rosario*. (*Courtesy of the Shipping Collection, Alexander Turnbull Library, Wellington, NZ*)

11. Missionaries and villagers at the landing place of Nukapu, Reef Islands, 1906. National Library of Australia, nla.obj-141117803, photographer John Watt Beattie. (*Courtesy of Dr Clive Moore*)

12. Markham's assault on the island of Nukapu. National Library of Australia, CDC-10634971, *Town and County Journal*, 21 February 1872.

13. The *Alert*'s winter camp. From Edward L. Moss, *Shores of the Polar Sea: A Narrative of the Arctic Expedition of 1875–6*, 1878. (*Courtesy of the Cleveland Public Library*)

14. A photograph of the *Alert* in its winter quarters on Floeberg Beach. From George Nares, *Narrative of a Voyage to the Polar Sea During 1875–6 in H.M. Ships 'Alert' and 'Discovery'*, 1878. (*Courtesy of the Cleveland Public Library*)

15. Sailors building snow halls at Floeberg Beach. From Edward L. Moss, *Shores of the Polar Sea: A Narrative of the Arctic Expedition of 1875–6*, 1878. (*Courtesy of the Cleveland Public Library*)

16. Morning inspection and prayers on the *Alert*'s deck. From Edward L. Moss, *Shores of the Polar Sea: A Narrative of the Arctic Expedition of 1875–6*, 1878. (*Courtesy of the Cleveland Public Library*)

17. Sledge travelling in the Arctic. From Edward L. Moss, *Shores of the Polar Sea: A Narrative of the Arctic Expedition of 1875–6*, 1878. (*Courtesy of the Cleveland Public Library*)

18. Markham's most northern camp. From Albert Hastings Markham, *The Great Frozen Sea: A Personal Narrative of the Voyage of the 'Alert' During the Arctic Expedition of 1875–6*, 1878. (*Courtesy of the Archives & Rare Books Library, University of Cincinnati*)

19. Markham, Radmore, Jolliffe and Maskell return with the *Marco Polo* after seventy-two days. (*Illustration by Zsuzsi Hajdu*)

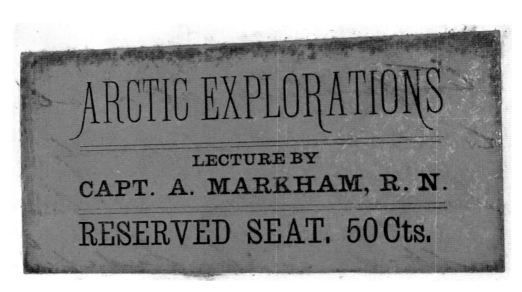

20. A ticket from one of Markham's lectures while he visited the United States. (*Courtesy of the 19th Century Rare Book & Photograph Shop*)

21. The Kiowa and Comanche Reservation near Fort Sill. (*Courtesy of the Clay County Historical Society, Inc*)

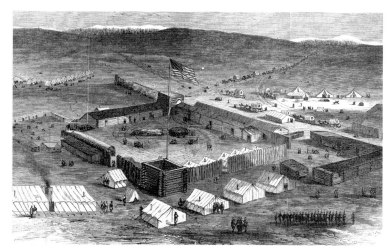

22. Camp Supply. From *Harper's Weekly*, 1869. (*Courtesy of the Library of Congress.*)

23. A watercolour from Markham's journal showing him hunting buffalo. (*Courtesy of the 19th Century Rare Book & Photograph Shop*)

24. A modern view of Clements Markham's residence at 21 Eccleston Square. (*Courtesy of Robert B. Stephenson, The Antarctic Circle*)

25. Markham dressed in his travelling outfit during his Hudson's Bay expedition. (*Illustration by Zsuzsi Hajdu*)

26. Sir Henry Gore-Booth (1843–1900) and some of the *Isbjörn*'s Norwegian crew during Markham's trip to Novaya Zemlya. From Albert Hastings Markham, *Polar Reconnaissance: Being the Voyage of the 'Isbjörn' to Novaya Zemlya in 1879*, 1881.

27. HMS *Triumph* in Esquimalt Harbour, Vancouver Island. City of Vancouver Archives, Out P303, photographer George W. Edwards.

28. The Battle of Miraflores. National Library of Chile, id Bnd: LE0000904, artist Ruperto Salcedo, available in Memoria Chilena/Biblioteca Nacional Digital. (*http://www.bibliotecanacionaldigital.cl/bnd/631/w3-article-334181.html*)

29. Entry of General Baquedano's victorious Chilean soldiers into Lima, 17 January 1881. National Library of Chile, id MC: MC0002340, available in Memoria Chilena/Biblioteca Nacional Digital. (*http://www.memoriachilena.cl/602/w3-article-98788.html*)

30. A modern aerial view of York Factory, Manitoba, established as a trading post by the Hudson's Bay Company in the seventeenth century. (*Courtesy of Parks Canada*)

31. A modern view of the Great Meteoron Monastery, Greece, established by St Athanasius of Alexandria in the fourteenth century. (*Courtesy of Visit Meteora*)

32. Markham climbing to the top of the Great Meteoron Monastery. From *Pearson's Magazine*, 1899. (*Courtesy of Herman B. Wells Library, Indiana University*)

33. Vice Admiral Sir George Tryon (1832–93). From William Laird Clowes, *The Royal Navy: A History from the Earliest Times to the Death of Queen Victoria*, 1903.

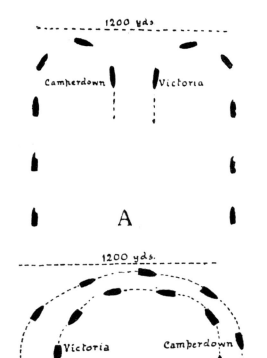

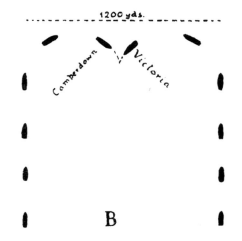

34. A) What should have happened on 22 June 1893; B) what happened; 3) what Markham thought Tryon intended. From *William Laird Clowes, The Royal Navy: A History from the Earliest Times to the Death of Queen Victoria,* 1903.

35. HMS *Victoria* moments after its collision with HMS *Camperdown*. (*Courtesy of Voyager Press Rare Books and Manuscripts*)

36. Theodora Chevallier Gervers Markham (1875–1962). (*Courtesy of the International Autograph Auctions Ltd*)

37. Admiral Sir Albert Hastings Markham (1841–1918). (*Courtesy of the International Autograph Auctions Ltd*)

38. Markham's retreat: Amat Lodge. (*Courtesy of the Tain & District Museum*)

39. Markham with his daughter, Joy Mary Minna (1900–35). From *The Sketch, A Journal of Art and Actuality*, 1904. (*Courtesy of the University of Minnesota*)

40. Markham's tombstone in Kensal Green Cemetery. (*Courtesy of the Henry Vivian-Neal, Kensal Green Cemetery*)

41. Markham's epitaph. (*Courtesy of the Henry Vivian-Neal, Kensal Green Cemetery*)

party strong enough to undertake such a march,' Markham reasoned. 'I have the utmost confidence in his judgment and ability to perform it.' Parr left his comrades with a note for Nares, food for only one day and a small spirit lamp. He took a quicker, but more perilous route, passing back over the melting pack. Parr's sledge motto was suitably *Faire sans dire* – to do without saying.

On 8 June, a day after Parr left to go off on his own, George Porter died. He never seemed to regain his strength after first falling ill. Markham gave an account of Porter's final hours:

Poor Porter is no more! After halting last night he was placed as usual in his tent, where I visited him before supper. He said, in answer to my inquiry, that he was easy and comfortable, and appeared to be more cheerful and talkative. Before I had quite finished my supper, I was called in haste to his tent, where I found him suffering from a spasmodic attack of some nature, and quite unconscious: this was about 8 o'clock (A.M.). He was revived by having his nostrils bathed with spirit of ammonia, and then a little rum, slightly diluted with water, was given [to] him, when he regained consciousness. His breathing was short and stertorous; he complained much of difficulty in breathing, and appeared to be sinking fast. Two hours after he had a similar attack, and was again brought round by the same means; but he seemed to be much exhausted, and although between the two attacks he had enjoyed a short doze. After this he sank rapidly, and expired, with my finger on his pulse, at 10 minutes past 12 (noon). He was sensible to within a few minutes of his death, and his end was calm and quiet. This is a sad calamity, although we were not totally unprepared for it, and I fear the depressing moral effect that this lamentable event will have on those who are very sick, and who consider themselves to be in nearly as precarious a condition.

'The corpse,' Markham recalled, 'which has swelled up considerably and was terribly disfigured after dissolution took place, was sewn up in a sleeping bag, and laid on a sledge.' Porter's companions draped his body in the Union Jack, read prayers and bid their farewells before the burial. A small procession of men clad in Arctic gear, with only the swollen skin of their faces visible, led the sledge to an 8-foot hole dug a few yards from their camp. They constructed a cross from an oar and a spare sledge batten and carved it with the inscription 'Beneath this cross lie buried the remains of Geo. Porter, R.M.A, who died June 8th, 1876. Thy will be done', placing it at the head of his grave. 'Of all the melancholy and mournful duties I have ever been called upon to perform,' Markham confessed, 'this has been the saddest.'

The same day that George Porter passed away, Parr staggered into Captain Nares's cabin on the *Alert*. He had walked about 30 miles in twenty-two and a half hours. Nares could hardly recognise the lieutenant's swollen and battered face. A relief party with medical provisions led by May and Moss immediately left camp to rescue Markham's men. A second relief party, commanded by Nares and Egerton, followed the next day. Before he left, Nares ordered the main deck cleared, bedding aired and dried, and hammocks made ready for the men's arrival.

The next morning, Markham's men spotted three figures among a field of hummocks in the distance. His men were ecstatic but did not have the strength to express their joy in their fragile condition. Dr Moss inspected the men that night. He afterwards reported that 'Rawlings, Simpson, Ferbrache, and Pearson [were] staggering along in advance. Captain Markham, Radmore, Joliffe, Maskell, Harley and Lawrence worked the drag belts pulling Hawkins, Francombe, Shirley and Pearce. Porter had died the day before. It was difficult to recognise any of the men, their faces so swollen and peeled and their voices so changed.' He administered a dose of lime juice and the little fresh meat he had on hand to each man, hoping this would give them enough strength to make it back to camp. He did not provide Markham, Joliffe and Radmore with lime juice or fresh meat since they appeared to be in the best shape.

Of the fourteen men, eleven were transported on the rescue sledges back to the *Alert*'s camp. On 13 June, May and Moss returned to the *Alert*'s camp with the two men most critically ill, Shirley and Pearson. That evening, May, with a dog sledge, went back out to retrieve Lawrence, Harley and Winstone. Nares's relief party arrived with the remaining men too sick to walk. In an admirable display of perseverance, Markham, Radmore, Joliffe and Maskell, with grimy, weather-beaten faces, dragged the *Marco Polo* into the *Alert*'s camp under their own power. Nares called for three cheers to salute their indomitable courage and devotion to duty.

After being away for seventy-two days, Markham described it as being an 'indescribable pleasure' to take a warm bath, eat a cooked meal and drink a glass of champagne. A day after his return, he wrote with satisfaction: 'Plenty to eat and drink and plenty of sleep!'

Markham's men were not the only ones who had suffered from a scurvy outbreak. On 25 June, Lieutenant Aldrich's sledge team returned to the *Alert*'s camp after an absence of eighty-four days. All of his crew, besides himself, was placed on the sick list. The illness had also broken out among the men who remained behind with Nares at the *Alert*'s camp while the sledges were away. The impact was as awful as it had been among Markham's and Aldrich's parties. By late June, only nine men from the *Alert* crew's were fit to work.

On 29 June, Nares invited his officers for dinner in the *Alert*'s wardroom to celebrate the safe return of both sledge parties. Champagne and other delicacies were served for dinner. Moss sketched a scene depicting the most northern point reached by Markham's team and had it reproduced on the dinner menus. The Reverend Pullen composed a poem in honor of the men, which was printed on the back. After dinner, Nares broke the news that he planned for the ships to return to England even though they had arranged to stay for at least two years. 'In deciding to return to England,' Markham wrote defending the decision, 'Captain Nares showed great moral courage, and exercised a sound and wise judgment, in the opinion of all officers.'

The *Alert*'s crew would have to move quickly if they planned to break the ship free from the ice and link up with the *Discovery* before winter. Markham supervised the gear being removed from the halls and had it stored on the ship's upper deck in the event that the ship should have to be evacuated. The men erected a 10-foot cairn on a summit with a note signed by the officers and sailors of the ship chronicling their accomplishments before departing. They detonated torpedoes and ignited gunpowder to blow up the heavy ice encasing the ship's hull. By 31 July, the ship broke loose and steamed south towards a lead after eleven months of captivity. Markham exclaimed with exhilaration in his journal, 'Ship free! Steamed

out of our "cradle" and shaped a course to the South!! Hoisted colours!!!
Forward to Floeberg Beach!!!!'

The voyage south was as challenging and dangerous as it had been
to reach Floeberg Beach the year before. On 1 August, the *Alert* barely
dodged a floeberg; instead, the massive block levelled some nearby
hummocks. This demonstrated to Markham 'what our fate would have
been if we had remained'. Smaller floes kept coming towards the ship as
fast as the men were able to demolish or dodge them. Seven days later,
another floeberg collided with the shore a quarter of a mile from the
ship, forcing chunks of ice in the direction of the *Alert*. The ship shot 3
or 4 feet into the air from the impact and it became pinned against the
shore. 'The noise of the cracking of the beams and the groaning of the
timbers was a sound that once heard will never be forgotten,' Markham
recalled. The men spent all morning and afternoon with pickaxes and
shovels chipping away at the masses of ice squeezed up against the ship's
hull. Three days later, they finally managed to break the ship free after
an explosive charge shattered the last hunk of ice holding them hostage.

The *Alert* continued to fight its way south until it joined its sister
ship in Discovery Bay on 11 August. The officers from the *Discovery*
came aboard the *Alert* and dined on sausages and sardines and indulged
themselves with brandy and whisky. The *Discovery*'s crew suffered
equally as badly from scurvy even though they had a fresh supply of
meat in close proximity and regularly consumed their lime juice rations.
Two hundred yards from their camp they discovered ancient Eskimo
remains, which were the first to have been recovered that far north. They
also uncovered a large supply of lignite (brown coal) 3 miles from camp.
Markham went with Nares and a few other officers in a 15-foot ice boat
to retrieve samples of the coal. When the coal was tested back home,
Markham said it was reported to be 'equal to the best Welsh coal'.

Lieutenant Beaumont's team had been sent out from the *Discovery*'s
camp to explore the northeastern coast of Greenland around the same
time as Markham's and Aldrich's sledges had left to go on their own
expeditions. On 14 August, Beaumont's sledge finally appeared outside
the *Discovery*'s camp. Shortly after 3.00 pm that same day, Markham took
a dinghy, sledge and six men to offer assistance and did not return with
Beaumont's team for another ten hours. Two of Beaumont's men, James

Hand and Charles W. Paul, had died from scurvy, whilst the remainder were wasting away from it. Now that Beaumont and his men had safely returned to camp, both the *Alert* and *Discovery* blasted their way out of Lady Franklin Bay and continued on their voyage to escape Smith Sound.

Ice remained tightly packed in the Arctic sea passage blocking the ships' advance and forcing them to wait for an opening. 'Our patience is sorely taxed,' Markham complained. Their patience paid off when, on 18 August, they spotted a lead and steamed towards it. For weeks, the two ships struggled to progress even a few hundred yards a day but now had a decent course for miles. On 9 September, after what Markham described as 'a glorious run' through a good lead, the ships punched through a barrier of ice and emerged into the open sea for the first time in a year. 'We had a fight,' Markham continued, '[B]ut perseverance and patience ultimately proved triumphant.'

When they reached the depot erected the year before at Cape Isabella, the men inspected the wooden casks. Inside they discovered letters from home deposited by some gutsy captain and his crew. The letters spoke of the 'Eastern Question' and the deteriorating relationship between England and Russia over what was transpiring in the Balkans. 'Wars, and rumours of wars, were prevalent,' Markham stated, 'for our latest news came from England at the time when all of Europe was disturbed and unsettled by the complexion of affairs in the East.' A potential war with Russia hastened the men's desire to return home.

On 4 October, the ships left the Arctic Circle a year and three months after they first crossed into it. Twelve days later, they spotted and exchanged signals with the yacht *Pondora*. It was the first ship they had made contact with since leaving Smith Sound. They found out that it was the ship that had deposited the letters in the casks at Cape Isabella. On 29 October, both ships reached Queenstown. Nares left the *Alert* and travelled the rest of the way by train to report to the Admiralty. He left Markham in command for the remainder of their voyage home. News spread along the coast as the ships made their way to Portsmouth, arriving there on 2 November.

For a time, the expedition's participants were the most popular men in England. Queen Victoria appreciated their 'valuable service' and requested that 'her thanks could be duly conveyed to these gallant men for what they have accomplished'. The expedition was applauded for its scientific discoveries: the men had recorded vast amounts of meteorological, magnetic and tidal observations, collected thousands of geological, zoological and botanical specimens, mapped 400 miles of uncharted coastline and uncovered traces of coal and ancient Eskimo remains. When it came to science, Clements Markham said the expedition was the 'most successful that ever crossed the Arctic Circle'.

A silver Arctic Medal was struck and presented to each man and at least nine banquets were held in their honour. Nares dined with Her Majesty at Windsor Castle, was made a KCB and was awarded the Royal Geological Society's Founder's Medal. Eleven officers received promotions, including Markham, who was elevated to captain. He also received a gold watch from the Royal Geographical Society for setting a new world record.

Everyone wanted to hear accounts of the expedition. The Royal Geographical Society hosted the senior officers, Nares, Markham and Stephenson, at St James's Hall in London on 12 December. At the end of his lecture on sledge travelling, Markham took a moment to recognise the expedition's sledge crews:

> In conclusion, I would desire, not only in my own name, but in the name of all those officers who commanded the several sledge-parties during the recent Expedition, to pay my tribute of praise to our gallant companions who bore the principal brunt of hard work whilst employed in their interesting work of exploration. These brave fellows, though suffering acute bodily pain and almost unheard-of hardships and privations, bore their suffering with manly fortitude and endurance, without a murmur or complaint; animated by the same praiseworthy zeal and devotion to achieve all that was possible for the credit of their profession and the honour of their flag.

The Prince of Wales, in attendance, rose and briefly addressed the audience, asking them to give the officers a round of applause that 'they have so thoroughly deserved'.

While those who took part in the expedition were treated like heroes for the dangers they encountered, the difficulties they overcame and their scientific discoveries, detractors criticised them for falling short of the North Pole. These critics accused Captain Nares of being too cautious, claiming that he had prematurely halted the *Alert*'s advance north and abandoned his camp on Floeberg Beach. However, the Admiralty supported Nares's decision to return to England, rather than having him uselessly risk the lives of his men – and avoiding the embarrassment of a second Franklin expedition – to reach the North Pole. Clements Markham called the craze to reach the North Pole 'a childish and useless quest, and quite unworthy of serious consideration', blaming the Admiralty for foolishly inserting this in Nares's orders. 'They might as well have inserted orders to go to the moon,' he grumbled. The truth was, the public had been oversold on how simple it would be for an expedition to reach the North Pole by the men so eager to initiate it.

The outbreak of scurvy among Nares's expedition generated another heated debate. Scurvy had never crippled an Arctic expedition like it did with this one. Most of the men on both ships, particularly their sledge teams, fell victim to scurvy during the summer of 1876. Ultimately, it led to the deaths of three men and cut the expedition short by at least a year. Someone had to be held responsible for what they suspected as negligence. 'It is a very disgraceful and discreditable thing to reflect upon,' Clements Markham angrily wrote, 'that our greatest explorers and travellers, by sea and land, from the time of James Bruce of Kinnaird, have been attacked on their return by a swarm of ignorant detractors.' Regardless of Clements's sentiment, the Admiralty wanted answers.

The Lords Commissioners were concerned enough with the scurvy outbreak during the expedition to order an investigation in January 1877. Twenty-two members of the expedition were called to testify in the ensuing weeks. Nares soon surfaced as the scapegoat, receiving rebuke for not ordering his sledge crews to carry bottles of lime juice on their expeditions. He defended his actions by arguing that his men carried the same equipment and stuck to the same diets as past Arctic explorers. Some of this blame even trickled down to Markham, who had ordered two bottles of lime juice to be packed on each of his sledges. Even though he ordered it to be taken on his own accord, he was criticised during the investigation for not having taken more. After hearing the officers' testimonies, the committee issued their final report three months later, concluding that the absence of lime juice in the sledge rations led to scurvy among the sledge crews and the untimely deaths of three men. The committee's ruling tainted Nares's legacy – he failed to receive a promotion for another two decades – and left a shadow over the expedition.

If a scurvy outbreak was caused by an inadequate amount of lime juice on the sledges, then why did it have the same devastating effects on the men who remained behind at the *Alert*'s camp taking regular doses of the antiscorbutic? There was a logical reason behind this, which was not uncovered until 1918. Humans are one of the few mammals unable to produce their own vitamin C, and it is necessary for them to consume at least 10 to 15 milligrams a day to prevent scurvy – producing symptoms of bruising, weakness, fatigue and bleeding gums if an individual fell below the daily required amount. The Royal Navy issued lemon juice beginning in 1803 to protect their sailors from this debilitating ailment. In 1860, cheaper West Indies limes replaced Mediterranean lemons. Nobody was aware of this at the time, but limes produce about half the amount of vitamin C as lemons, making its juice practically useless as an antiscorbutic. Drs Kenneth J. Carpenter, E.J.C. Kendall and John Edwards Caswell explained the devastating consequences this switch would have to the Arctic Expedition of 1875–76 fifteen years later.

Nares's men had a small amount of fresh meat when they arrived at the Arctic in the autumn of 1875, but they primarily relied on canned food, which lost most of its nutrition during the cooking and canning process. If they were lucky, they were getting somewhere between 3 to 5 milligrams of vitamin C per day – 10 milligrams less than the human body required. Symptoms caused by a vitamin C deficiency generally appear after thirty-four weeks. The sledge crews began to suffer from a deficiency weeks before they even headed out on their spring/summer expeditions but only began to notice its debilitating symptoms weeks later. Contrary to the inquiry's ruling, it did not matter if Nares had ordered lime juice taken by his sledge crews or if Markham had packed a few extra bottles. It was useless. The 'John Henry mange' already began to compromise the sledge crews' strength before they set out from the *Alert*'s camp.

During the investigation, Markham was asked another unsettling question: Why did he continue north for eight more days after he first expressed a concern that his men may be suffering from scurvy? One of the reasons he noted in his journal on 2 May that the further his sledges advanced away from the land, the more confident he was that they would find larger and more level floes and less snow, making travel easier for the men. He provided his other motives for continuing forwards in his official report submitted to Nares in July:

It may be necessary for me to offer some explanation as to why, with so many sick men on the sledges, I did not immediately turn back and endeavour to reach the ship as speedily as possible. To this my reply must be, that we were for some considerable time totally unacquainted with the character of the malady with which our party were attacked, and that we naturally concluded they were suffering only from swollen knees and ankles, which were aware was of frequent occurrence amongst the sledging crews of former expeditions, and was only what we had been led to expect; but we hoped, with a little rest and judicious treatment, they would soon recover and be able to resume their places on the drag-ropes. The short distance also that we were from the land was another reason for not turning back, for we felt confident of being able to reach the depots in a few days, provided our sick list did not increase at an alarming rate, little dreaming that the entire party would be afflicted and rendered nearly helpless – a case without precedent. I may perhaps mention that the men themselves, before the nature of disease was communicated to them, regarded their ailment as only temporary; and I must say, in justice to themselves, they shared, equally with their officers, the same eager desire to advance and carry out, to the utmost of their powers, the charge entrusted to them.

The other two sledge commanders, Aldrich and Beaumont, like Markham, were reluctant to accept that their men could actually be suffering from scurvy and waited until days after to halt their advance. Should Markham have continued on once he suspected scurvy? No. Was he willing to recklessly jeopardise the lives of his men to reach the highest northern latitude possible? Not at all. He specifically chose the motto of 'I dare do all that may become a man; Who dares do more is none' to be engraved on his flagstaff, exuding wisdom instead of rashness, which tells us for which trait he had a greater admiration. Markham was ambitious like every other officer on that expedition, but he was not impetuous or vain. He felt it his duty to continue with his mission until it was no longer reasonably viable to accomplish it. When he reached this point, even when he felt 'the ball apparently at my feet asking only to be rolled on', he put the welfare of his men above his own ambition and ordered a halt to their advance, knowing it 'would be folly, nay sheer madness' to push on. If Markham was guilty of anything, it was his eagerness to fulfill his duty.

While Parry's record of reaching the highest northern latitude remained unbroken for four decades, Markham's record was shattered in only six years. The American Lieutenant James B. Lockwood's dog sledge team, part of Lieutenant Adolphus W. Greely's expedition, passed Markham's most northern point by a mere 4 miles in 1882. After that, the records began to tumble in quick succession. Lockwood's success was trumped by the Norwegian explorer Fridtjof Nansen in 1895, then eclipsed by two Italians, Prince Luigi Amedeo and Umberto Cagni, five years later. The American Robert E. Peary finally reached the North Pole in 1909, three decades after Markham's expedition. (It is still debated whether Peary actually did accomplish this feat.) By the early twentieth century, Markham's achievement had been pretty much forgotten.

However, Markham always remembered the Arctic Expedition with pride. He stayed in contact with his comrades and continued to eulogise the endurance and sacrifice of the men under his command equally to his own role as the leader. Decades after the expedition, while serving in the Mediterranean Station, he invited John Radmore, one of the three men who dragged the *Marco Polo* with him back to the *Alert*'s camp, who was then serving as his ship's carpenter, to dine with him on the anniversary of their glorious achievement even though the record no longer stood or mattered. For Markham, 12 May remained a day to cherish and celebrate for the remainder of his life.

Chapter 6

The American Frontier and Novaya Zemlya

'Geographical exploration is one of the most fascinating pursuits to which a man can devote his energies and his abilities. This fascination is most powerful when investigations are made in those regions which have hitherto been regarded as almost inaccessible – where nature, assisted by the severity of the climate, combines with all her forces to repel the mortal intruders who strive to solve the mysteries of the Pole.'

Albert H. Markham, *A Polar Reconnaissance:*
Being the Voyage of the "Isbjörn" to Novaya Zemlya in 1879

When he was between naval assignments, Albert Markham stayed with Clements and his wife, Minna, in their home at 21 Eccleston Square, just six doors away from where Winston Churchill's family resided from 1908 to 1913. Relics from around the world lined the hallway and staircase of the Markhams' home. These included a statue Albert had carried off from Ningpo during the Taiping Rebellion, regalia and weapons collected from the South Pacific, and animals and birds captured in the Arctic.

It was in his cousin's home that Albert, energised from his trip to the Arctic and craving exploration, planned a trip to the American Frontier. He dreamed of seeing its remote army posts, vast prairies, wild Indians and herds of roaming buffalo. 'For some years I had regarded with longing eyes this portion of North America,' Markham confessed. His opportunity came in September 1877 when the Admiralty granted him eight months' leave to travel to America.

On 22 September, Markham departed London aboard the steamer *Algeria* and arrived in New York City in early October. After spending two days in New York City, he travelled to Chicago and called on Lieutenant General Philip H. Sheridan, head of the Military Division of the Missouri, and expressed his desire to tour American military posts and hunt buffalo in Indian Territory (Oklahoma). Sheridan was familiar with Europeans wanting to see what the American West had to offer. The general granted Markham's wish and furnished him with a letter of introduction to Colonel Ranald S. Mackenzie, commander at Fort Sill.

En route to Caddo from St Louis, Markham found his train ride through Southwest Missouri dull but kept his eyes glued to the window once he crossed into Indian Territory. He was captivated by the landscape. 'It is almost impossible to describe the beauties of the country,' he wrote. 'Amidst such scenery books were abandoned, and I feasted my eyes on the truly lovely and wild panorama that was continually passing before me, and which exists in no other part of the globe ...'

His reverie was broken when a passenger cautioned him about the dangers he faced on the lawless frontier. He told him how only six weeks earlier, six men had robbed a similar train. Gamblers, prostitutes, whiskey peddlers and outlaws – such as the famed James, Dalton and Doolin Gangs – rode wild in this 70,000 square mile region. The Five Civilized Tribes (Cherokee, Chickasaw, Choctaw, Creek and Seminole) administered the territory. They were responsible for enforcing the laws, but their courts had no jurisdiction over whites who committed crimes. Markham took heed to the man's warning and kept his revolver and rifle easily accessible for the rest of his travels.

After reaching Caddo, Markham paid a man to drive him the remaining 163 miles to Fort Sill in a rickety wagon. They encountered continuous thunderstorms for most of the journey. 'Never do I recollect witnessing, even in the tropics,' Markham swore, 'such a commotion in the heavens, or such a severe storm as this that assailed us on the open prairie.'

Fort Sill – named in honor of Brigadier General Joshua W. Sill, killed during the American Civil War – included a barracks, officers' quarters, large parade ground, hospital, quartermaster's store, cattle corral, stables and two sutler's stores. It consisted of a garrison of 500 soldiers and cavalrymen. When he arrived, Colonel Ranald S. Mackenzie invited Markham to his quarters. Nicknamed 'Bad Hand' after losing two fingers on his right hand in battle, Mackenzie had distinguished himself as an Indian fighter. The two got along well. Mackenzie, an avid hunter like

Markham, invited him on a hunt where they managed to corner and kill an impressive 29-pound bobcat.

Markham expressed an interest in visiting the Kiowa and Comanche Reservation located 11 miles north of the fort. Mackenzie arranged for a wagon to take him there. After a two-hour ride, Markham arrived at the base of Mount Scott. 'I was agreeably surprised at the appearance of these people,' Markham indicated of the 1,000 Indians encamped there. '[F]or they were undoubtedly finer and more intelligent-looking than any I had hitherto seen.' He watched a group of Indian boys place a five cent piece on a stick and hit it with a bow and arrow at 12 to 15 yards without taking aim. 'The skill of the red man with a bow and arrow has always been proverbial,' he declared after observing this feat. 'I can testify to the fact that they have not deteriorated as marksmen since those days so graphically described by [James] Fenimore Cooper.'

When he heard that a detachment of cavalrymen would be travelling on a hunting and scouting mission to the Texas border, Markham asked to go. Mackenzie granted his request. The party consisted of Lieutenant William Alexis 'Hurricane Bill' Thompson, who was the leader of the group, Lieutenant Alexander K. 'Sandy' Rodgers, Lieutenant James Parker and sixteen troopers of the 4th Cavalry Regiment. One of the troopers, an Englishman originally from Eccleston Square named Cook, was assigned to Markham to act as his orderly. A black servant and two teamsters were in charge of the wagons loaded with camp supplies and provisions. Three Comanche Indians (two men and one woman), two of whom had fought against Mackenzie during the Red River War and were the sons of Comanche Chief Mow-way, also accompanied the party to act as interpreters.

Markham especially enjoyed the company of Thompson. The pair rose each day at daybreak to hunt deer and buffalo while Rodgers and Parker, two recent graduates of the United States Military Academy, would sleep in. Parker described Markham as a 'dapper little Englishman of pleasant manner'. Compared to his own modest frock coat and pantaloons, he said Markham 'was always carefully and neatly clothed in sporting equipment'. The officers were equally impressed with the naval officer's array of rifles and shotguns and spirit for adventure.

After eating wild turkey steaks or grilled duck for breakfast, the men were packed and ready to hunt by 8.00 am each day. They hunted duck, wild turkey, antelope, deer or buffalo. 'To a lover of the chase this country offers such attractions as are seldom to be found equalled in any part of the globe,' Markham declared. The officers usually returned to their temporary campsite around 4.00 or 5.00 pm to indulge in venison steaks and share the best stories from the day around the campfire. Markham typically excused himself earlier than the rest and headed to his tent to write in his journal before bed.

To Markham, hunting buffalo on the open prairies was one of the greatest experiences of his life. He admired the energy, practice and nerve hunters needed to master it. When the Englishman and his companions spotted a fleeing herd, they enthusiastically pursued it. Each man picked out an animal, steadied his aim and emptied his revolver. After being pierced in the lungs multiple times, the buffalo fell dead to the ground. It was then butchered and stripped of its hide. A portion of the meat was cooked and eaten by the men, some was dried to be taken back to Fort Sill, and the remainder, including the hide, given to their Indian comrades.

As much as he relished in these hunts, Markham realised that the buffalo – and the Indian's way of life – was quickly disappearing. As the party travelled further west, Markham noticed the prairie was strewn with thousands of bleached white buffalo skulls and bones. The officers revealed to him that millions of buffalo had roamed the same area two years before. From 1872–74, 4 million buffalo were killed on the southern plains. 'It can only be a work of time,' Markham calculated, 'when the red man, with the buffalo and other animals that used to range the boundless prairies in numbers innumerable, will become extinct as the dodo, the moa, and the great auk.' He was precise: less than 100 buffalo roamed the prairies by the 1880s.

While they were predators in most instances, Markham and the cavalry officers encountered some hostile wildlife on the plains. One of the most obnoxious and dangerous creatures on the prairie was the skunk. It was rumored that its bite could lead to rabies. The men stayed in their tents if they smelled its familiar odor. Another foe was the rattlesnake. While crawling on all fours towards a pond to take a shot at a group of ducks,

Markham dodged a rattlesnake before it could deliver a venomous bite. He knew that these reptiles liked to curl up in warm places, so he made sure to check his tent and blankets each night before bed, and turned his boots upside down before sticking his feet inside each morning.

On 1 December, the hunting party returned to Fort Sill. Their wagons were weighed down by hundreds of pounds of dried meat. They had killed 50 buffalo, 150 turkeys and 300 wildfowl within four weeks. Markham spent a few more days hunting and attending dinner parties before departing the fort. 'Nothing could exceed the kindness and hospitality extended towards me,' he wrote of the officers of the garrison. 'I felt a pang of regret when the time came to say farewell to the kind friends who had taken such good care of me, and who had caused the time spent on those lone bleak prairies to pass so pleasantly.'

Instead of returning by the same route he had taken from Caddo, Markham chose to travel another 300 miles north by a more scenic route to catch a train in Kansas destined for St Louis, Missouri. A lieutenant from Fort Sill's garrison drove Markham in a horse and buggy 60 miles north to Fort Reno. They passed through the Wichita Reservation where Indians of the Wichita, Caddo, Delaware and Pawnee tribes congregated. Due to a heavy rainstorm, Markham and the lieutenant stayed the night at the home of Major Sho-we-tat, also known as George Washington, the chief of the Whitehead Caddo on the Wichita Reservation.

Chief Sho-we-tat had fought for the Confederacy during the American Civil War. Markham described his Indian host as 'a very intelligent old man' and 'a most original character'. The 61-year-old chief still retained supreme authority over his tribe. Speaking in broken English, he introduced to Markham his daughter Cindie, a name he assumed was short for Cinderella. Much to his satisfaction, she boiled the Englishman some coffee and lent him buffalo robes for the night.

Markham left Chief Sho-we-tat's home and pushed on to Fort Reno the next day. Major John K. Mizner, commander of the garrison, and his fellow officers greeted Markham with the same warmth he had received from Mackenzie and the officers at Fort Sill. He was humbled by how he had been treated by the American officers of these isolated posts. 'From all I received the greatest kindness and the most unbounded hospitality,' Markham stated. '[B]y them nothing was left undone that could in any way conduce to my comfort or pleasure.' Markham spent two days at Fort Reno, dedicating one day to visiting the Cheyenne-Arapaho Reservation, made up of about 5,000 Cheyenne and Arapaho Indians.

On 7 December, he hitched a ride in a wagon headed for Camp Supply, the northernmost military station in Indian Territory. During this 130-mile journey, he shared the wagon with Captain William H. Clapp of the 16th Infantry Regiment. He described 41-year-old Clapp as 'a most agreeable and pleasant companion'. Ironically, seven years later, Clapp volunteered to lead an Arctic expedition to rescue Lieutenant Adolphus W. Greely and his starving men trapped on Cape Sabine in Smith Sound. Markham and George Nares would also lend support in this rescue effort.

Camp Supply had been established in 1868 by General Sheridan as a supply base during one of his Indian campaigns. Around 8,000 to 9,000 Cheyenne and Arapaho Indians lived outside of the post. Markham spent more time mingling with the Indians here than in any of the other reservations he visited. He was introduced to the distinguished Arapaho chiefs Little Raven, Big Wolf and Yellow Bear. The Indians were nearly starving because of the dwindling supply of buffalo meat. He was appalled when he witnessed them bartering their clothes away for food and begging the soldiers for scraps of meat and bread.

Markham left Camp Supply and hitched a ride in a wagon headed 90 miles north towards the nearest railway station located in Dodge City, Kansas. The stretch of land he passed through on his way to Dodge City had a reputation for being a haven for robbers and drifters. After crossing over the Cimarron River and entering Kansas, two armed strangers emerged from the darkness and demanded a ride. The frightened driver agreed to take the two raggedly clothed cowboys to Dodge City.

The men climbed into the wagon and sat next to Markham. He later described the cowboys as 'the roughest specimens of humanity' he had ever met. One of them, a white man named Jack, sported a beard, moustache and long, greasy hair. The other cowboy, a heavyset black man named Bob King, wore a shabby beard on his face. Markham learned that the two men had belonged to a group of twenty-six cowboys driving a herd of 7,000 cattle from Texas to Kansas. After a dispute with their boss, they shot him through the heart and fled, but not before he put a bullet in King's thigh.

The wagon halted for the night at a crude ranch made of mud and logs called Bear Creek Station, the halfway point to Dodge City. A stagecoach relay station was located close by. When Markham strolled through the front door, he saw about a dozen or so rough-looking cowboys gathered around a fireplace. He quietly sat down next to them and listened in on their conversation. 'I soon found out that we were in a regular den of murderers and thieves,' he recalled. Each man boasted about how many men he had killed or how many times he had been shot or stabbed. Markham claimed that these stories were 'enough to curdle one's blood'. He got what little sleep he could on the ranch's dirt floor wrapped up in a buffalo robe, while King, spread out in his tattered blanket, slept next to him.

The wagon pulled into Dodge City on 14 December. Markham checked into the Dodge House Hotel at the end of Front Street, close to the notorious Long Branch Saloon. Most of the wooden buildings lining the streets were saloons, gambling houses or dance halls filled with drifters, prostitutes and gamblers. The city officials were controlled by the saloon keepers and gamblers. Markham walked the cattle town's dirt streets, and described it as 'the sink of iniquity' and 'perfect "hell upon earth"'. He even compared it to Sodom and Gomorrah. He could not have been happier when he boarded his train to St Louis and left this den of debauchery for good.

Three weeks after leaving Dodge City, while glancing over a newspaper, Markham came across a column mentioning the cowboy Bob King. He had shot and killed a woman, Laura Barnhill, in Memphis. When the officer heard the screams of Barnhill and rushed over to apprehend her assailant, King shot the lawman in the jaw, nearly killing him, and fled the scene. A reward of fifty dollars was offered for King, and two men hunted him down and brought him back to stand trial. Markham found it strange to think that he had slept next to this murderer only a few weeks before.

From St Louis, Markham travelled to his family's farm and arrived on 20 December. He spent some time there before concluding his tour of the United States. Over a six-week period, he visited cities in Wisconsin and Minnesota, even taking his mother to St Paul for a few days. Word rapidly spread that an English Arctic explorer was in the area and he capitalised on this fame by conducting several presentations in front of local audiences for a small fee. He then travelled to Washington, D.C. on his way to New York, where he met up with Dr Emil Bessels, working at the Smithsonian Institution, who had been rescued by the *Arctic* in 1873. After touring some notable attractions in the city, he headed to New York and left for England. On 8 March 1878, he arrived back home after a six-month trip.

Markham returned to find England on the brink of war. In April, the Russians invaded the Balkans and defeated the Ottoman Empire within nine months, forcing them to sign an embarrassing peace treaty in March. England, fearing the risk Russia posed to the Suez Canal and India, threatened to take action if the Russians did not amend the treaty and relinquish some of the territory taken from the Ottomans. On the home front, a squadron of ships under Admiral Sir Astley Cooper Key was mobilised for service in the Baltic Sea in the event of an Anglo-Russian war. Markham temporarily took command of a turret ship in the squadron, HMS *Hydra*, but diplomats successfully hammered out a revised peace treaty in July, ending the threat of an international war. With the risk of war over, the *Hydra* was decommissioned in August and Markham was without a command.

This period between assignments allowed him to pursue some of his other pastimes. Besides spending time travelling, Markham continued to write. Between 1878 and 1880, he published three books. The first was a lengthy history of the Arctic Expedition, titled *The Great Frozen Sea: A Personal Narrative of the Voyage of the "Alert" During the Arctic Expedition of 1875–6*, published in March 1878. This was followed by a monograph that dealt with past English expeditions to the North Pole. In 1880, he edited and provided notes for a book on the collected writings of the sixteenth-century English navigator John Davis.

In September 1878, Albert vacationed in France and the Netherlands with Clements and Minna. While in Amsterdam, they met two distinguished Dutch Arctic explorers, Lieutenants A. de Bruyne and Koolemans Beynen, who had returned from exploring the Barents Sea four months earlier. The Dutch officers had taken the schooner *Willem Barents* to erect memorials to fallen Dutch navigators on the islands of Jan Mayen, Spitsbergen and the archipelago of Novaya Zemlya. They also collected scientific data and reported on the condition of the ice. Fascinated by what he had learned from the Dutch officers, Albert published an account of their expedition in the monthly periodical *Good Words* the following year. This meeting left him longing to visit this uninhabited Arctic region.

Few subjects of the British Empire had ventured into the Barents Sea before, with the exception of the 5th Baronet of Sligo, Sir Henry Gore-Booth. The wealthy Irish baron had made several salmon fishing cruises to the Barents Sea in the decades before. He chartered a 40-ton Norwegian cutter, the *Isbjörn*, and intended to go on a hunting, fishing and sightseeing trip that summer along the coast of Novaya Zemlya. His wife, Georgina, had a stream dammed on their 32,000-acre estate and filled it with fish hoping that it would satisfy her husband's restlessness. It did not work. Like Markham, he had fallen under the Arctic spell and nothing could hold him back from pursuing the irresistible call of the north.

Gore-Booth's travelling companion for this trip had dropped out at the last minute and Georgina insisted that he find a replacement. He hurried to London in April and came to 21 Eccleston Square hoping that Clements Markham could recommend a suitable substitute at such short notice. Clements was away when he arrived, but Albert Markham was there to greet him. While the two sat down and were 'cogitating over the glorious field that lies open to the explorer in the Arctic regions, and bitterly lamenting the apparent decadence of spirit of enterprise' in England, Gore-Booth, impressed with his background and knowledge, bluntly asked Markham to join him on his cruise. He agreed to go if Gore-Booth promised to dedicate part of the voyage to scientific research and exploration. The baronet accepted Markham's wishes, and he left without delay to request leave from the Admiralty.

The Lords Commissioners granted Markham's request under the condition that he would report back the condition of the ice between Novaya Zemlya and Spitsbergen and the navigability of the Barents Sea. He packed his bags and left with Gore-Booth for Norway on 1 May on the steamship *Tasso*. They reached the city of Tromsø, Norway, nine days later.

There they encountered the cutter that they would call home for the next eighteen weeks. Markham described the black and yellow *Isbjörn* as being a trim and rakish ship. The 43-ton cargo ship had been strengthened with bands of iron and timber to allow for it to easily cut through ice. It had acquired renown for carrying the Austro-Hungarian explorers Julius von Payer and Carl Weyprecht on their expedition to the Barents Sea in 1871.

Captain Frederick C. Mack, acting as Gore-Booth's agent in Tromsø, had handled the arrangements for chartering the *Isbjörn*. He allowed Markham and Gore-Booth to store their luggage in his office and hang around in his hotel until the schooner departed. Also accompanying the two men were Gore-Booth's hunting collie Gouch, as well as his valet and butler, Thomas Kilgallon. Kilgallon was not a typical butler and remained a faithful companion to Gore-Booth on his numerous trips over the years. Dubbed 'the faithful one' by the *Isbjörn*'s crew, Kilgallon made sure Gore-Booth and Markham always had a hot meal and dry clothing. 'A more useful or willing man for such a cruise it would have been impossible to find,' Markham fondly wrote of the baronet's loyal butler.

Markham and Gore-Booth had the good fortune to bump into Captain Elling Carlsen, a well-known Norwegian explorer, before leaving Tromsø. He had accompanied Payer and Weyprecht when they discovered a mysterious landmass to the north of Novaya Zemlya, christened Franz Josef Land. The Norwegian captain gave them valuable information about the condition of the ice and pointed out the best spots to hunt seals, walruses and bears. He warned them to be wary of the *Isbjörn*'s owner and captain, Lors 'Old Jog' Jorgensen, who knew little about navigating through ice or captaining a ship.

Just as Carlsen had cautioned him, Markham found 'Old Jog' to be an incompetent sailor and captain. 'His qualifications for the command were *nil*,' Markham complained. He relied on his two harpooners to make most of the decisions relating to navigation. He doubted if Jorgensen had ever seen a sextant or chronometer before. Like the *Isbjörn*'s crew, he did not speak a word of English. Even worse, his crew questioned his sanity. He would suddenly burst out in song and dance while at the wheel as if he had gone mad.

While Markham had Jorgensen to worry about, the *Isbjörn*'s crew did not help to ease his concern. He described the nine Norwegians as a 'very rough and uncouth set of men'. He found them also to be lazy and lacking in discipline. They would never compare to the men that made up his sledge teams in 1876.

Markham regarded the most reliable man on the ship to be Jorgensen's second-in-command, a sailor named Sorensen, who had served on English, Russian, German and Norwegian ships in the past. He spoke English well and served as the interpreter.

Just before the *Isbjörn* left Tromsø's harbour, a creditor showed up demanding payment of past due debts owed by Jorgensen. The debt collector threatened to seize the *Isbjörn* if Jorgensen did not pay up. Luckily, Gore-Booth's agent, Captain Mack, intervened and told the creditor that the *Isbjörn* was no longer the property of the captain, but was now under English control. Gore-Booth and Markham had no legal authority from their government to hoist the English colours on the ship but remained silent on the matter. This ruse stalled the creditor long enough for the *Isbjörn* to flee and head northeast on 18 May 1879.

Originally built to store goods instead of passengers, space was limited on the Norwegian cutter. Markham and Gore-Booth shared a 6-foot-wide cabin with little room for storage besides cupboards located under their bunks. Markham hated the amount of area available to exercise on the gangway and compared it to that which was allotted to the bears in their cages at London's Zoological Gardens. Four funnels, from 2 to 6 feet in height, spewed black clouds of smoke, making it nearly impossible to exercise in this cramped area without inhaling these toxic fumes.

On their way to Novaya Zemlya, the men shot birds, reindeer, walruses, seals and even a few polar bears. Markham and Gore-Booth tried a fried walrus tongue. Markham claimed it was not that bad except for the fact that it was as tough as boot leather. The crew collected and hung the skins of birds to dry along the front of the ship. Haunches of venison, duck, geese and other birds were scattered in stinking piles on the upper deck. The ship looked and smelled like a slaughterhouse.

When he was not indulging in hunting, Markham spent his time collecting animals, plants and insects indigenous to the Arctic zone. He skinned sixty birds of twenty-three species so that they could be stuffed and donated to natural history collections. He also dissected carcasses to examine their insides. He cut open the stomach of a reindeer to determine if it lived off willow or moss during the winter. He catalogued a total of eighty-nine types of flora, grasses, mosses and lichens. Besides collecting animal and plant life, he gathered notes on the wind and weather patterns, the condition of the ice and the navigability of the Barents Sea.

Markham and Gore-Booth got their first glimpse of the Arctic archipelago of Novaya Zemlya on 9 June. Three days later, the ship anchored in Nameless Bay to replenish its provisions. Thousands of loons nested nearby. 'Never before had I ever seen such a "living mass" of the feathered denizens of the air assembled in one place,' Markham recalled. The birds flew in a pack as thick as bees and came close enough to the ship that the crew could strike them down with their oars. Markham and Gore-Booth grabbed their guns and killed them by the dozens in a matter of minutes – a total of 600 were killed in two hours.

On 18 June, the ship left Nameless Bay and entered Matochkin Shar. The 60-mile-wide fjord cut through the center of Novaya Zemlya and led to the Kara Sea on the other side of the archipelago. 'It seemed difficult to realise that we were really in the Matyushin [Matochkin] Shar,' Markham declared. He said it was 'almost as fabulous and out of reach as some of those mythical places visited and described by the fictitious heroes of our boyhood'. The fjord was so narrow – its narrowest point was 660 yards across – and bendy that ships were reported to have sailed 10 or 15 miles in and then turned around thinking they were in a landlocked bay. The *Isbjörn* only made it about 12 miles before it was stopped by a barrier of ice that ran from shore to shore. The ship had arrived too early in the season to advance further.

The *Isbjörn* turned back and anchored off Cross Island on the coast of Novaya Zemlya on 11 July. The crew went ashore and discovered the graves of the Norwegian walrus hunter Captain Sivert Tobiesen and his son. Both had died of scurvy after the schooner *Freya* was trapped in ice in 1872. 'It was indeed a melancholy and dreary scene that we gazed upon, on that cold, cheerless July day,' Markham stated as he stared upon the two mounds of stones marked by pieces of driftwood. 'In the foreground were the two graves, typical of loving affection, united in life, unsevered in death.' Fragments of Tobiesen's ill-failed schooner and its cargo were scattered along the beachline.

Since they were unable to pass through Matochkin Shar, Markham appealed to Jorgensen to push further north along the coast of Novaya

Zemlya. But the captain and his crew did not share Markham's desire for exploration and discovery. They had been paid to take two passengers on a hunting and sightseeing trip, not to risk their lives in the heavy northern ice. With the exception of the two harpooners, none of the men had navigated these icy waters before. Jorgensen's harpooners saw Markham and Gore-Booth as 'mad hair-brained Englishmen' and convinced the others of the foolhardiness of attempting to go further north into uncharted waters.

To appease his passengers, Jorgensen said he would again try to force his way through Matochkin Shar. The ship re-entered the fjord on 21 July and this time rammed its way through the ice barrier. After spending twenty-eight days in the Kara Sea on the eastern coast of Novaya Zemlya, they re-entered Matochkin Shar on 18 August. There they encountered Lieutenant Bruyne, whom Markham had previously met in Amsterdam, in his ship *Willem Barents*. Markham and Bruyne continued to correspond after this meeting the previous year, and before he departed Tromsø, Markham received a letter from Bruyne telling him when he expected to arrive at different points along the archipelago during his own expedition.

Bruyne and his officers came aboard the *Isbjörn* but found its quarters too cramped, so they invited its crew to come to their more spacious ship. For three days the two ships remained anchored side by side and their crews enjoyed each other's company. An English photographer, William J.A. Grant, who accompanied the Dutchmen, took several photographs of their crews. Bruyne and his officers kindly offered cups, plates and tumblers to replace the *Isbjörn*'s broken tableware. The *Isbjörn*'s crew traded fresh meat for boots and arsenical soap. (Markham used the soap to preserve his bird skins.)

Bruyne brought news from Europe of the untimely death of the Prince Imperial, the son of the exiled Emperor Napoleon III, killed after being speared by Zulus in South Africa. The news deeply affected Markham, who had been raised for a time in France and was fond of the French imperial family. He recalled Empress Eugénie and her now deceased son visiting Portsmouth before the *Alert* and *Discovery* left the port for the Arctic in May 1875. 'I not only remembered the honour that was conferred upon us, when fitting out in the *Alert* and *Discovery*, by a visit from his mother and himself,' Markham wrote, 'but also the thoughtful present sent to the ships' companies of those vessels by the Empress [Eugénie presented each man of the expedition with a knitted wool cap], and the kind words with which she wished us success on our mission and bade us God-speed.'

The *Isbjörn* and *Willem Barents* returned to the Barents Sea after exiting Matochkin Shar on 22 August. Bruyne intended to sail north around Novaya Zemlya and visit the location on its tip called Ice Haven, where Willem Barents and his crew passed the winter of 1596. Barents's claim to fame was his discovery of Spitsbergen and the Barents Sea before his death a year later. Markham, an admirer of the sixteenth-century Dutch explorer, hoped that hearing this news would motivate Jorgensen to do the same. Maybe, if they were lucky, they could even get a clear view of Franz Josef Land.

To his astonishment, the usually timid captain agreed to follow the Dutch schooner to Ice Haven. But the further north Jorgensen took his ship, the less enthusiastic he became to proceed into the Arctic unknown. The ship had four weeks of provisions left, and Jorgensen feared that they would not have enough food to sustain the crew and his passengers if the ship was entombed in ice. His nerves got the better of him, and after consulting his harpooners, he gave the order to turn back. The captain's announcement aggravated Markham who afterwards accused 'the chicken-hearted harpooners' for Jorgensen's sudden change of heart.

After spending eighteen weeks exploring Novaya Zemlya's coast and Matochkin Shar, the *Isbjörn* returned to Tromsø on 22 September. A few days after their return, to Markham's displeasure, he learned that the *Willem Barents* had not only reached Ice Haven but its crew also got a glimpse of the mysterious archipelago to the north he desired to see so badly.

Markham was dissatisfied with the results of the cruise but tried to make the best of it. Considering the *Isbjörn*'s fainthearted captain and crew, he was grateful for what he had been able to achieve. He presented an impressive collection of notes to the Admiralty. Still, the voyage was nothing more than a glorified hunting and fishing trip. It did not unearth anything that was not already discovered. Others saw the trip as a wasted effort unworthy of praise as an Arctic expedition. 'It is not wise ... to claim for this dashing trip any importance as a voyage of Arctic exploration,' an article published in *The Saturday Review* declared. 'He [Markham] deserves all credit as an energetic English sailor, but not in this case as an explorer.'

In 1881, Markham published a lengthy narrative titled *A Polar Reconnaissance: Being the Voyage of the "Isbjörn" to Novaya Zemlya in 1879* chronicling his voyage. He used the book as a means to encourage English exploration in the northwest portion of the Arctic Ocean, chiefly dominated by Dutch and Austro-Hungarian explorers. 'I am more than ever convinced,' he stated, 'that a greater amount of success will be gained by the exploration of the region in the vicinity of Franz Josef Land than in any other part of the Arctic regions.' He reasoned that the route between Spitsbergen and Novaya Zemlya could provide the closest approach to the North Pole. While Clements Markham snubbed an attempt to reach the North Pole as 'a childish and useless quest', Markham remained dedicated to it. As other explorers began to inch closer to attaining this 300–year-old quest, he felt that someone, hopefully an Englishman, would be the first to do so.

Since there were still over a million square miles of unexplored land in the Arctic, Markham argued that the English should continue to explore this remote region. Other parts of the world, such as Africa and Australia, had been investigated while this vast area remained virtually untouched. While a renewal of Arctic exploration may not bring the English financial gain, Markham proclaimed, it would certainly lead to greater glory for the empire and further scientific discoveries imperative to civilisation. 'To my mind England, as a great maritime nation, should not be content with the unimportant role which she has of late years played in the grand work of geographical discovery,' Markham reasoned. '[S]he should equip expeditions, not only for the exploration of that region culminating at the North Pole, but also for the complete discovery of the whole terrestrial globe!'

The disappointing voyage to Novaya Zemlya would be Markham's last trip that far north. An American, not an Englishman, eventually did reach the North Pole. While Markham's voyages exploring uncharted Arctic regions may have ended for good, he continued to encourage it, later turning his attention, like his cousin, to Antarctica and the South Pole. But Markham's globetrotting did not end with his trip to Novaya Zemlya. He focused his energy instead on the Americas.

Chapter 7

A Gentleman Adventurer

'I wanted to get away out of the reach of posts and telegraph, to bury myself for a time from the civilised world, and to be free from receipt of all official letters and documents.'

Albert H. Markham, *Good Words*

Albert Markham returned from his cruise to Novaya Zemlya at the beginning of October 1879. Shortly after, he received orders to report to his old commander, Rear Admiral Stirling, who was now in command of the Pacific Station. His orders were to proceed to Peru and assume command of Stirling's flagship, HMS *Triumph*. Less than a month after returning from the frozen waters of the Barents Sea, Markham departed England for the Caribbean.

He reached the island of St Thomas on 15 November. In Port Royal, Jamaica, he ran into the former head surgeon on the *Alert* during the Arctic Expedition of 1875–76, Dr Thomas Colan. The doctor was serving as the deputy inspector general in charge of the Royal Navy Hospital. Markham left this old pirate stronghold and journeyed overland to Panama and waited for a steamer to take him to Lima, Peru. There he joined the *Triumph*, anchored in Callao, caught in a war that had broken out during the spring of 1879 between Chile, Bolivia and Peru over a territorial dispute in the Atacama Desert.

A desert may not seem like an area worth fighting a war over, but millions of tons of bird guano (used as chemical fertiliser by farmers) and sodium nitrate (used in munitions) were being harvested from the Bolivian-controlled part of the region and exported to Europe and North America for a hefty profit. Thousands of Chilean peasants working in the Bolivian nitrate mines felt justified in their share of this revenue. To prevent a bloody confrontation between the two sides, Bolivia and Chile signed the Treaty of Mutual Benefits in 1866. In February 1878, the Bolivian President Hilarión Daza violated this treaty when he placed a ten cent tax on the Chilean mining companies. The owners refused to pay and a pugnacious Daza seized the mines. The Chilean government responded by dispatching a fleet and landed 200 sailors and soldiers in the Bolivian city of Antofagasta on 14 February. After a breakdown in negotiations, Chile officially declared war on Bolivia, and its ally Peru, on 15 April 1879.

The Peruvians – pulled into the conflict by their alliance with Bolivia – shouldered the brunt of the fighting against Chile. The Peruvians were able to delay a Chilean ground invasion for at least six months due to the bold tactics of Captain Miguel Grau. The Peruvian captain terrorised Chilean transports along the South American coast with his ironclad, *Huáscar*. Manufactured by the Laird Brothers of Birkenhead in 1866, the menacing ironclad weighed 1,130 tons, carried two 10-inch, 250lb Armstrong guns with a range of 2,200 yards and was reinforced with 4-inch thick armour plating on its sides. The *Huáscar* singlehandedly bullied the Chilean Navy into inaction.

After months of being intimidated by the *Huáscar*, Chilean ships trapped the ironclad at Angamos on 8 October and killed Grau and most of his crew. The Chileans captured the ironclad and converted it for services in their navy. This seizure gave the Chileans a major confidence boost and changed the fortunes of the war in their favour by allowing the Chilean Navy to freely transport soldiers up and down the western coast of South America and blockade Peruvian ports.

English, American, French and Italian warships stayed neutral in the conflict but remained close by to protect the lives of foreigners and their economic investments in Peru. Of the then 100,156 inhabitants living in Lima, 17,922 were foreigners employed as merchants or shopkeepers, or in other trades. Millions of pounds were invested in Peru's infrastructure – railways, port facilities and mining companies – by English businessmen and entrepreneurs so that they could more easily and efficiently export guano and nitrates from the Atacama Desert to European markets. The war threatened to disrupt this business, and Prime Minister Gladstone even considered intervention to quickly end the war.

When Markham arrived at Callao in December, he found the discipline of the *Triumph*'s crew not up to the standards he expected of a ship on the brink of war. The lure of strong drink and women in Lima led some sailors to go on unauthorised leave and to engage in other acts of disobedience. Markham reprimanded them severely but also felt remorseful for doing so. 'I wonder if the men have any idea that I feel the punishment I inflict upon them as much as they do themselves,' he privately confessed. 'I was very much distressed to-day at having to punish those who have been otherwise well-behaved, but I am determined to put a stop if I possibly can to leave-breaking.'

In one instance of insubordination that took place on the *Triumph*'s quarterdeck, a young sailor, Louis Price, thought to be drunk, struck a superior officer. For this offence, the boy was sentenced to three years' hard labour by a court martial. Feeling sympathetic for Price, Markham intervened in his defence. He said that Price was one of his most promising men leading up to the incident. Taking into account Price's youth and good standing, Markham asked for the sentence to be commuted. The Admiralty approved his request and reduced Price's prison time by one year.

After the loss of the *Huáscar* and Chile's capture of the Peruvian province of Tarapacá, morale in Lima plummeted. 'Since the loss of the *Huáscar* the nation has gone into mourning,' Lieutenant Rudolph de Lisle of HMS *Shannon* observed. '[N]o parties or gaiety of any sort, no dances, for the populace would break anyone's windows who permitted it.' Chilean ships blockaded Callao and Arica – with the *Huáscar* added to their ranks – just out of range of the Peruvian guns and torpedoes but clearly visible to their citizens. The Peruvian President Mariano Ignacio Prado abruptly left for Europe on 18 December to buy armaments and ironclads to gain an advantage over the Chileans. A former finance minister in the Peruvian government, Nicolás de Piérola, took advantage of the discontent and Prado's absence and stormed the presidential palace on 23 December. Piérola's successful coup allowed him to take control of the country.

The crews of the neutral warships did what they could to pass the time as this internal strife unfolded in Lima and a war was being fought on the mainland. They competed in sailing races, held cricket and baseball games, hunted wildlife, visited botanical gardens and attended dances and banquets. Markham collected plants and insects and hunted at least

600 birds, including a rare species of gull. As usual, he sent specimens back to museums in England to be studied and for safekeeping.

On 24 January 1880, the *Triumph* left Callao for Esquimalt Harbour on Vancouver Island to be refitted. The Bolivians, Peruvians and Chileans were in talks discussing ending the war and it seemed like an opportune time to handle these repairs. Admiral Stirling permitted Markham to stop at the Galapagos Islands en route to the Pacific Station base. Due to the shallowness of the water between the islands, Markham was restricted where he could take his 6,640-ton ship. Assisted by his junior officers, he made several excursions and collected birds, insects and shells. Afterwards, he sent the birds to Osbert Salvin, a noted naturalist and ornithologist. Grateful for Markham's contribution to the British Museum, Salvin named a rare storm petrel recovered from the islands after him.

After leaving the Galapagos Islands, the *Triumph* steamed north and stopped at Acapulco, Mexico, in March, where Markham collected more insects. The ship then arrived in San Francisco on 2 April, where it remained for a period of ten days before anchoring at Vancouver Island on 17 April. Markham kept himself occupied during the eight months his ship underwent repairs by giving a lecture on the Arctic at the Mechanics Institute; overseeing the construction of the Seaman's Club House and Recreation Ground; serving as Justice of the Peace for the district; and collecting birds native to Vancouver Island and British Columbia. In November, negotiations between the South American countries broke down and a Chilean expeditionary force of 26,000 soldiers under General Manuel Baquedano landed south of Lima and marched on the Peruvian capital, forcing the *Triumph* to leave Esquimalt Harbour and hurry back to Callao.

When the ship returned to the Peruvian capital, Admiral Stirling selected two officers from the *Triumph*, Commander William Dyke Acland and Lieutenant Reginald Carey Brenton, to act as observers and report on the troop movements of both armies. Markham afterwards commended both Brenton and Acland for their service, praising the 'admirable manner in which they have fulfilled such delicate and serious duties' despite the 'many risks and the many situations of extreme danger in which they found themselves'. Days before the Chilean victory at

Chorrillos in January 1881, Stirling wished to communicate with the Chilean commander and ordered Markham to convey a message to his headquarters. He passed through both the Peruvian and Chilean lines, having a chance to see soldiers from both armies for himself. Markham later described the Chilean soldiers as being 'of fine physique, intelligent, and full of energy and enthusiasm, well clothed and fed, and in the best of spirits', compared to the 'dispirited, wretched, and apathetic' Peruvian soldiers entrusted with the defence of Lima.

Word reached Lima of the atrocities committed by the Chilean soldiers after their victory at Chorrillos. The report sent Lima's residents into a frenzy. The Chilean soldiers had raped, robbed, destroyed and killed everything in sight. One of the civilians murdered by this mob included Dr Maclean, a 77-year-old English physician. Commander Acland, attached to the Chilean army, gave a horrific account of what he had witnessed at Chorrillos:

> Soon after the fighting was over, the troops broke into the grog shops and wine cellars, getting rapidly drunk, and becoming entirely out of control, and there ensued a scene of destruction and horror that I hope has rarely been witnessed in modern times; houses and property destroyed, men quarrelling and shooting each other for amusement, women violated, innocent civilians of any age murdered. The cemetery turned into a place where drunken soldiers held their orgies and even broke open the graves in order that the corpses might be removed to make way for their own drunken companions.

When the Chileans occupied a position 8 miles from Lima and prepared to break through the Peruvian entrenchments, civilians and their families living in Lima looked to the foreign ministers and warships for protection. The lucky ones boarded warships and boats anchored in Callao. However, thousands of refugees turned to foreign legations, convents and other neutral buildings in the city to seek shelter. At least 600 women and children of all classes, colours and nationalities crammed into the British Legation hoping that the English would protect them when the city fell. Admiral Stirling and Minister Spencer St John did all that they could to guarantee the safety of the citizens and their families.

In a rare display of unity, the Italians, French and English, led by Stirling and St John, worked together to navigate the dicey political situation and negotiate a ceasefire with the Chileans.

President Piérola allowed St John to send a delegation to the Chilean camp. On 14 January, Admiral Stirling sent Lieutenant Brenton and Italian Lieutenant Conde Royck by train to the Chilean camp to see if Baquedano would be willing to discuss the surrender of Lima. Acland, with the Chileans, stopped Brenton before he returned to the Peruvian line and told him to inform St John that it would be dangerous for any woman or child to remain in the capital if the Chileans broke through the Peruvian defences and stormed the city. When the leading ministers and naval commanders gathered at the British Legation before departing to meet with Baquedano, Stirling assured all that he would not hesitate to 'take or sink the Chilean fleet' if the neutral embassies or compounds were attacked. He directed Markham, at Callao with the *Triumph*, to be ready at a moment's notice as these events unfolded.

The next day, St John and the diplomatic corps met with General Baquedano. The Chilean general demanded the unconditional surrender of Lima and Callao. The English minister assured Baquedano that he would do whatever was necessary to protect the English subjects in the city, even if it meant firing on Chilean ships. Stirling and some of his officers planned to stay at the British Legation to ensure that the refugees were not harmed. Baquedano agreed to respect any buildings distinguished by foreign flags and would only enter Lima with a well-disciplined detachment to avoid what had happened at Chorrillos. The two sides agreed to an armistice and St John left to meet with Piérola to discuss the terms of surrender. It appeared for a time as if the city would be handed over without further bloodshed.

Piérola met with the foreign ministers and senior naval officers over lunch at his headquarters to discuss Baquedano's terms. Their meeting abruptly ended with the outbreak of gunfire. Peruvian soldiers had shot at Baquedano and his staff when he rode within range of their lines, causing the fighting to resume. The foreign ministers, admirals, secretaries and aides-de-camp, only 200 yards or so from the front line, made a humiliating retreat to escape being killed in the crossfire. Those unable to catch a train headed to Lima had to flee 8 miles on foot back to the capital. Even though exposed to heavy fire, the foreigners returned to Lima unharmed, with the exception of St John, who was wounded when a Chilean shell exploded nearby causing a piece of rock to slice open his hand.

As Chilean and Peruvian soldiers fought the Battle of Miraflores, marines from the foreign warships were dispatched to defend the refugees being evacuated by train out of the city. The foreign ministers and naval commanders, and the remaining Peruvian government officials who had not fled, met and agreed it was in the best interests of Lima's citizens to attempt to reach Baquedano so that they could surrender before his troops rampaged through the streets of the city. Stirling sent Brenton, Royck and French Lieutenant Roberjot to the Chilean headquarters to find Baquedano. When they located him he agreed to a ceasefire. The Peruvians handed over Lima to the Chileans on 17 January 1881. On the same day, Stirling asked Markham to come up to the British Legation from Callao by train to assist with the transfer of the city to Chilean hands.

Besides a nasty guerilla war that ensued until the Treaty of Ancón was signed in October 1883, things remained quiet for the foreign warships. This peacefulness was interrupted when, less than a month later, an explosion rocked the *Triumph* while anchored at Coquimbo. On 23 November at 8.00 am, Gunner Thomas H.T. Davies went below deck to grab a can of yellow paint, and as he unscrewed the hatch to the glory hole, everything below his abdomen was nearly torn away from a blast. Two other men, Able Seaman William N. Foxon and Gunner Charles Legg, were instantly killed. Seven sailors nearby sustained severe burns and internal injuries. 'It is with deep regret I have to inform you that an explosion occurred in one of the paint rooms,' Markham wrote in shock to Admiral Stirling. 'The explosion was of such violence as to completely wreck (I have no better word to describe the ruin it effected) the lower sickbay, in which were several sick men confined to their beds.'

Stirling ordered a formal investigation to be conducted to determine what had caused the explosion. Markham speculated that it had been caused by a reaction from a keg of xerotine siccative stored under the paint room. The three officers assigned to the investigation found this to be the case, determining that the explosion had been caused by a leaky

6-gallon tin of xerotine siccative – a liquid mixed with paint to make it dry quicker. Toxic vapours in the ship's hold ignited the moment they came into contact with the light of Davies's lantern. As a result, the unfortunate gunner was torn to shreds.

No one could have fathomed how destructive xerotine siccative was, including Markham. He was angered that such a deadly substance was on his ship without knowing the danger it posed to his men. 'I deeply regret,' he stated, 'that for some *incomprehensible reason*, we on board, were not in possession of more explicit information regarding the exceedingly dangerous and explosive nature of this composition (xerotive siccative) before it was authorised to be issued to us as ship's stores.' A similar explosion involving xerotive siccative had taken place on HMS *Doterel* in April, which sunk the ship and killed its crew of 145 men. The sailors on the *Triumph* had been fortunate. The Admiralty banned the use of xerotive siccative on all English ships after the *Triumph*'s accident.

Markham returned to England in February and was assigned to the command of the torpedo training school in Portsmouth based on a floating hulk, HMS *Vernon*. This was an uneventful assignment for him, with the exception of when one of his torpedo boat tenders, HMS *Hecla*, collided with a steamship, the *Cheerful*, on its way from Falmouth to Liverpool in July 1885. The collision left a gaping 8-foot hole in the *Hecla*'s bow, but its crew stretched a sail over the opening and worked tirelessly to pull thirty-six of the *Cheerful*'s passengers from the water before it limped back to Portsmouth. An investigation by the Admiralty found neither ship at fault and blamed the accident on thick fog.

While stationed at the torpedo training school, Markham received word of a proposed American rescue operation to save Lieutenant Adolphus W. Greely and his crew stranded on Ellesmere Island in Smith Sound. Four American officers of the Greely Relief Board, established in December 1883 by President Chester A. Arthur, reached out to the leading experts overseas who had navigated Smith Sound: George Nares, Albert H. Markham, Henry F. Stephenson and Otto Nordenskjöld. One of the board members, Captain George W. Davis, believed Markham was the most important of these men to enlist. 'The three first-named [Nares, Markham and Stephenson] are probably better acquainted with the navigation of the upper part of Baffin Bay and Smith Sound than any persons now living, Commander Markham, particularly,' Davis stated. 'If I were going up there myself in command of the expedition, I should request this government to ask leave of that of Great Britain to have Commander Markham accompany the party as an advisory officer, if he would do so.' Markham did not accompany the rescue expedition, but he and George Nares sent a detailed report to the Americans providing suggestions for the organisation, equipment and conduct of a relief expedition. The President of the Greely Relief Board, Brigadier General William B. Hazen, forwarded the 'very interesting and instructive' report to Secretary of Navy William E. Chandler. Taking these suggestions into consideration, an American rescue expedition under Commander Winfield Scott Schley reached Cape Sabine in June 1884 and saved Greely and five survivors of the original twenty-five men.

Markham was relieved when his assignment came to an end after three and a half years of being cooped up on the *Vernon*. He immediately applied for six months' leave. 'I wanted to get away out of the reach of posts and telegraph,' he declared, 'to bury myself for a time from the civilised world, and to be free from receipt of all official letters and documents.' He planned a retreat to North America and made arrangements to leave for the United States on 5 June 1886. Days before leaving he was introduced by a friend to a dapper Canadian named Hugh Sutherland, of the Winnipeg and Hudson Bay Railway and Steamship Company. The timing of the meeting could not have been better for both men.

Sutherland came to England in search of financial support for his scheme to connect Manitoba and the Northwest Territories to Europe by rail and sea. Completing a railway line from Winnipeg to the Hudson Bay, as well as constructing a seaport on the massive body of saltwater (470,000 square miles), would allow goods to pass more efficiently and quickly through the Hudson Strait to the Atlantic Ocean instead of being transported overland. Not only saving money and time, Sutherland also reasoned his new route would help to bolster commerce and industry in Canada.

Three years earlier, the Canadian government authorised Lieutenant Andrew Robertson Gordon, a retired Royal Navy officer, to establish meteorological stations along the coast to further investigate the navigability of the Hudson Strait. Gordon's subsequent report found that the low temperatures in the region from November to April made navigation *impossible*; the ice was too heavy to permit steamers to enter the Hudson Strait until at least 1 July; even in July, the ice could cause considerable delay to ships; travel was only practical for three months out of the year (15 July to 15 October); and during these months, ships would be at risk of being damaged by the ice. Gordon's findings posed a major roadblock to Sutherland's initiative since most Eastern Canadian businessmen refused to back his scheme, finding the financial risk greater than the reward.

Of course, Sutherland dismissed Gordon's report and decided to send his own expert to conduct a similar investigation. Markham, regarded as one of the leading experts in Arctic travel, already planned to vacation in North America and made an ideal candidate. Sutherland agreed to cover the expenses of Markham's voyage to Nova Scotia. The Canadian government also granted Sutherland special permission to send one of his representatives on Gordon's ship travelling from Halifax to the settlement of York Factory. Markham would only have to pay for the trip from York Factory to Winnipeg.

Sutherland's proposal to explore a remote region, collect data and make observations – sweetened by a chance to be reunited with his old ship, the *Alert*, on loan to the Canadians – was too tempting an offer for Markham to refuse. 'The very idea of again ploughing the icy seas of the north in my old ship, although only as a passenger, was too fascinating and too delightful to be resisted,' he revealed. 'I felt also that a certain amount of responsibility would be vested in me, and that on my report the question of a Hudson's Bay railroad would be, in a certain degree, for the present decided.' At around the same time that Sutherland presented him with this opportunity, Markham received an offer from the Admiralty to take command of HMS *Imperieuse*. He turned it down in favour of this chance to escape to Canada. 'This offer suited me exactly, and I had no hesitation in accepting it,' he later admitted.

Markham left London two days after meeting with Sutherland. On 8 June, he departed on the Allan Line steamer *Carthaginian* and arrived in Halifax eleven days later. He was reunited with the *Alert* and travelled aboard the steamer as it passed along the Labrador coast. He found the voyage refreshing, allowing him to focus his efforts on science and exploration for the first time in seven years.

On 9 July, the *Alert* entered the entrance of the Hudson Strait after being delayed by ice and heavy fog. They stopped at a bay called Ashe Inlet and encountered a handful of men at the station house adjacent to an Eskimo campsite. Markham observed a few heavy pieces of ice in the area but saw nothing to cause him any concern. The steamer easily sliced through any frozen chunks they encountered. The conditions were nothing compared to what he had experienced in Smith Sound in 1876 or the Barents Sea in 1879.

The *Alert* arrived eight days later to Digges Island located at the mouth of the Hudson Bay. It anchored at a station house in Port De Laperriere and remained there for a few days so that the crew could make some repairs to the engine as well as replenish the ship's water supply. Markham spent this time gathering Arctic flowers from the island's hills to add to his botanical collection. While out exploring, he noticed a strange black film stretched across a pond. Upon closer examination, he realised that it was actually millions of mosquitoes lying on its surface. While at anchor, the insects latched onto the ship and snuck into every room, making it nearly impossible for the men to get a moment's rest. Despite every effort to get rid of these annoying pests – they even resorted to burning paper in their rooms to attempt to smoke them out – the crew could do little but swat them away, squash them or complain. 'I never met with such voracious and insatiable musquitoes in all my life,' Markham declared of this troublesome adversary.

On 25 July, the *Alert* steamed out of the harbour and reached the open waters of the Hudson Bay. The men were overjoyed to escape this insect hell. They encountered some scattered ice and easily reached Churchill four days later. Compared to the 'sterile aspect of the land in the Hudson's Strait', Markham found Churchill's grassy plains, pine forests and diversely coloured wildflowers to be a pleasing change of scenery. By examining old records of the Hudson's Bay Company, founded in 1670 as a fur trading company, he discovered that ships had used this route for the last 150 years.

The *Alert* left Churchill on 4 August and reached the settlement and trading post at York Factory two days later. The Scottish author Robert

Michael Ballantyne visited the settlement in 1845 and described it as 'a monstrous blot on a swampy spot, with a partial view of the frozen sea'. It had been intentionally built at the confluence of the Hudson Bay and the Hayes River to serve as a convenient location for a trading post. Compared to Churchill, it was larger and more populated with fifty buildings and a Cree village located half a mile away. Its most prominent feature was a towering white depot protected by a palisade wall and gate.

Markham left the *Alert* here and made arrangements to travel alone by canoe through the heart of Manitoba to Winnipeg. The chief trader sold him enough food to last him for twenty days. He also purchased some extra equipment and accessories, such as a coat with a hood, colourful sash, sealskin moccasins and an old Zulu straw hat with a veil attached to it to help shield his face from bugs. With the help of the chief trader, Markham hired two experienced Indian canoeists. Jem, a man of mixed Indian and European descent, served as his interpreter and cook. The other man, Biquatenac – better known as Tom to Markham – was a full-blooded Cree who did not speak a word of English, but was an excellent canoeist. Both Indians agreed to accompany Markham as far as Oxford House for the price of one dollar a day and the guarantee to leave enough food behind to feed their wives and children.

The three men departed York Factory on 9 August and spent the first four or five days paddling south on the Hayes River. They rose each morning at about half-past four and travelled until sundown, only stopping to eat breakfast and dinner. One Indian tracked the canoe, while the other one did the paddling and steering. Markham sat in the center of the canoe and helped them as much as he could. Navigating the whitewater rapids required advanced paddling skills, which Markham lacked. 'It is certainly a most exciting moment when the rapid is entered, and the water is seething and whirling around, when, for a second perhaps, it is even doubtful whether the torrent will not overwhelm us altogether,' Markham later wrote with exhilaration. The bottom of the canoe frequently scraped the riverbed, forcing them to halt several times in a day to repair its hull.

The journey became more difficult and miserable the deeper they advanced into Manitoba's interior. They ran into ten to twelve portages (paths used to transport boats and supplies overland between two navigable waterways) each day. Some of these portages were 20 or 30 yards in length whilst others were up to a mile long with menacing nicknames such as 'Devil's Portage' and 'Dead Man's Portage'. 'Of all the uninteresting, and I may safely say disagreeable, work that can be imagined,' Markham declared, 'that of pushing a canoe for miles in a black muddy ditch, redolent with the odours of decomposed vegetable matters, or through long and thickly clustered reeds in shallow stagnant water, is perhaps the worst.' He described walking along the banks of the river to be 'execrable' since he had to scale rocky boulders, cut his way through thick pine forests or wade through marshy quagmires. Hundreds of mosquitoes, bulldog flies (horse flies) and fleas terrorised him, and he kept his head wrapped with a handkerchief and his face shielded at all times.

They only made about 60 miles in the first three days despite working from dawn until dusk. At that rate, they would run out of provisions before reaching Oxford House. Jem and Tom left in the canoe and headed in the direction of an Indian village located 25 miles downriver to recruit extra help. They left Markham behind with most of the provisions and equipment on the riverbank to lighten their load and make better time.

For three days the Englishman patiently hunkered down under a tattered piece of canvas hung from a tree to shield him from the wind and heavy rain. He sipped on a cup of warm tea and swatted away mosquitoes while lost in his thoughts as he waited for their return. He joked to himself that he was like Robinson Crusoe. Despite these miserable conditions, he embraced the solitude and being surrounded by nature. This was at least better than being stuck behind a desk tackling mounds of paperwork.

On the third night, Jem and Tom returned with a recruit, a Cree Indian named Nichi. He did not speak any English, but Markham said he 'was a first-rate fellow, worked like a horse, was as merry as a cricket, and was an excellent and experienced canoeist'. The addition of Nichi helped to speed up their progress.

On the night of 21 August, the men reached Oxford House after a gruelling sixteen hours of traversing portages, rapids and lakes. Oxford House, surrounded by a wooden stockade fence, consisted of a trader's house, office and store, and peltry and lumber shop. The chief trader invited Markham into his small home for supper, also occupied by his wife and five children. For the first time in nearly two weeks, Markham got a good night's sleep in a soft bed, and ate a homemade meal prepared by the trader's wife that included sweet jam, creamy butter and freshly baked bread.

Jem, Tom and Nichi took the canoe and headed back in the direction of Churchill, leaving Markham behind to find a new crew and canoe for the next leg of his journey to Norway House. It took him two days to locate and hire two Cree Indians. He rented another canoe and replenished his provisions. Neither of the Indians spoke any English, forcing Markham to communicate with them by hand gestures. They shoved off from the pier at Oxford House on 23 August and paddled southwest across Oxford Lake.

They rowed for three days and watched as a forest fire seared thousands of acres of woods along Oxford Lake's coast. The smoke from the fire was so thick that it blotted out the sun for hours at a time. 'It was a sad sight to see all the trees charred and burned to cinders and the bush totally consumed,' Markham lamented as he rowed along the coast, 'whilst the poor birds would be flying about in a most melancholy and utterly depressed manner, vainly seeking for a place to alight and rest, but finding none.' He also noticed dozens of dead rabbits floating in the river, evidently drowned while trying to escape the flames. While the smoke from the fire stung his eyes, it at least protected him for a time from the mosquitoes. After four days of paddling past this scorched land, they arrived at Norway House.

The locals at Norway House informed Markham that the winds and tides on Lake Winnipeg would make it too dangerous for him to cross it in a canoe. The final leg of the trip would have to be made by boat. Therefore, Markham hitched a ride on a 40-foot flat-bottom barge with a dozen Indians – four men, two women and six children – heading to Selkirk. He operated the barge's heavy steering oar as they sailed from Norway House on 30 August. The group ran short of provisions before they reached Selkirk and had nothing but flour to eat for two days. When they finally reached Selkirk on 11 September, Markham hopped on a train bound for Winnipeg.

He arrived at the bustling city looking more like a voyageur than an English naval officer. He was bombarded by visitors, reporters and dinner invitations. Everyone wanted to hear about his 600-mile trip through Manitoba's backwoods. He checked into a hotel and sent a brief telegram to Sutherland on 13 September. 'I think route practicable four months, possibly five or more. Nature of ice in Strait favourable for navigation. Report follows. –MARKHAM.'

Markham challenged Gordon's findings and maintained that the Hudson Strait was navigable for nearly half a year. He stated that when the *Alert* reached the entrance of the strait on 5 July, the scattered floes did little to prevent the steamer from making progress. From 9 to 11 July, he said he scarcely saw any ice, and the ship made 200 miles in about thirty-six hours. Therefore, he concluded that the roughly 500-mile long strait was navigable for at least four months or more every year. 'There will, I have no doubt, be many years when navigation can be carried out safely from the first of June to the end of November.' He endorsed Sutherland's scheme for a railroad and seaport and deemed the Hudson Strait to be a practical commercial waterway.

While Markham received acclaim from some individuals, others questioned the accuracy of his report. The Scottish explorer Dr John Rae, who had decades of experience exploring the Northwest Passage and the Canadian Arctic, said that Markham's single voyage was not sufficient to determine the navigability of the Hudson Strait. One summer in the region was hardly enough time to determine if it was navigable for the same number of months each year. Its weather patterns were some of the most unpredictable in the world. One year it could be jammed up with ice and impassable, and the next it could be free with only scattered floes.

Some critics even went so far as to question Markham's integrity and intent. 'We all know that the evidence of a gentleman of that sort is to be taken with a certain allowance,' Canadian Parliament member William Power indicated. 'Without at all saying that Capt. Markham would state what he did not believe to be true, it is always expected that a gentleman who goes out with a strong desire to find certain things will generally find that thing. He does not take the impartial view of what he observes that a person should take in case of this kind.' Power accused Markham of going to the Hudson Bay so that the Winnipeg and Hudson Bay Railway and Steamship Company 'would be able to place its bonds advantageously in the money markets of the world'. In the face of these allegations,

Markham vowed that he was 'perfectly impartial and unbiassed' in his report and that he 'was untrammelled by orders or suggestions' from Sutherland. Fortunately, most accepted he was objective in his report and he received the official thanks of the Canadian government for conducting the expedition even though Sutherland's grand scheme did not receive the support he hoped for.

While Markham made sure to jot down notes for his final report to Sutherland, he also filled his journals with observations on birds and plants native to the region. Natural history was always in the back of his mind. He lent these notes to Henry W. Feilden, an old comrade from the Arctic Expedition of 1875–76, who presented them to the Norfolk and Norwich Naturalists' Society on 25 January 1887. While Feilden handled the presentation on animal life, Herbert D. Geldart, a noted botanist, lectured about the information collected by Markham on the thirty-eight different types of plants. 'During all his voyages, and in the midst of professional duties,' Feilden declared to his audience, 'Captain Markham has invariably interested himself in the cause of science, and his diligence in collecting objects of natural history, and care in recording observations, is equalled by his readiness to impart the information thus obtained to others.'

On 9 October 1887, the Admiralty telegraphed Markham offering him command of the Training Squadron with the rank of commodore. The squadron had been organised in 1885 to train young naval officers on seamanship and tactics. This was accomplished by taking the officers out to sea on winter and spring cruises to ports in South America, the Caribbean, the Mediterranean and Northern Europe. Captain Gerard H. Noel, the commander of HMS *Rover* in the squadron, stated that service in this unit provided the young officers with a healthy balance of 'work, interest, and pleasure'. He accepted the position and joined his flagship, HMS *Active*, at Portsmouth on 10 November. The Training Squadron was a dream assignment for Markham and proved to be his most enjoyable appointment.

As commander of the squadron, Markham was able to invite Clements to come along as a guest on his cruises. He became a favourite visitor among the squadron's officers, including Midshipman Robert Falcon Scott. Albert and Clements dined with the 18-year-old midshipman after winning a boat race held while the squadron was anchored at St Kitts. 'Although only a comparatively young officer,' Albert later commented, 'Scott at once assumed responsibility, and evinced a grasp of his duties that was most remarkable.' He may have seen some of himself in Scott when he praised him for his 'active and capable mind blended with sound judgment' and as being 'an excellent organiser, sympathetic to those serving under him, and a born leader of men'. Clements was equally mesmerised by Scott and afterwards recruited him to lead two expeditions to Antarctica, where he tragically perished on his return journey from the South Pole in 1912. Before his death, Scott named the tallest peak in Antarctica's Churchill Mountains after his old commodore in the Training Squadron.

Markham met and befriended important heads of state and their families while visiting various ports with his squadron. Lieutenant Sydney R. Fremantle recalled that his commander was 'very hospitably inclined, and made the ship popular wherever we went'. Markham's courteous and friendly personality, along with his enthusiasm for history, exploration and the arts, made him an excellent envoy and host. He invited the Queen Regent of Spain, Maria Christina of Austria, aboard the *Active* while anchored at Barcelona; he dined with King Christian IX of Denmark and his wife, Queen Louise of Hesse-Kassel, at Copenhagen; he hosted the widowed Empress Frederick (Queen Victoria's eldest child), on his ship at Schleswig-Holstein; and the Prince and Princess Henry of Prussia entertained him at their castle in Kiel. The evening before the Royal Navy Review was held at Spithead to celebrate the fiftieth anniversary of Queen Victoria's accession to the throne, Markham dined with the Royal Family at Buckingham Palace. (A year later, he served as Queen Victoria's aide-de-camp.)

This satisfying time with the Training Squadron quickly came and went. He held the position of Captain of the Steam Reserve at Portsmouth until August 1891, when he was promoted to the rank of rear admiral. In January 1892, the Admiralty selected him to replace the popular Rear Admiral Walter Talbot Kerr as the second-in-command of the Mediterranean Fleet, under the overall command of Rear Admiral Sir George Tryon. A few years earlier, Vice Admiral John K.E. Baird and Markham had been outfoxed by Tryon during the naval war games when he evaded their blockade and 'attacked' Glasgow and Edinburgh, earning a reputation among his colleagues as a master strategist and tactician.

Markham arrived at the Mediterranean Station on the cusp of an international crisis brewing in Egypt. Khedive Tewfik had died, and his son, Abbas II, succeeded to the throne in January. The Ottoman Sultan Abdülhamid II issued a *firman* (decree) and inserted a clause in it demanding that the new khedive withdraw Egyptian soldiers from the Sinai Peninsula, which included the Suez Canal. Sir Evelyn Baring, the English consul general in Cairo, had no intention of allowing the Ottomans to take control of the Suez Canal. Baring requested Markham to remain in Alexandria with HMS *Australia* and his seven warships to demonstrate English strength and their unwillingness to yield. Admiral Tryon sent Markham a telegraph advising him to avoid becoming involved in the matter, but Markham understood the importance of his presence and disregarded Tryon's recommendation, remaining there for ten days. The bellicose stance by the English in Egypt contributed to the Ottomans ultimately dropping their claim to the Suez.

When the crisis in Egypt passed, Albert Markham continued to indulge in his sightseeing trips, exploring coastal cities and ancient sites along the Mediterranean Basin. Clements again joined Markham on HMS *Trafalgar*. 'It was delightful to be with him on these occasions,' Albert wrote of his cousin, 'for he was thoroughly versed in the mythological chronicles of each place visited, as well in the actual history.' Accompanied by officers from the *Trafalgar*, the pair visited the ruins of the 400-year-old fortress of the Knights of St John and the battlefields of Marathon and Thermopylae. Lieutenant Edward F.B. Charlton wrote to his mother telling her of his visit to these ancient battlefields with his chief:

> We spent one day at Marathon Bay where Xerxes fought his great battle and I wandered all over the plain. ... On Sunday I made up a big picnic of Mids. [midshipmen] etc. for a walk to Thermopylae. The cutter had some difficulty getting in and we all had to 'off breeks' and wade ashore, carrying our breeks round our necks and trudging two miles through a marsh. After walking 6 miles and thinking we had four to go I heard a hail from a neighbouring mound. 'Hi! you fellows. this is where Leonidas stood,' and found Rear-Admiral

Markham calling us. The place where the 300 Spartans made their stand was once 50 feet only from the sea, but the Bay has so silted up that it is now five miles of well cultivated plain and marsh.

The following year in January 1893, the *Trafalgar* anchored at the Greek port city Volos. With a few days to spare before heading back to sea, Markham decided to visit the famed 'Monasteries in the Air'. Accompanied by six officers, he left by rail for the town of Kalabaka, where the governor assigned the Englishmen with a guide and interpreter to take them to the remote monasteries.

The Great Meteoron Monastery was the highest and oldest of all the Meteoron monasteries and the one Markham desired to visit most. Their guide fired his gun into the air when the party reached its base to get the attention of the Orthodox monks living in isolation on top of the rocky cliff. In order to maintain their seclusion and to protect them from bandits, the only way to get to the top was by a single net suspended from an iron hook hanging over the north side of the cliff. The monks had a large capstan stored inside an old wooden shed to pull the net to the top. The holy men shouted to the guide that they needed help turning the capstan in order to lower the net down. They dropped a wooden ladder against the face of the cliff so that a couple of the visitors could climb up to help them operate the device. 'It was with some curiosity, not unmixed with qualms of apprehension, that we gazed up to the top of the rock,' Markham recalled. '[F]or we were well aware that the only modes of obtaining access to a place that seemed fitted for the habitation of eagles than of human beings, were by climbing up an excessively rickety wooden ladder, swinging perpendicularly against the face of the cliff, or the more undignified method of being packed into a net, and being wound up by a rope attached to a capstan, a height of over 150 ft., by monks above.'

Markham and another officer volunteered to climb the ladder. Markham's hands went numb from the ice caked on its rungs as he made his way to the top. Losing his grip and falling would mean certain death. The ladder had a large gap in the middle, so he had to grip the second section with one hand and pull himself up from the lower half. Monks dressed in black robes with long flowing beards greeted him when he reached the top. He helped lower the net down to his companions, pulling them up one by one. After touring this magnificent site and viewing the gorgeous sixteenth-century iconostases and frescoes, the Englishmen drank wine from the monastery's cellars that night and initiated 'the monks into the mysteries of hot whisky toddy'. These were the kind of experiences Markham lived for.

Early in February, Markham contracted the Mediterranean fever, crippling him for several months. It afflicted many sailors in the fleet, causing symptoms of chest and lung inflammation and painful, swollen joints. This sickness, combined with his rheumatism acting up, forced the 51-year-old rear admiral to go on extended sick leave. He rejoined the *Trafalgar* at the Greek port of Piraeus about a month later and was ordered to proceed to Malta to take command of HMS *Camperdown* while his flagship underwent repairs. But he had not fully recovered and spent another few weeks on sick leave in Sicily with Clements, who was there vacationing with Minna. He felt well enough to return to duty on 22 May. Had he been absent for four more weeks he would have avoided taking part in one of the worst naval disasters in English history. Rather, he would spend the remainder of his life tormented by the tragic events that occurred on 22 June 1893.

Chapter 8

The Fiend of Misfortune

'He was crucified alive for another man's blunder.'
Admiral Lord Charles Beresford,
Admirals in Collision

On 21 June 1893, the evening before the Mediterranean Fleet was scheduled to leave Beirut, Rear Admiral Markham wished to discuss the next day's agenda with Vice Admiral Tryon after dinner. Tryon planned to take out his ships the next morning to practise his new system of signals – dubbed the T.A. System – on their way to Tripoli. Markham was feeling feverish that night, his temperature rising to 100°F. He was still suffering from the effects of the Mediterranean fever since going on sick leave. 'I thought it prudent to remain on board and have a quiet night,' he wrote that evening in his journal after cancelling his meeting with Tryon so that he could get some rest in preparation for the busy day ahead.

At 9.30 am, eleven of Her Majesty's ships and two light cruisers left Beirut and proceeded north along the African coast in the direction of Tripoli. Around 2.00 pm, Tryon intended to divide the ships into two columns with 6 cables (1,200 yards) between them, before anchoring in Tripoli's harbour. Markham, who commanded HMS *Camperdown*, headed one column – composed of HMS *Edinburgh*, HMS *Sans Pareil*, HMS *Edgar* and HMS *Amphion* – while Tryon, in his flagship, HMS *Victoria*, headed the other – HMS *Nile*, HMS *Dreadnought*, HMS *Inflexible*, HMS *Phaeton* and HMS *Collingwood*. They were arranged in this formation:

Camperdown		*Victoria*
Edinburgh		*Nile*
Sans Pareil	1,200 yards	*Dreadnought*
Edgar		*Inflexible*
Amphion		*Phaeton*
		Collingwood

This seemingly straightforward manoeuvre left the *Victoria*'s staff commander, Thomas Hawkins-Smith, restless. He knew that at 6 cables, the two columns would be too close when they turned inwards towards each other before anchoring. They needed to be at least 8 cables (1,600 yards) apart to safely conduct the manoeuvre. Few officers dared to challenge the imperious Tryon, who had a reputation for being one of the greatest admirals and tacticians since Nelson. While in Tryon's cabin, Hawkins-Smith spoke up and remarked to his commander, 'I will require at least eight cables for that, sir.' Tryon unexpectedly agreed with his junior officer's recommendation and replied, 'Yes, it shall be eight cables.' Hawkins-Smith left Tryon's cabin satisfied that he had diverted a disaster.

Flag Lieutenant Richard Charles Lord Gillford entered Tryon's cabin to receive the order for dividing the fleet into two lines. Tryon handed him a scrap of paper with the number 6 scribbled on it, the distance that the two columns should be separated. Hawkins-Smith spotted the signal to form the two columns at 6 cables, not the 8 cables that Tryon had agreed upon. He raced over to Gillford on the ship's bridge after leaving Tryon's cabin and asked, 'Haven't you made a mistake?' Gillford calmly handed him Tryon's note and said, 'No, I think not.' Agitated when he saw the number 6 written on a scrap of paper, Hawkins-Smith exclaimed, 'I am sure the admiral intended it to be eight. Will you please go down to his cabin to again make certain?'

Flag Lieutenant Gillford reluctantly agreed and made his way back to Tryon's cabin to ask about the signal. 'The staff commander asked me to remind you that you had agreed to eight cables, sir,' Gillford stated to his commander. Thirty-nine-year-old Captain Maurice Archibald Bourke, second-in-command of the *Victoria*, who happened to be in the cabin when Hawkins-Smith entered on the first occasion, intervened after noticing the dissatisfaction on his commander's face. 'You certainly said it was to be more than six cables, sir,' Bourke added. 'Leave it at six cables,' Tryon barked to Gillford after being provoked by both officers.

Captain Bourke left Tryon's cabin to find Hawkins-Smith and broke the news to him. 'He won't go to more than six cables,' Bourke told the anxious staff-commander. Despite their reservations about the order, all three officers failed to challenge Tryon. 'Open criticism to one's superior is not quite consonant with true discipline,' Bourke later reasoned when questioned why he had not pressed the issue again with Tryon. He claimed insubordination was a 'dangerous course, striking deep at the foundation of discipline and responsibility'. In other words, it was better for an officer to follow through with his orders regardless of how much he may disapprove of them rather than to question his superior and threaten a breakdown of discipline. This blind obedience would have tragic consequences.

Half an hour after Tryon gave the order for his ships to form into two columns, the vice admiral left the comfort of his cabin and joined his jittery officers on deck. The sun was out, and it could not have been a more pleasing afternoon to be on a cruise in the Mediterranean Sea. Tryon gave the order for the two columns to reverse their direction so that they could proceed with the manoeuvre. Each ship acknowledged the signal sent out from the *Victoria*, except for one: the *Camperdown*.

There was alarm among the *Camperdown*'s officers. 'As the columns were only 6 cables apart I saw that this was not only a dangerous manoeuvre, but one that it was impossible to <u>execute</u> without a <u>certainty</u> of collision,' Markham later wrote in his journal, including these underlines. When he realised the two columns were too close to safely conduct the manoeuvre, Markham turned to his flag lieutenant, Henry Buller Bradshaw, and whispered to him so that he could not be overheard by others nearby, 'It is impossible, as it is an impractical manoeuvre.'

Markham ordered Flag Lieutenant Bradshaw to keep the *Camperdown*'s signal three quarters up or 'at the dip' to indicate that the *Victoria*'s order had not been understood. He marched to the fore bridge and met Captain Charles Johnstone, his second-in-command, who was equally concerned with Tryon's signal. Johnstone asked his commander what he should do. 'It is alright. Don't do anything. I have not answered the signal,' Markham told his perplexed second-in-command. He then returned to the bridge and directed Bradshaw to send a semaphore signal to Tryon with this message: 'Am I to understand that it is your wish for the columns to turn as indicated by signal now flying?'

Before Bradshaw had a chance to send Markham's semaphore signal to the *Victoria*, the *Camperdown* received this curt message from the vice admiral: 'What are we waiting for?' Markham was perturbed by

Tryon's message. In that same moment, Markham had an epiphany that Tryon intended to do something else. 'It then flashed across me,' he later recorded, 'that he [Tryon] wanted my division to turn 16 points in succession and that he intended to wheel round my ships which would have been a perfectly safe maneuver, although at first I was unable to conceive the object that would be gained. … Acting under this impression and having the utmost confidence in the tactical skill of the C. in C. (who devotes much time to working out tactical problems) I ordered the signal to be answered.' He stopped Bradshaw from sending the semaphore signal questioning Tryon's original order and instead acknowledged that it was understood. It was a decision that Markham would regret for the rest of his life.

The two columns steamed parallel of one another, and the *Camperdown* and *Victoria* proceeded to turn inwards. As the two lead ships neared each other, it quickly became clear that a collision was inevitable. To lessen the impact, Markham ordered the *Camperdown*'s engines full speed astern. But it was too late. Moments later, the *Camperdown*'s ram pierced the *Victoria*'s hull on its starboard side at an 80° angle. John Baggett, yeoman of signals on the *Victoria*, compared the *Camperdown*'s ram going through the *Victoria*'s hull to 'a plough turning the soil'. The *Victoria* began to fill with water as soon as its hull was punctured.

The captains of the other ships dispatched rescue boats when they saw the *Camperdown* and *Victoria* collide. Tryon ordered the rescue boats back, either thinking it was not necessary yet to abandon the ship or to avoid the boats from littering the *Victoria*'s path to the shallow water. Many of the rescue boats did turn back, but luckily some did not. 'I think she's going down,' Staff Commander Hawkins–Smith stated to the fleet commander when he realised that the *Victoria* had begun to capsize. 'Yes, sir, I think she is,' admitted Tryon.

Hundreds of sailors crowded the *Victoria*'s upper deck before it capsized. The men in the boiler and engine rooms had no idea that the order for evacuation had been given and drowned at their stations. The Reverend Samuel Morris, the *Victoria*'s chaplain, reassured the men crowding the deck by calmly calling out, 'Steady men, steady.' The *Victoria*'s sailors remained as composed as the 93rd Highlanders at Balaclava, or the 74th Regiment during the HMS *Birkenhead* wreck, as the ship began to keel over. At the last moment, the order was given to abandon ship. Bourke later recalled with pride the scene before the ship was evacuated:

> There was absolutely no panic, no shouting, no rushing aimlessly about. The officers went quietly to their stations, and everything was prepared, and the men were all in their positions, for hoisting out boats or performing any duty that may have been ordered. … This order to turn about was given apparently about a minute before the end; and I can hear of not one single instance of any man rushing to the side. … Not one was found who had not that control over himself which characterises true discipline and order.

Tryon remained at his station and went down with his ship. John Baggett recalled how he 'saw the Admiral facing bravely up to meet his doom' clinging to a rail as the ship rolled over. 'He was perfectly calm and collected to the last,' Hawkins-Smith later reported of Tryon. 'I never expected to see him again, as I am sure he, being a short-breathed man, could not have kept the water out of his lungs as long as I was able to do, and I could not have done so a second or two longer. … He died as he had lived, a brave man.' For all his faults, no one could question Tryon's devotion to duty or courage.

Markham watched in horror as the *Victoria*'s gold funnels disappeared into the sea and its hull turned bottom up. 'Within ten minutes after the fatal blow had been struck,' Markham somberly declared, 'she was observed to be fast settling by the head and heeling over considerably to starboard and then within a very few seconds she turned bottom upward and disappeared beneath the water, her screws continuing to revolve as she took her last fatal plunge. It was a terrible and awful spectacle!' All that remained after was 'a large circle fringed by a mass of human heads'. Assuming command of the fleet, Markham sent a signal to the other ships to send all their rescue boats to the scene of the wreck with all haste.

The rescue boats fought to save as many of the *Victoria*'s survivors as they possibly could. Some of the men were sucked into the sinking ship's vortex and drowned, while others drifted into the *Victoria*'s spinning propeller and were cut to pieces. Wood and metal fragments shot up from the water like projectiles, killing and maiming many men. The survivors were so tightly packed together after evacuating that some could not stretch their arms out in the open water to gain traction and sank.

The rescue boats managed to pull twenty-nine officers and 262 sailors from the water. Vice Admiral Tryon, twenty-two officers, and 336 sailors drowned. The *Victoria*'s commander, Captain Bourke, managed to survive the debacle. 'It would have been better I think had I not been saved,' he wrote to a fellow naval officer while despairing over the loss. 'This is an awful cross to bear. ... And those poor little midshipmen, 8 gone. Why oh why?' When reflecting upon some other unfortunate events that had occurred during his naval career, Bourke began to wonder if some kind of phantom was stalking him. 'What is this fiend of misfortune which follows my steps whenever I am at sea?'

Another officer who managed to escape the *Victoria* before it sank was Commander John 'Jack' Jellicoe, who went on to command the Grand Fleet during the Battle of Jutland in 1916. Suffering from a fever, Jellicoe was in his bed when the two ships collided. He managed to stagger to the upper deck and slid down from the ship's hull into the sea. Feverish and weak, he fought to keep his head above the water. Midshipman Philip Roberts-West spotted him struggling, and allowed Jellicoe to rest his hand on his shoulder while they trod water. This act saved Jellicoe's life. Both men were rescued ten minutes later by one of the *Nile*'s boats.

For those who survived, it was an affair indelibly etched into their minds. As he fought to survive, John Baggett recalled that the 'cries for help drowned everything'. He told a friend in the same letter recounting this experience, 'I am rehearsing it again & am all of a shake so dear friend please excuse the writing, hand trembling, & again dear friend thanks for sympathy.' Captain John Brackenbury, in command of the *Edinburgh* at the time of the collision, watched the events unfold from the deck of his ship. He confessed four years later that, 'The scene haunts one to this moment. ... It is too sad!' The night of the collision, Markham mourned the death of his 'gallant and ever to be lamented chief' and the *Victoria*'s crew 'dragged down in the waters never again to be seen alive'. He described what he had witnessed that day as 'a frightful sight and one that I shall never forget'.

Markham ordered the *Camperdown*'s watertight doors closed and kept it at the wreck site for as long as he could. The impact tore a 10 by 4-foot hole in the ship's hull and flooded several rooms on its lower deck. The men fought valiantly to keep the ship afloat by placing a collision mat over the breach and by pumping out the excess water. Markham ordered the *Camperdown* to port at about 5.30 pm to ensure it did not meet a similar fate to the *Victoria* and directed the two light cruisers of the fleet, HMS *Fearless* and HMS *Barham*, and the *Amphion* to remain near the wreck site late into the night, distinguished by the bubbling sea and cross bearings.

Markham prepared a lengthy telegram to the Admiralty that evening. At 12.30 am, he sent his telegraph from the British Consul at Tripoli to the Secretary of the Admiralty Ughtred Kay-Shuttleworth:

> It is with the most profound regret that I have to report for the information of their Lordships the total loss of H.M.S. 'Victoria', involving the irreparable loss of the Commander-in-Chief, Sir George Tryon, K.C.B., together with 22 officers and 336 men. … I cannot express to their Lordships the deep grief and sorrow that is felt in consequence of this lamentable catastrophe by myself, and the Captains, the Officers, and men of the Mediterranean squadron; a sorrow that is very materially enhanced by the great and irreparable loss that the Navy and the Nation has sustained in the death of our beloved Commander-in-Chief, Sir George Tryon, K.C.B.

Markham was up until the early morning hours recording the day's accident in his journal:

> A terrible and appalling disaster has occurred. I know not how to describe, or write about, it. The *Victoria* has ceased to exist and now lies in 80 fathoms of water, dragging down with her, our Com. in Chief Sir George Tryon and 22 officers and 336 men! It is too dreadful to contemplate, and I can hardly even now believe, or realise, that such a cruel and ghastly accident has actually occurred.

He tried to get some rest but found it impossible to sleep with his mind still racing. After tossing and turning for four and a half hours, he was up again at daybreak to supervise the search for bodies.

The *Fearless* combed the North African coast for two days. An Ottoman cavalry patrol offered assistance on land, riding up and down the 14-mile beachline in search of bodies that may have washed ashore. Sultan Abdülhamid II afterwards offered a plot of land to the English to bury the remains recovered. The Admiralty later erected a monument in the cemetery to their memory. (It is still maintained by the Commonwealth War Graves Commission.)

A funeral was held the evening after the disaster to honour those who had perished. Shortly before sunset at 6.45 pm, the *Sans Pareil* – the *Victoria*'s sister ship – fired a salute and its band played the *Dead March*. Tryon's flag, hoisted at half-staff, was hauled down one last time.

All of England was in a state of shock after receiving Markham's telegram reporting the catastrophe. 'It would be hard to describe the feeling that prevails in regard to the calamity by all the country through the loss of the battle ship *Victoria* and the drowning of so many of her officers and crew,' reported the American newspaper *Los Angeles Herald*. 'Sorrow for the dead and sympathy for the relatives and friends is widespread.' The day after the disaster, Queen Victoria noted the appalling news in her private journal:

> When I was dressing the following dreadful telegram was given to me. ... Too awful! Poor excellent, distinguished Sir G. Tryon, so much liked by all and the fittest Admiral going—to perish like this! And the ship bearing my name! We can talk and think of nothing else but this fearful catastrophe. Decided to put off the State ball, which was to have taken place to-night, owing to this dreadful news. Heard the confirmation of it from the Admiralty.

The queen expressed her condolences in a letter sent to the widowed Lady Tryon the next day:

> Dear Lady Tryon,—You will I trust forgive my intrusion on your terrible grief, as I cannot refrain from telling you how deeply I feel for you, and how truly I mourn your distinguished and excellent husband. His loss to his Sovereign and country is very great, and to be thus cut off in the prime of life is too terrible.

He looked so well when I saw him only two months ago at Florence, and was the picture of health and strength. I have always taken such interest in your dear husband's career from his having served on board the *Victoria* and *Albert* now many years ago.

That God may support and comfort you in this hour of overwhelming affliction and bereavement is the sincere prayer of yours very sincerely, Victoria R.I.

The *Victoria*'s survivors reached Malta three days after the disaster. They were confined to the *Edgar* and the *Phaeton* once they arrived in port. No one was allowed to talk to them or visit the ships for fear of what they may disclose to the public. Grief-stricken mothers, fathers, sisters and brothers crowded the Admiralty's London office and demanded that a list of those who had perished or who survived the wreck be released. The *Los Angeles Herald* described what took place when the list was finally delivered:

> Crowds of people remained all night before the admiralty office in hopes of getting definite information in regard to the fate of relatives on board the ill-fated battleship. At 6 o'clock this morning a list of those saved was posted on a bulletin board in front of the office. When the list was read to the crowd, many touching scenes resulted. Some, overwrought by the strain of anxiety, fainted with joy when the name of a loved one was mentioned among the saved. Others, overcome with grief when the list was completed and the missing one's name was not mentioned, swooned and fell to the ground.

Markham received dozens of telegrams from distinguished individuals and friends telling him how stunned they were by the demoralising news and wishing him their deepest sympathy. Writing back to Rear Admiral Charles Frederick Hotham on 10 July, Markham spoke of the shadow that hung over the Mediterranean Fleet, his empathy for the families of the deceased and his grief for Tryon's death. He hardly finished the letter before he broke down:

We are all overwhelmed with grief and distress at the terrible and appalling calamity that has befallen us. Even now I can hardly realise its magnitude—it was all so sudden, so unexpected and came upon us with such awful and astounding rapidity my heart bleeds for the poor widows and orphans of those who are no more, and who they will never see again in this world. I can hardly trust myself to write about my beloved chief—He was a great personal friend of mine, and always treated me with such kindness and consideration. On public grounds his loss is irreparable. He was the most able man on the admirals [*sic*] list—a man of sound judgment, a first rate officer and a skillful and consummate tactician. I am unable to write more.

A court martial – headed by Admiral Sir Michael Culme-Seymour and nine other officers – convened in Malta on 17 July to determine who was responsible for the loss of the *Victoria*. The surviving senior officers gave lengthy testimonies and it became evident that Tryon gave the order that led to the disaster. Captain Bourke admitted that he was aware that the distance of 6 cables was not suitable to conduct the manoeuvre but did nothing to stop it. 'My impression was that something was going to happen,' he testified during the trial. 'I had confidence in the Commander-in-Chief, and nobody ever questioned him. I never questioned him.' Both Flag Lieutenant Gillford and Staff Commander Hawkins-Smith, who were also conscious of the fact that their commander was making a fatal error, incriminated Tryon by testifying that he had admitted that the collision was his fault before the ship went down.

Rear Admiral Markham was summoned to testify and arrived at the island on the third day of the court martial. Even though initially perturbed at Tryon's order, Markham told the officers of the court that he realised that the vice admiral planned to have the *Victoria* wheel around the *Camperdown*, instead of turning inwards. 'I had some sort of idea of that in my head at the time,' Markham explained to the court. 'I thought he was going to wheel round me and come up somewhere on the other side and re-form his squadron.' He admitted that it was not uncommon for the unpredictable Tryon to 'carry out many evolutions in the Mediterranean Squadron of which at the time, I must acknowledge, I hardly knew what was the object, and they were only afterwards fully explained to me by the Commander-in-Chief, in his cabin'. This realisation, combined with Tryon's curt signal, led Markham to stop Bradshaw from sending the signal to the *Victoria* questioning this order.

Markham appeared foolish in front of the court martial when Bradshaw testified that he never reported Tryon's semaphore signal to Markham. The conflicting statement made Markham appear as if he was either negligent or had been caught in a half-truth. Despite this testimony from his flag lieutenant, Markham stuck by his original statement:

> My reason for stopping the semaphore was because the semaphore signalled from the Commander-in-Chief was reported to me. I said to the Flag Lieutenant, and I thought it was by my Flag Lieutenant, and I think now it was by the Flag Lieutenant. It was certainly reported to me by somebody. Perhaps I may have heard it taken in by the signalman writing it down, but at any rate it came to my knowledge that the signal was made.

Markham retired that night exhausted and frustrated from the day's events. 'I was the first witness examined today,' he noted with displeasure, 'and by no means happy at the result of the examination. My position was a peculiarly painful one, for it was difficult for me to justify the course I took without, in a measure, implying culpability to Sir George Tryon.' He felt that he had been treated unfairly as a defendant by the court. He continued:

> I was simply a witness and nothing else, and I had no opportunity of informing myself of the evidence of the other witnesses, until that evidence was pointed in the London papers and had come out again, to Malta. I did not have the ordinary privileges and indulgence that are invariably granted to a prisoner assigned before a Court Martial, nor was I afforded the opportunity of defending myself in any way.

After a total of ten days of questioning the witnesses and survivors, the court came to a verdict. They exonerated the *Victoria*'s survivors, and found Tryon responsible for the disaster:

[I]t is with the deepest sorrow and regret that the Court further finds that this collision was due to an order given by the then Commander-in-Chief, the late Vice Admiral Sir George Tryon, to the two Divisions in which the Fleet was formed to turn sixteen points inwards, leaders first, the others in succession, the columns at that time being only six cables apart.

Queen Victoria was satisfied with the court's ruling even though she had admired Tryon. She wrote on 28 July:

[Y]esterday evening Lord Spencer brought down with him the telegrams giving the finding of the Court Martial. It is very sad and incomprehensible that so brilliantly clever a man [Tryon] should have made such a fatal mistake. I also forgot to mention, that in Lord Gillford's examination, when he was obliged, much against his will, to state all he knew, he said that at the last, when he was near the Admiral, he heard him very distinctly say 'It is all my fault,' which was very noble and fine, and a certain satisfaction.

Not everyone involved escaped criticism. The court expressed its displeasure that Markham had not followed through with sending his message to Tryon and scolded him for it. But the court did not want to promote disobedience among its officers, so they lessened the blow to Markham by adding that 'it would be fatal to the best interests of the service to say he was to blame for carrying out the directions of his Commander-in-Chief present in person'. Still, censuring him left him feeling embittered.

Markham privately wrote 'Who does not?' regarding the court's statement that they regretted he had not sent the signal. 'No person perhaps regrets it more than I do,' he complained. 'But this is judging of events after they occurred, and is really a matter of sentiment. It is the condition of the affairs at the moment that should be considered.' If the court disapproved of Markham's conduct, Bourke, Gillford and Hawkins-Smith – all aware of the flaw in Tryon's order well before Markham – should have shared in some of this criticism.

Revealing a little more detail than he presented at the court martial of how Tryon's brusque order influenced his decision to proceed with the manoeuvre, Markham wrote:

> The signal made to me by Sir G.T. 'What are you waiting for?' made it perfectly clear to me, that after due reflection that it would have been both useless and improper for me to have questioned him further. His semaphore signal to me was in itself conclusive proof that no further argument on my part would have been tolerated by him.

Similar to Bourke, Markham insisted that it would have been an 'insubordinate act' to protest Tryon's order, and that 'time did not admit of long argument by signal' since all the other captains had acknowledged the signal and the two columns were quickly steaming towards each other. Markham felt his 'hands were fettered' and compelled to obey his superior's demand, leading to terrible consequences. 'Most people say that Admiral Markham should have refused to obey the signal,' one unidentified midshipman expressed in a letter printed in *The Times*. '[B]ut I think that Admiral Tryon infused so much awe in most of the captains of the Fleet that few would have disobeyed him.' There is no question that Tryon carried much clout over his officers and that obedience was their priority.

Markham's colleagues were divided over whether his conduct had been proper or negligent. The eminent Admiral Geoffrey Thomas Phipps Hornby was one notable officer who publically denounced Markham in August 1893. 'My cousin will, I am sure, be deeply grieved to find that you have tried and condemned him in the *Fortnightly Review*,' Clements Markham wrote to Hornby after reading his scathing remark. 'I am sure you will feel how excessively sensitive a naval officer ought to be on such a point; especially if the censure is undeserved. … Poor Tryon would, with his generous large heralded nature, have been the first to denounce these attempts to blame others for his error.' Other senior naval officers – such as Admirals Edmund Commerell, Richard Vesey Hamilton, Philip Colomb, William Dyke Acland and Lord Charles Beresford – supported Markham and told him that under similar circumstances they would have acted precisely as he had. The support from his brother officers provided Markham with some solace during these embarrassing attacks.

It appears as if the same 'fiend of misfortune' that haunted Bourke may have also cursed Markham. The rear admiral had experienced an uncomfortable number of run-ins with controversy and misfortune during his naval career – an explosion that could have destroyed his vessel, the accidental collision with a cargo ship, an official investigation into his conduct at Nguna and Nukapu and nearly losing his sledge crews to scurvy in the Arctic – but the *Victoria* disaster proved to be the *coup de grâce*. The Admiralty reviewed the proceedings of the *Victoria* court martial held three months earlier and came to a damning conclusion.

Markham was devastated when he read the Lords Commissioners' statement in *The Times* on 28 October:

> Their Lordships concur in the feeling expressed by the Court that it is much to be regretted that Rear Admiral A.H. Markham did not carry out his first intention of semaphoring to the Commander-in-Chief his doubts as to the signal; but they deem it necessary to point out that the Rear Admiral's belief that the Commander-in-Chief would circle round him was not justified by the proper interpretation of the signal.

The Lords Commissioners not only expressed their displeasure that he had not sent his signal, but they also publicly questioned his judgment.

Markham badly wanted to write to the Admiralty to justify his conduct in more detail than he was permitted to do during the court martial. Both Admiral Culme-Seymour and George Joachim Goschen, later the First Lord of the Admiralty, confidentially advised him against it. Culme-Seymour assured him that it would be hopeless to attempt to get the Lords Commissioners to overturn this final ruling, especially after it had been published in the papers. Markham reluctantly followed the advice of both men and suppressed his desire to vindicate his name. Lieutenant, later Admiral, Sydney Robert Fremantle, who served under Markham, said he admired 'the dignity which he faced the very difficult and invidious position in which he was placed'.

Markham found the sinking of the *Victoria* to be 'a most painful and distressing subject' to discuss. Once exalted for his exploits in the Arctic, the vice admiral's name became synonymous with the tragedy, making it impossible to distance himself from it. Those closest to Markham observed a change in his temperament. His original biographers said he lost his usual 'boyish light-heartedness' characteristic of his earlier years. After the disaster, he became a 'grave and at times silent man'. Still, he tried to conceal his heartache. 'He was a fine character,' declared Jack Jellicoe, who befriended the dejected admiral. '[H]e never shewed that better than in the days which brought him so much sadness.'

Markham found an escape from this melancholy by starting a family. In 1894, one of his midshipmen, Charles Tiedeman Gervers, fell gravely ill and it was feared that he would not live long. Markham telegraphed his father, Francis Theodore Gervers, advising him to come immediately to the *Trafalgar* to see his dying son. Mr Gervers soon arrived with his wife and 19-year-old daughter, Theodora Chevallier. Midshipmen Gervers made a full recovery and Markham began courting his sister. Thirty-three years his junior, she was born in the same year Markham planted the Union Jack within 400 miles of the North Pole. The 52-year-old bachelor presented the teenager with a ring originally made by the *Alert*'s armourer in 1876 and asked her to marry him.

The wedding was held in St Michael's Church in London on 11 October 1894, after Markham's commission in the Mediterranean Fleet ended. Admirals and generals, junior officers of the *Trafalgar*, friends, family and random spectators crowded the church for the ceremony. Theodora's eight bridesmaids wore white dresses trimmed with naval lace and white caps with an insignia of Markham's sledge flag and the Union Jack sewed on them. Rear Admiral Edward Hobart Seymour acted as Markham's best man. The most impressive spectacle of the reception was the couple's Arctic-themed wedding cake. Markham was pleased with his accomplishments in the Arctic and thought it fitting to embody it on their cake, spending three weeks designing a 5-foot-tall, 80-pound masterpiece. A massive mold of the *Alert* with Markham's sledge flag and motto sat on top of the cake, while around its base were dozens of capstans, anchors, boats, davits, lifebuoys, sledges, oak leaves, acorns and flowers made of sugar.

The newlyweds travelled as guests of Sir Charles William Cayzer, owner of the Clan Line of Steamers Ltd., on his steamer *Clan Matheson* during the summer of 1895. They attended the ceremonial opening of the Kaiser

Wilhelm Canal in Kiel, which was christened by Emperor Wilhelm II. They spent that winter in Malta. On Christmas Day, Admiral and Mrs Markham were invited by the officers of the *Trafalgar* to join them on the ship for their holiday celebration. To Mrs Markham's surprise and amusement, portraits of her husband were attached to the top of each dish of plum pudding being served as the dessert. He was still beloved by the officers on his old flagship, and his young bride was considered to be 'the reigning beauty of Naval circles'. For a short period of his life after the *Victoria* disaster, Markham was able to take his mind away from this tragic incident.

But his period of happiness was followed by two painful blows in the span of two years. In April 1897, Markham's mother died at the age of 87. Four months later, Markham was advanced to vice admiral but still remained on half-pay without a command. He offered his services to the Admiralty during the Second Boer War, which broke out in October 1899, but to his grief, he was turned down. For a man who found his self-worth through his accomplishments, the idleness was tormenting. He deeply took to heart the maxim 'Idleness is the enemy of the soul'. Work, or at least a feeling that he had a purpose, meant everything to him, and without it, he was nothing.

Markham lingered for seven years on half-pay and remained unemployed. When he inquired why, the First Lord of the Admiralty John Poyntz Spencer, 5th Earl Spencer, gave the excuse that 'there were so many officers on the rear admiral's list who had never hoisted their flags' waiting to receive an assignment ahead of him. In truth, he had been blacklisted. He found this out from Goschen. 'There was not a whisper from any one in authority at the Admiralty that my non-employment was due to the cloud that was accidentally hanging over me in consequence of my association with the *Victoria* disaster until Mr. Goschen revealed the fact,' Markham declared. 'After 40 years faithful service in the Navy in all parts of the world, and in positions some of great responsibility,' he wrote with anguish, 'I am now curtly informed that I have been practically condemned, for having committed an error in judgment which I feel confident I can explain and clear myself of ...'

Markham did whatever he could to stay occupied as he languished in ignominy. He served on the board of directors of several companies – such as the Cape Electric Tramways Limited and the Mexico Electric

Tramways Co. – and was an active member of the Freemasons. He stayed at his father-in-law's home at Amat Lodge, in Ardgay, Scotland, on a plot of land enclosed by 3,000 acres of forest and moorland. This retreat allowed him to indulge in his appetite for nature. A daughter, Joy Mary Minna, was added to the family on 3 June 1900, and became his pride and joy, helping to fill the void. Markham's friend, the Prince of Wales (King George V in 1910), born on the same day as his daughter twenty-five years earlier, was selected to be her godfather. But as much as he cherished these diversions, they were only temporary distractions, and could not stave off the shame and worthlessness gnawing away at him with each passing year.

His depression became so bad that Theodora wrote to the Prince of Wales, pleading for him to use his influence to find her husband an assignment. 'I beg your Royal Highness to forgive me if I am taking an unheard of liberty in daring to address you,' she stated. 'If such is the case I can only plead ignorance and inexperience having heard and knowing of your many kind acts.' Theodora then told the prince that even though her husband applied over and over again for an assignment, nothing ever came of it. She confessed that the 'cruelty and injustice of the Admiralty is breaking his heart'. She ended her passionate letter by expressing that 'Should your Royal Highness think it very wrong on my part writing please please forgive me my heart is aching for my Admiral no one knows of this letter Admiral Markham least of all.'

Theodora Markham's plea did not fall on deaf ears. In November 1901 – eleven months after Queen Victoria died and the young prince's father, Edward VII, became king – Albert H. Markham was appointed Commander-in-Chief, The Nore by the First Lord of the Admiralty William Waldegrave Palmer, 2nd Earl of Selborne. It was the first command he held in nearly a decade. 'After a long weary wait of 7½ years,' he wrote with a sigh of relief, 'a spell of professional idleness that had been compulsorily forced upon me, I have at last the satisfaction and the gratification of seeing my flag flying again, and of knowing and feeling that a most regrettable episode in my naval career, had practically come to an end.'

In January 1903, Markham was promoted to the rank of admiral, over forty years after first entering the service as a naval cadet. Eleven months later, he was made a Knight Commander of the Bath (KCB) by King Edward VII and had the privilege of adding the title of 'Sir' before his forename. When he turned 65 years old in November 1906, he retired after five decades of service in the Royal Navy. Besides serving faithfully wherever he was stationed in the world, he explored and discovered uncharted Arctic lands, made contributions to natural history and aided in developing a new generation of naval officers. Few of his colleagues could claim to have achieved as much as he did during a career that spanned almost half of the nineteenth century.

When Europe went to war in August 1914, the 72-year-old retired admiral offered his service to the Admiralty. The war impacted the Markham family just as it did millions of other families across the British Empire. A cousin, 44-year-old Major Ronald Anthony Markham of the Coldstream Guards, was mortally wounded on 25 October 1914 at the Battle of Ypres and died two days later. Even though Albert's health had rapidly declined in his old age and he had grown stout, he offered to waive his rank and serve in any capacity the Admiralty saw fit. His offer was politely turned down.

Although he was not able to contribute to the war effort by serving on active duty, Albert Markham offered to serve as the treasurer of the Minesweepers' Fund, a charitable organisation that collected thousands of pounds from donations for the families of men who had died in the war. Mrs Markham opened a Canadian Officers' rendezvous at Prince's Gardens, South Kensington with the wife of Brigadier General Henry Page Croft and other influential women in London. The Markhams regularly entertained officers of the Canadian Expeditionary Force at their home at 19 Queen's Gate Place in South Kensington. In September 1916, Markham wrote the introduction for George Herbert Rae Gibson's book, *Maple Leaves in Flanders Fields*, which provided a graphic account of Canadian soldiers serving on the Western Front. 'I am proud to number many Canadians among my friends at the front,' Markham declared in the introduction, 'for all of whom I entertain a profound respect, love, and admiration; and I am therefore delighted, and honoured, in being afforded the opportunity of assisting in the launch of this latest Canadian venture on the stormy sea of literature.'

Markham suffered the greatest loss next to his parents' deaths when his mentor, role model and confidant Clements Markham unexpectedly passed away. The 86-year-old geographer accidentally knocked over a candle resting on a pedestal next to his bed, causing his sheets to catch fire. Sarah Crank, his wife Minna's maid, heard screams coming from his bedroom and rushed to the scene, but the smoke was so heavy that she was not able to enter his room. The butler, Thomas Henry Crees, heard Crank yelling for help, and as he ran over, Clements burst out of the room and collapsed into his arms, faintly gasping, 'Put it out'. Cress dragged Clements's lifeless body to the library and Minna called for a doctor.

Clements suffered severe burns to his chest, back of his head, side of his face and on his arms and hands. He remained unresponsive for about twenty hours before passing away on 29 January 1916. Albert Markham thought it only appropriate that he write a biography of the man who had such a great impact on his life from an early age. He published his last and arguably his best book, *The Life of Sir Clements R. Markham, K.C.B., F.R.S.*, in 1917.

Albert only outlived his project by about a year. He contracted bronchitis on 23 October 1918 and died five days later at his home at the age of 77. Dr P.P. Whitcombe noted on his death certificate that syncope, or the loss of consciousness due to restricted blood flow to the brain, also contributed to his death. 'The death of Admiral Sir Albert Markham,' *The Globe* declared upon receiving word of his passing, 'removes from general society one of the most arresting figures of his time.'

The Lords Commissioners of the Admiralty – whom Markham had been at odds with at various times during his life – sent a sympathetic letter to Mrs Markham on 29 October to pay homage to her deceased husband's lengthy service in the Royal Navy:

Madam,

My Lords Commissioners of the Admiralty have received with deep regret the intelligence of the death of your husband—Admiral Sir Albert H. Markham, K.C.B., on the 28th instant.

On several occasions during his long career My Lords had the satisfaction of expressing their appreciation of your husband's services, both in the appointments which he held in His Majesty's

Navy, and in the field of Arctic exploration, and it only remains for them to express their sincere sympathy with you and your family in bereavement.

Letters of sympathy poured in from his friends and colleagues. These included letters from Admirals Pelham Aldrich, Jack Jellicoe, George A. Giffard, William H. May, Lord Charles Beresford and Captain (later Admiral) William Munro Kerr. Each wished the widowed Mrs Markham their sympathy and spoke of her husband's gentle, unselfish and pleasant character. 'I was indeed a devoted admirer of Sir Albert,' Admiral Sir Frederick Samuel Inglefield, nephew of Admiral Sir Edward Augustus Inglefield, wrote, 'and have always thought him quite the best officer and finest man that I ever met in the Navy, and his most charming personality and delightful voice will be a vivid remembrance to the end of my days.' His long-time acquaintance, Admiral Jellicoe, was equally troubled by his loss. 'I always felt that I had in him a true friend,' he wrote, 'and his friendship was indeed worth having.'

Dr Fridtjof Nansen wrote from Norway to express his condolences. The successful Norwegian Arctic explorer appreciated their friendship and the advice Markham had given to him on exploration in the years leading up to his death. 'I cannot tell you what I feel, he was always, since the first time we met, so good and dear to me,' Nansen wrote to his widow. 'A splendid type of a man, whom I always admired, and was proud to call my friend and whom it always was [a] joy to meet.' In the same letter, Nansen agreed to write a chapter about Albert's expedition to the North Pole for a book Theodora must have planned to publish. The Norwegian at one time declared Markham's 1876 expedition to be 'the most energetic attempt ever made to reach high latitudes'. Unfortunately, the book never came to fruition.

Letters from Markham's comrades spoke of the impact he had on their early naval careers. Sydney Robert Fremantle revered the deceased admiral 'whom I always feel that I owe my start in the Service, as he was the first Captain under whom I served any position of responsibility'. Another officer, Rear Admiral Reginald C. Prothero – nicknamed 'Prothero the Bad' for his terrifying and hostile disposition to distinguish him from his more likable cousin, Admiral Arthur W.E. Prothero – recalled how

Markham took him as a spirited youth under his wing and helped to shape him into an efficient naval officer:

> Sir Admiral A.H. Markham was so good to me in my Midshipman days when serving in the 'Victoria' in the Mediterranean 1864–67 that I have always considered him my 'Sea Daddy' as midshipmen in those days always termed a senior who was good enough to take an interest in us boys at the crucial stage of one's early career.

Admiral Markham's funeral was held at Brompton Parish Church on 1 November 1918, ten days before Germany signed the Armistice. His coffin, draped with the Union Jack, was drawn on a gun carriage to the church and escorted by a detachment of sailors. Twenty admirals attended the funeral, including Jack Jellicoe, William H. May, Stanley Colville (Commander-in-Chief at Portsmouth), Edward Seymour, Lewis Beaumont and George Le Clerc Egerton, along with members of the Royal Geographical Society. His guests included men who had served alongside him four decades before on the British Arctic Expedition, all greyed and wrinkled with age. Markham's dying wish was that his comrades from the expedition still living should be invited to his funeral. Aldrich was not able to attend, but wrote to Theodora, 'I am very much touched at his having expressed a wish that I should be invited to attend—it is a mark of his kindness to me even up to the last.' Excluded during the ceremony was any mention of the *Victoria* disaster that haunted him until his last breath. Rather, he was remembered as a capable naval officer, distinguished explorer and dear friend.

Markham's remains were interred at the Kensal Green Cemetery and his tombstone was inscribed with this touching tribute:

IN

LOVING AND THANKFUL

MEMORY OF

ALBERT HASTINGS MARKHAM

ADMIRAL K.C.B.

BORN NOV 11th 1841

PASSED OVER OCT 28th 1918

AFTER A GOD-FEARING LIFE SPENT IN THE

SERVICE OF HIS SOVEREIGN AND COUNTRY.

He was buried among other Arctic luminaries who had either vehemently encouraged the exploration of the vast, uncharted region or risked their lives by braving the elements and journeying there themselves – Sir Clements Markham, Rear Admiral Sir John Franklin's widow Lady Jane Franklin, Vice Admiral Sir Robert McClure and Admiral Sir John Ross. Sir Albert Hastings Markham would not have wanted it any other way.

While his tombstone currently lies on its back 100 years after his death, and continues to deteriorate with the passage of time, Markham has other memorials scattered throughout the world to honour his efforts in exploration. Besides Scott christening a mountain in Antarctica after him in 1908, the admiral has at least two other Arctic geographical features in remote regions carrying his name. The first was one of the five largest ice shelves in Canada's Arctic, the over 4,500-year-old Markham Ice Shelf (which broke from Ellesmere Island and was cast adrift in 2008), and the second, Cape Albert Markham, located on the northern part of Franz Josef Land's Hooker Island. The cape was named by the English Arctic explorer and army officer Frederick George Jackson in honour of his zealous predecessor who stirred fellow explorers and adventurers to emulate his deeds in the Arctic.

Epilogue

Markham's only child, Joy, married a Canadian officer, 31-year-old Captain William Sidney McCann of the Canadian Field Artillery, in November 1919. She was 19 when they were married. Unfortunately, Markham was not able to be with his beloved daughter on the happiest day of her life. Joy passed away in July 1935 at the age of 35 and is buried in Wanborough's St Bartholomew's churchyard.

The widowed Theodora Markham married a 34-year-old Dutch lieutenant, James Knell, in October 1921. She was twelve years his senior. Knell died during the Second World War at the age of 59. His grave marker, also in the same cemetery as his stepdaughter, is inscribed with this tribute:

IN MEMORY OF
MY BELOVED HUSBAND
COLONEL JAMES KNELL
ROYAL NETHERLAND HUSSARS
BORN APRIL 26TH 1887
DIED JULY 14TH 1945
WHO GAVE HIS LIFE FOR ENGLAND AND HOLLAND

Enduring the death of her daughter and two husbands, Theodora lived on for almost another two decades, passing away on 3 October 1962 at the age of 87. Richard Hough, the naval historian and author of *Admirals in Collision* (1959), chronicling the tragic tale of the 1893 *Victoria* disaster, found it astounding that the former Mrs Markham was still alive when his book was published. The author of this book finds it equally as remarkable.

A Complete List of the Officers and Men of the British Arctic Expedition of 1875–76

HMS *Alert*
Officers

Captain George S. Nares
Commander Albert H. Markham*
Lieutenant Pelham Aldrich
Lieutenant Alfred A.C. Parr*
Lieutenant George A. Giffard
Lieutenant W.H. May
Sub Lieutenant George Le C. Egerton

Fleet Surgeon Thomas Colan, MD
Surgeon Edward L. Moss, MD
Engineer James Wootton
Engineer George White
Naturalist, Captain H.Wemyss Feilden
Chaplain, Reverend Henry H. Pullen

Crew

Joseph Good
John R. Radmore*
George L. Burroughs
Vincent Dominics
Ice Quartermaster, David Deuchars
Ice Quartermaster, John Thores
Ice Quartermaster, James Berrie
Edward Lawrence*
Daniel W. Harley*
Thomas Stuckberry
Thomas Rawlings*
James Doidge
Thomas Joliffe*
Spero Capato
George Kemish
John Hawkins*
Frederick Cane
William F. Hunt
Robert Joiner
John Simmons
Adam Ayles

William Ferbrache*
George Cranstone
William Lorrimer
George Winstone*
Reuben Francombe*
Thomas H. Simpson*
David Mitchell
Alfred R. Pearce*
James Self
William P. Woolley
John Pearson*
William Maskell*
William Malley
Robert D. Symons
Henry Mann
William I. Gore
John Shirley*
Edward Stubbs
George Norris
Eskimo dog driver and interpreter, *Neil Christian Petersen*

Eskimo dog driver and hunter,
    Frederick
Marine, William Wood
Marine, William Ellard
Marine, Thomas Smith

Marine, John Hollins
Marine, Elias Hill
Marine, *George Porter**
Marine, Thomas Oakley

HMS *Discovery*
Officers
Captain Henry F. Stephenson
Lieutenant Lewis A. Beaumont
Lieutenant Robert H. Archer
Lieutenant Wyatt Rawson
Lieutenant Reginald B. Fulford
Sub Lieutenant C.I.M. Conybeare
Surgeon Richard W. Coppinger

Staff Surgeon Belgrave Ninnis
Engineer Daniel Cartmel
Engineer Matthew R. Miller
Chaplain Charles E. Hodgson
Naturalist, Chichester Hart
Assist Paymaster, Thomas Mitchell

Crew
George R. Sarah
George W. Emmerson
E.C. Eddy
Ice Quartermaster, Alexander Gray
Ice Quartermaster, William Dougall
Ice Quartermaster, Edward Taws
George Bryant
Frank Chatel
David Stewart
Thomas Simmons
George Bunyan
William Ward
James Shepherd
John E. Smith
Jonah Gear
George Stone
James Cooper
Henry W. Edwards
Benjamin Wyatt
Daniel Girard
Michael Regan
Thomas Chalkley
James Hodges
James Thornback

Alfred Hindle
Peter Craig
George Leggatt
Robert W. Hitchcock
John S. Saggers
James J. Hand
Charles Paul
Henry Windser
James Phillips
Jeremiah Rourke
Frank Jones
Samuel Bulley
William R. Sweet
Greenlander dog driver, Hans
    Hendrik
Marine, William C. Wellington
Marine, Wilson Dobing
Marine, John Cropp
Marine, Elijah Rayner
Marine, William Waller
Marine, Thomas Darke
Marine, John Murray
Marine, Henry Petty

* The sailors from the *Alert* who made it to within 400 miles of the North Pole.
The names of the men who died during the expedition are in *italics*.

Albert Hastings Markham's Books and Articles

Books

A Polar Reconnaissance: Being the Voyage of the "Isbjörn" to Novaya Zemlya in 1879 (C. Kegan Paul & Co., London, 1881).

A Whaling Cruise to Baffin's Bay and the Gulf of Boothia, and an Account of the Rescue of the Crew of the "Polaris" (Sampson Low, Marston, Low, & Searle, London, 1874).

Life of Sir John Franklin and the North-West Passage (George Philip & Son, London, 1891).

Northward Ho! Including a Narrative of Captain Phipps's Expedition, By a Midshipman (MacMillan & Co., London, 1879).

The Cruise of the "Rosario" Amongst the New Hebrides and Santa Cruz Islands, Exposing the Recent Atrocities Connected with the Kidnapping of Natives in the South Seas (Sampson Low, Marston, Low, & Searle, London, 1873).

The Great Frozen Sea: A Personal Narrative of the Voyage of the "Alert" During the Arctic Expedition of 1875–6, 4th ed. (C. Kegan Paul & Co., London, 1880).

The Life of Sir Clements R. Markham, K.C.B., F.R.S. (John Murray, London, 1917).

The Voyages and Works of John Davis, the Navigator (printed for the Hakluyt Society, London, 1880).

Articles

'Among Chinese Pirates', in *The Idler: An Illustrated Monthly Magazine. August, 1896, to January 1897*, edited by Jerome K. Jerome, 40–44, Vol. 10 (Chatto & Windus, London, 1897).

'Antarctic Exploration', in *The North American Review*, edited by David A. Munro, 431–40, Vol. 164 (The North American Review Publishing Co., New York, 1897).

'A Diplomatic Scramble', in *The Living Age, Seventh Series. January, February, March, 1899*, 548–53, Vol. 2 (The Living Age Company, Boston, 1899).

'A Visit to the Galapagos Islands in 1880', in *Proceedings of the Royal Geographical Society and Monthly Record, 1880*, 742–58, Vol. 2 (Edward Stanford, London, 1880).

'Hudson's Bay and Hudson's Strait as a Navigable Channel', in *Proceedings of the Royal Geographical Society and Monthly Record of Geography*, 549–67, Vol. 10 (Edward Stanford, London, 1888).

'Monasteries in the Air', in *Pearson's Magazine* 7, no. 41 (May 1899): 211–17 (Pearson Publishing Co., New York, 1899).

'Sketches on the Prairies', in *Good Words for 1878*, edited by Donald Macleod, 343–9, 415–22, 455–61 & 525–32 (Daldy, Isbister & Co., London, 1878).

'The Arctic Campaign of 1879 in the Barents Sea', in *Proceedings of the Royal Geographical Society and Monthly Record of Geography, 1880*, 1–40, Vol. 2 (Edward Stanford, London, 1880).

'The Road to the Pole: A Yachting Cruise to Novaya Zemlya and Seas Adjacent', in *Good Words for 1881*, edited by Donald Macleod, 89–205 & 277–82 (Ibister & Co., London, 1880).

'Through Hudson's Strait and Bay: A Naval Officer's Holiday Trip', in *Good Words For 1888*, edited by Donald McLeod, 23–8, 116–23, 187–94 & 256–64, Vol. 29 (Isbister & Co., London, 1888).

Bibliography

Unpublished

The British Library, London, Western Manuscripts
Expedition Journals of Sir Albert Hastings Markham

General Register Office (GRO), Southport
Albert Hastings Markham Death Certificate

National Maritime Museum, Greenwich
Admiral Sir Albert Hastings Markham Collection

National Museum of the Royal Navy, Portsmouth
Letter from Admiral Sir A.H. Markham (RNM 1982/100)
Letter from Yeoman of Signals John Baggett (RNM 2009/74)

Newspapers

Daily Globe (United States)
Dundee Courier (Scotland)
The Dundee Courier and Argus (Scotland)
Eastern Daily Press (England)
The Globe (England)
Gloucester Citizen (England)
Hampshire Telegraph (England)
The Illustrated London News (England)
Los Angeles Herald (United States)
The New York Herald (United States)
The New York Times (United States)
Manchester Evening News (England)
Marlborough Express (New Zealand)
The Maryborough Chronicle (Australia)
Memphis Daily Appeal (United States)
The Mercury (Australia)
Morning Advertiser (England)
The Morning Post (England)
Newcastle Courant (England)
The Ohio Democrat (United States)
Otago Daily Times (New Zealand)
The Pall Mall Gazette (England)
The Public Ledger (England)
Reading Mercury (England)
The Royal Leamington Spa Courier (England)
The Scotsman (Scotland)
The Sketch (England)
The Spectator (England)
The St Paul Daily Globe (United States)
Tamworth Herald (England)
Truth (Australia)
Waikato Times (New Zealand)
Weekly Times (Australia)

Books

Abruzzi, Luigi Amedeo of Savoy, Duke of the, *On the "Polar Star" in the Arctic Sea*, Vol. 1, translated by William Le Queux (Hutchinson & Co., London, 1903).

Appleton, Paul C., *Resurrecting Dr Moss: The Life and Letters of a Royal Navy Surgeon, Edward Lawton Moss, MD, RN, 1837–1880*, edited by William Barr (University of Calgary Press, 2008).

Appendix to the Journals of the House of Representatives of New Zealand. Legislative, Political, and Native, Vol. 1 (printed for the House of Representatives, by George Didsbury, Government Printers, Wellington, 1870).

Ballantyne, Robert M., *Hudson's Bay, Or, Every-day Life in the Wilds of North America: During Six Years' Residence in the Territories of the Honourable Hudson's Bay Company*, 2nd ed. (William Blackwood & Sons, Edinburgh & London, 1848).

Batres, Milla, ed., *Testimonios Británicos de la Ocupación Chilena de Lima* (Milla Batres, Lima, 1986).

Belich, James, *The Victorian Interpretation of Racial Conflict: The Maori, the British, and the New Zealand Wars*, 2nd ed. (Auckland University Press, 2015).

Berton, Pierre, *The Arctic Grail: The Quest for the North West Passage and the North Pole, 1818–1909* (Penguin Books, New York, 1988).

Bruner, Katherine F., Fairbank, John K. & Smith, Richard J., eds., *Entering China's Service: Robert Hart's Journals, 1854–1863*, Vol. 1 (Harvard University Asia Center, Cambridge, MA, 1986).

Buckle, George E., ed., *Letters of Queen Victoria 1891–1895, Third Series: A Selection from Her Majesty's Correspondence and Journal Between The Years 1886 and 1901*, Vol. 2 (Longmans, Green & Co., London, 1931).

Burke, Bernard, *A Genealogical and Heraldic History of the Landed Gentry of Great Britain & Ireland*, Vol. 2, 5th ed. (Harrison, Pall Mall, London, 1871).

Burke, John, *A Genealogical and Heraldic History of the Landed Gentry of Great Britain & Ireland, M to Z*, Vol. 2 (Henry Colburn, London, 1847).

Burr, Robert N., *By Reason Or Force: Chile and the Balancing of Power in South America, 1830–1905* (University of California Press, Berkeley, 1974).

Burton, Art T., *Black, Red and Deadly: Black and Indian Gunfighters of the Indian Territory* (Eakin Press, Austin, TX, 1991).

Carpenter, Kenneth J., *The History of Scurvy and Vitamin C* (Cambridge University Press, 1986).

Carter, Jennifer M.T., *Eyes to the Future: Sketches of Australia and her Neighbours in the 1870s* (National Library of Australia, Canberra, 2000).

Clowes, William L., *The Royal Navy: A History from the Earliest Times to the Death of Queen Victoria*, Vol. 7 (Sampson Low, Marston, & Co., London, 1903).

David, Robert G., *The Arctic in the British Imagination, 1818–1914* (Manchester University Press, 2000).

Davis, Charles H., ed., *Narrative of the North Polar Expeditions U.S. Ship Polaris, Captain Charles Francis Hall Commanding* (Government Printing Office, Washington, 1876).

Douglas, Mary, *The Frozen North: The Story of North Polar Expeditions with Nordenskiöld, Nares, Greely, De Long, Nansen and Jackson-Harmsworth* (DeWolfe, Fiske & Co., Boston, 1895).

Dunbabin, Thomas, *Slavers of the South Seas* (Angus & Robertson, Sydney, 1935).

Elgin, James B, Earl of, *Correspondence Relative to the Earl of Elgin's Special Missions to China and Japan, 1857–1859* (Blue Book, London, 1859).

Esposito, Gabriele & Giuseppe Rava, *Armies of the War of the Pacific 1879–83: Chile, Peru & Bolivia* (Osprey Publishing, Oxford & New York, 2016).

Farcau, Bruce W., *The Ten Cents War: Chile, Peru, and Bolivia in the War of the Pacific, 1879–1884* (Praeger, Westport, CT, 2000).

Farwell, Byron, *The Encyclopedia of Nineteenth-Century Land Warfare: An Illustrated World View* (W.W. Norton, New York, 2001).

Felton, Mark, *China Station: The British Military in the Middle Kingdom 1839–1997* (Pen & Sword, Barnsley, 2013).

Fitzgerald, Charles C.P., *Life of Vice-Admiral Sir George Tryon, K.C.B.* (William Blackwood & Sons, Edinburgh & London, 1897).

Fleming, Howard A., *Canada's Arctic Outlet: A History of the Hudson Bay Railway* (University of California Press, Berkeley & Los Angeles, 1957).

Fortune, Robert, *Three Years' Wanderings in the Northern Provinces of China*, 2nd ed. (John Murray, London, 1847).

Fox, Grace E., *British Admirals and Chinese Pirates 1832–1869* (Kegan Paul, Trench, Trübner, London, 1940).

Franklin, Jane, *As Affecting the Fate of My Absent Husband: Selected Letters of Lady Franklin Concerning the Search for the Lost Franklin Expedition, 1848–1860*, edited by Erika B. Elce (McGill-Queen's University Press, Montreal, 2009).

Gillmore, Parker, *Leaves from a Sportsman's Diary*, 2nd ed. (Gibbings & Co., London, 1896).

Gordon, Andrew, *The Rules of the Game: Jutland and British Naval Command* (Naval Institute Press, Annapolis, MD, 1996).

Gordon, Charles G., *Events in the Taeping Rebellion*, edited by A. Egmont Hake (W.H. Allen & Co., London, 1891).

Graham-Yooll, Andrew, *Imperial Skirmishes: War and Gunboat Diplomacy in Latin America* (Olive Branch Press, Brooklyn, NY, 2002).

Greely, Adolphus W., *True Tales of Arctic Heroism in the New World* (Scribner's Sons, New York, 1912).

Gregory, John S., *Great Britain and the Taipings* (Australian National University Press, Canberra, 1969).

Grier, C. Sydney, ed., *The Letters of Warren Hastings to His Wife* (William Blackwood & Sons, London, 1905).

Heath, Ian, & Perry, Michael, *The Taiping Rebellion, 1851–66* (Osprey, London, 1994).

Hedren, Paul L., *After Custer: Loss and Transformation in Sioux Country* (University of Oklahoma Press, Norman, 2011).

Heywood, Benjamin A., *Memoir of Captain Prescot William Stephens*, 2nd ed. (James Nisbet & Co., London, 1886).

Holthouse, Hector, *Cannibal Cargoes: The Story of the Australian Blackbirders* (Angus & Robertson, North Ryde, NSW, 1969).

Huxley, Elspeth, *Scott of the Antarctic* (Antheneum Books, New York, 1978).

Journals and Proceedings of the Arctic Expedition, 1875–76, Under the Command of Captain Sir George S. Nares, R.N., K.C.B. (Printed for Her Majesty's Stationary Office, by Harrison & Sons, London, 1877).

Kobalenko, Jerry, *The Horizontal Everest: Extreme Journeys on Ellesmere Island* (Penguin Books, Toronto, 2002).

Lane-Poole, Stanley & Dickins, Frederick Victor, *The Life of Sir Harry Parkes: Consul in China*, Vol. 1 (MacMillan & Co., London, 1894).

Levere, Trevor H., *Science and the Canadian Arctic: A Century of Exploration 1818–1918* (Cambridge University Press, 1993).

Lindley, Augustus F., *Ti-ping Tien-kwoh: The History of the Ti-ping Revolution* (Day & Son, Lithographers & Publishers, London, 1866).

Lisle, Gerard de, ed., *Royal Navy and the Peruvian-Chilean War 1879–1881: The Rudolph de Lisle's Diaries and Watercolors* (Pen & Sword, Barnsley, 2008).

List of the Private Secretaries to the Governors-General and Viceroys from 1774–1908 (Superintendent Government Printing, Calcutta, 1908).

Lowis, Geoffrey, *The Fabulous Admirals* (Putnam & Co. Ltd., London, 1957).

Mackenna, Benjamin V., *Historia de la campaña de Lima, 1880-1881* (Rafael Jover, Santiago de Chile 1881).

MacEwan, Grant, *The Battle for the Bay: The Story of the Hudson Bay Railroad* (Western Producer Book Service, Saskatoon, 1975).

Markham, Albert H. *A Polar Reconnaissance: Being the Voyage of the "Isbjörn" to Novaya Zemlya in 1879* (C. Kegan Paul & Co., London, 1881).

Markham, Albert H. *A Whaling Cruise to Baffin's Bay and the Gulf of Boothia, and an Account of the Rescue of the Crew of the "Polaris"* (Sampson Low, Marston, Low, & Searle, London, 1874).

Markham, Albert H. *Life of Sir John Franklin and the North-West Passage* (George Philip & Son, London, 1891).

Markham, Albert H. *Northward Ho! Including a Narrative of Captain Phipps's Expedition, By a Midshipman* (MacMillan & Co., London, 1879).

Markham, Albert H. *The Cruise of the "Rosario" Amongst the New Hebrides and Santa Cruz Islands, Exposing the Recent Atrocities Connected with the Kidnapping of Natives in the South Seas* (Sampson Low, Marston, Low, & Searle, London, 1873).

Markham, Albert H., *The Great Frozen Sea: A Personal Narrative of the Voyage of the 'Alert' During the Arctic Expedition of 1875–6*, 4th ed. (C. Kegan Paul & Co., London, 1880).

Markham, Albert H., *The Life of Sir Clements R. Markham, K.C.B., F.R.S.* (John Murray, London, 1917).

Markham, Albert H., ed., *The Voyages and Works of John Davis, the Navigator* (Printed for the Hakluyt Society, London, 1880).

Markham, Clements R., *A Memoir of Archbishop Markham, 1719–1807* (Clarendon Press, Oxford, 1906).

Markham, Clements R., *A Naval Career During the Old War: Being a Narrative of the Life of Admiral John Markham* (Sampson Low, Marston, Searle, & Rivington, London, 1883).

Markham, Clements R., *The Arctic Navy List; or, A Century of Arctic & Antarctic Officers, 1773–1873. Together with a List of Officers of the 1875 Expedition, and Their Services* (Griffin & Co., London, 1875).

Markham, Clements R., *The Threshold of the Unknown Region*, 4th ed. (Sampson Low, Marston, Searle, and Rivington, London, 1876).

Markham, David F., *A History of the Markham Family* (John Bowyer Nichols & Sons, London, 1854).

Mayers, William F. & Dennys, Nicholas B., *The Treaty Ports of China and Japan: A Complete Guide to the Open Ports of Those Countries, Together with Peking, Yedo, Hong Kong and Macao: Forming a Guide Book & Vade Mecum for Travellers, Merchants, and Residents in General* (Trübner & Co., London, 1867).

Minutes of Proceedings at a Court-Martial Held on Board Her Majesty's Ship 'Hibernia', at Malta, On Monday, the Seventeenth day of July 1893; and, by Adjournment, Every Day Afterwards (Sunday Excepted) to the Twenty-seventh day of July 1893, to Enquire into the Loss of Her Majesty's Ship 'Victoria' (Darling & Son, London, 1893).

Nares, George S., *A Voyage to the Polar Sea During 1875–76 in H.M. Ships 'Alert' and 'Discovery'*, Vol. 2 (Sampson Low, Marston, Searle, & Rivington, London, 1878).

Nares, George S., *The Official Report of the Recent Arctic Expedition* (John Murray, London, 1876).

Nicol, Donald M., *Meteora: The Rock Monasteries of Thessaly* (Chapman & Hall, London, 1963).

Papers and Correspondence Relating to the Equipment and Fitting Out of the Arctic Expedition of 1875, Including Report of the Admiralty Arctic Committee (Printed by George Edward Eyre & William Spottiswoode, For Her Majesty's Stationary Office, London, 1875).

Parker, James, *The Old Army: Memories, 1872–1918* (Dorrance & Company, Philadelphia, PA, 1929).

Parliamentary Papers. China: Hong Kong, Session 24 January to 28 August 1860, Vol. 48 (The House of Commons, London, 1860).

Pezet, Federico A., *The Question of the Pacific* (Press of George F. Lasher, Philadelphia, PA, 1901).

Pierce, Eben D., ed., *History of Trempealeau County, Wisconsin* (H.C. Cooper jun., & Co., Chicago & Winona, 1917).

Platt, Stephen R., *Autumn in the Heavenly Kingdom: China, the West, and the Epic Story of the Taiping Civil War* (Alfred A. Knopf, New York, 2012).

Quiller-Couch, Arthur, *The Story of the Sea* (Cassell & Co., London, Paris, & Melbourne, 1895).

Rae, Herbert, *Maple Leaves in Flanders Fields* (E. P. Dutton & Co., New York, 1916).

Report of the Board of Officers to Consider an Expedition for the Relief of Lieut. Greely and Party (Government Printing Office, Washington, 1884).

Report of the Proceedings of H.M. Ship "Rosario", During Her Cruise Among the South Sea Islands, Between 1st November 1871 and 12 February 1872 (George Edward Eyre & William Spottiswoode, for Her Majesty's Stationery Office, London, 1872).

Robb, Graham, *Victor Hugo* (W.W. Norton & Company, New York, 1998).

Ross, Stewart, *Admiral Sir Francis Bridgeman: The Life and Times of an Officer and a Gentleman* (Pearson Publishing Ltd., Cambridge, 1998).

Rusden, George W., *History of New Zealand*, Vol. 2. (Chapman & Hall Ltd., London, 1883).

Samson, Jane, *Imperial Benevolence: Making British Authority in the Pacific Islands* (University of Hawaii Press, Honolulu, 1998).

Sherriff, John L., *Australia Almanac, for the Year 1873* (John Ferguson, Sydney, 1873).

Shillingberg, William B., *Dodge City: The Early Years, 1872–1886* (The Arthur H. Clark Company, Norman, OK, 2009).

Smith, Joseph, *Illusions of Conflict: Anglo-American Diplomacy Toward Latin America, 1865–1896* (University of Pittsburgh, PA, 1979).

Speight, Harry, *Lower Wharfedale: Being a Complete Account of the History, Antiquities and Scenery of the Picturesque Valley of Wharfe, From Cawood to Arthington* (Elliot Stock, London, 1902).

Sykes, William H., *The Taeping Rebellion in China. Its Origin, Progress, and Present Condition, in a Series of Letters Addressed to the 'Aberdeen Free Press' and the London 'Daily News'* (Warren Hall & Co., London, 1863).

Taylor, Richard V., *The Biographia Leodiensis; or, Biographical Sketches of the Worthies of Leeds and Neighbourhood* (Simpkin, Marshall, & Co., London, 1865).

Urban, Frank, *Ned's Navy. The Private Letters of Edward Charlton from Cadet to Admiral: A Window on the British Empire from 1878 to 1924* (Airlife Publishing Ltd., Shrewsbury, 1998).

Walch's Tasmanian Almanac for 1871 (J. Walch & Sons, Tasmania, 1871).

Weeks, Willy F., *On Sea Ice* (University of Alaska Press, Fairbanks, 2010).

Welch, Joseph, *The List of the Queen's Scholars of St Peter's College, Westminster* (G.W. Ginger, London, 1852).

Wong, John Y., *Deadly Dreams: Opium, Imperialism, and the Arrow War (1856–1860) in China* (Cambridge University Press, 1998).

Chapters and Articles

'A Comet Observed From H.M.S. *Triumph*', in *Nature: A Weekly Illustrated Journal of Science, November 1879 to April 1880*, 515, Vol. 21 (MacMillan & Co., London & New York, 1880).

'Address in Answer to Her Majesty on Her Most Gracious Speech, February 6, 1872', in *House of Commons. Hansard's Parliamentary Debates, Third Series: Commencing with the Accession of William IV. Comprising the Period from the Sixth Day of February 1872 to the Fourteenth Day of March 1872. First Volume of the Session*, 41–90, Vol. 204 (Cornelius Buck, London, 1872).

'Address to the Royal Geographical Society, delivered at the Anniversary Meeting on the 27th May, 1872: Obituary – John Markham', in *Proceedings of the Royal Geographical Society of London. Session 1871–1872*, edited by Henry W. Bates, 311–13, Vol. 16 (William Clowes & Sons, London, 1872).

'Admiral Sir A.H. Markham', in *The Sketch: A Journal of Art and Actuality, January 20th to April 13th, 1904*, 230, Vol. 45 (Illustrated London News & Sketch Limited, London, 1904).

'Another Arctic Voyage', in *The Saturday Review of Politics, Literature, Science and Art*, 278–79, Vol. 51 (Published at the Office, London, 1881).

'Appendix III: Xertoine Siccative. Correspondence Relating to Accidents on Board *Cockatrice* and *Triumph*, And the Pacific Steamer *Coquimbo*; Also Admiralty Instructions as the Xerotine Siccative', in *Reports from Commissioners, Inspectors, and Others: Twenty-Three Volumes. Naval Professional Officers; Navy (Education of Seamen and Marines); Navy (Gas Explosions); Uniform System of Buyage. Session 15 February to 25 August 1883*, 25–51, Vol. 15 (printed by Henry Hansard & Son, London, 1883).

'Arctic Exploration. Interesting Reminiscences – Preparations for the New American Expedition – A Letter from Captain Howgate', in *The Saliors' Magazine and Seamen's Friend; And the Life Boat, From the Year Ending December, 1877*, 301–305, (American Seamen's Friend Society, New York, 1877).

'Births, Marriages, and Deaths: Captain John Markham, R.N. and Marianne Georgiana Davies', in *The Lady's Magazine and Museum of the Belles-Lettres, Fine Arts, Music, Drama, and Fashions, etc.*, 126, Vol. 5 (J. Page at the Office of the Ladies Magazine & Museum, London, 1834).

'Births, Marriages, and Deaths: William Markham to Elizabeth Bowles', in *The Lady's Magazine; or Entertaining Companion for the Fair Sex, Appropriated Solely to Their Use and Amusement*, 440, Vol. 26 (G.G. & J. Robinson, London, 1795).

Brooke, Charles H., 'The Summer at Norfolk Island', in *Mission Life; Or Home and Foreign Church Work*, edited by John J. Halcombe, 124–43, Vol. 4 (W. Wells, Gardner, London, 1873).

Burke, John B., 'Seats of Great Britain: Becca Hall', in *A Visitation of the Seats and Arms of the Noblemen and Gentlemen of Great Britain*, 249, Vol. 2 (Hurst & Blackett, London, 1853).

'Campaigning in China', in *The Cornhill Magazine: January to June, 1860*, edited by William M. Thackeray, 537–48, Vol. 1 (Smith, Elder & Co., London, 1860).

'Cape Electric Tramways', in *The Railway News Finance and Joint-Stock Companies' Journal, July to December, 1899*, 831, Vol. 72 (published at the Office of the *Railway News*, London, 1899).

Caswell, John E., 'The RGS and the British Arctic Expedition, 1875–76', in *The Geographical Journal*, 143, No. 2 (July 1977), 200–10.

'Chinese Gordon', in *Donahoe's Magazine: January, 1884, to July, 1884*, 346–9, Vol. 11 (Thomas B. Noonan & Company, Boston, 1884).

Clark, Frank I., 'The True Northwest Passage', in *The Pacific Monthly, July to December, 1906*, 575–83, Vol. 16 (Pacific Monthly Publishing Co., Portland, OR, 1906).

Deacon, Margaret, 'George Strong Nares (1831–1915)', in *Arctic* 38, No. 2 (1985), 148–9.

Dickens, Charles, 'Opium', in *Household Words. From July 4, 1857 to December 12, 1857*, 104–108, Vol. 16 (Office 16, Wellington Street North, London, 1857).

'Fatal Explosion on British Warships', in *Marine Engineering. January to December, 1898*, 13–14, Vol. 2 (Marine Publishing Company, New York, 1898).

Feilden, Henry W., 'On the Zoology of Captain Markham's Voyage to Hudson's Bay in the Summer of 1886', in *Transactions-Norfolk and Norwich Naturalists' Society. 1884–85 to 1888–89*, 344–53, Vol. 4 (Printed by Fletcher & Son, Norwich, 1889).

FitzGerald, William G., 'Illustrated Interviews: Rear-Admiral A.H. Markham, R.N., F.R.G.S.', in *The Strand Magazine. July to December, 1895*, edited by George Newnes, 548–59, Vol. 10 (George Newnes Ltd., London, 1895).

Geldart, Herbert D., 'Notes on Plants Collected by Captain Markham, R.N., at Fort Churchill, Hudson's Bay, and West Digges Island, Hudson's Straits, in July and August, 1886', in *Transactions-Norfolk and Norwich Naturalists' Society. 1884–85 to 1888–89*, 354–66, Vol. 4 (Printed by Fletcher & Son, Norwich, 1889).

'Geographical Notes: Hudson's Bay and Hudson's Strait as a Navigable Channel', in *Journal of the American Geographical Society of New York*, 517–19, Vol. 20 (Printed for the Society, New York, 1888).

'George H. Markham', in *Biographical History of La Crosse, Trempealeau and Buffalo Counties, Wisconsin*, 717–19 (The Lewis Publishing Co., Chicago, 1892).

'George Twisleton Colvill', in *Biographical Dictionary of Eminent Men of Fife: Of Past and Present Times. Natives of the Country, or Connected with it By Property, Residence, Office, Marriage, or Otherwise*, edited by M.F. Conolly, 126 (Inglis & Jack, Edinburgh, 1866).

Gordon, Charles G., 'Paper XIII. Notes on the Operation Round Shanghai in 1862–63–64', 109–31.

Gregory, John S., 'British Intervention Against the Taiping Rebellion', in *Journal of Asian Studies* 19 (November 1959), 11–24.

G.T., 'The Cruise of the "Rosario" in Melanesia', in *The Colonial Church Chronicle, and Missionary Journal*, 301–303 (John & Charles Mozley, London, 1872).

Guly, Henry R., 'Snow Blindness and Other Eye Problems During the Heroic Age of Antarctic Exploration', in *Wilderness & Environmental Medicine* 23 (2012), 77–82, https://www.wemjournal.org/article/S1080-6032(11)00327-9/pdf.

Halcombe John J., 'In Memoriam: Joseph Atkin', in *Mission Life; Or Home and Foreign Church Work*, 131–45, Vol. 3 (W. Wells Gardner, London, 1872).

Hashimoto, Mitsuru, 'Collision at Namamugi', translated by Betsey Scheiner, in *Representations* 18 (Spring 1987), 69–90.

Hornby, Geoffrey T.P., 'The Loss of the "Victoria"', in *The United Service. A Monthly Review of Military and Naval Affairs*, 334–40, Vol. 10 (L.R. Hamersly & Co., Philadelphia, 1893).

Jastrzembski, Frank, 'Avenging the Martyr: Markham's Raid on Nukapu', in *Soldiers of the Queen*, no. 168 (Autumn 2017), 3–7.

Kendall, E.J.C., 'Scurvy During Some British Polar Expeditions, 1875–1917', in *The Polar Record* 7, no. 51 (September 1951), 467–85.

Kolshus, Thorgeir & Hovdhaugen, Even, 'Reassessing the Death of Bishop John Coleridge Patteson', in *The Journal of Pacific History* 45, no. 3 (December 2010), 331–55.

Lalonde, Suzanne, 'Post-1918 Europe and the Near East', in *Determining Boundaries in a Conflicted World: The Role of Uti Possidetis*, 61–102 (McGill-Queen's University Press, Montreal & Kingston, 2002).

'Last Lessons from the Victoria', in *The Speaker: A Review of Politics, Letters, Science, and the Arts. July 8 to December 30, 1893*, 125–26, Vol. 7 (London, 1893).

'Masonic and General Tidings', in *The Freemason, A Weekly Journal of Freemasonry, Literature, Science and Art*, 150. Vol. 32 (George Kenning, London, 1894).

Markham, Albert H., 'A Diplomatic Scramble', in *The Living Age, Seventh Series. January, February, March, 1899*, 548–53, Vol. 2 (The Living Age Company, Boston, 1899).

Markham, Albert H., 'Among Chinese Pirates', in *The Idler: An Illustrated Monthly Magazine. August, 1896, to January 1897*, edited by Jerome K. Jerome, 40–4, Vol. 10 (Chatto & Windus, London, 1897).

Markham, Albert H., 'Antarctic Exploration', in *The North American Review*, edited by David A. Munro, 431–40, Vol. 164 (The North American Review Publishing Co., New York, 1897).

Markham, Albert H., 'A Visit to the Galapagos Islands in 1880', in *Proceedings of the Royal Geographical Society and Monthly Record, 1880*, 742–58, Vol. 2 (Edward Stanford, London, 1880).

Markham, Albert H., 'Hudson's Bay and Hudson's Strait as a Navigable Channel,' in *Proceedings of the Royal Geographical Society and Monthly Record of Geography*, 549–67, Vol. 10 (Edward Stanford, London, 1888).

Markham, Albert H., 'Sketches on the Prairies', in *Good Words for 1878*, edited by Donald Macleod, 343–9, 415–22, 455–61 & 525–32, (Daldy, Isbister & Co., London, 1878).

Markham, Albert. H., 'The Arctic Campaign of 1879 in the Barents Sea', in *Proceedings of the Royal Geographical Society and Monthly Record of Geography*, 1880, 1–40, Vol. 2 (Edward Stanford, London, 1880).

Markham, Albert H., 'The North Polar Problem', in *The North American Review*, edited by Lloyd Bryce, 486–96, Vol. 162 (New York, 1896).

Markham, Albert H., 'The Road to the Pole: A Yachting Cruise to Novaya Zemlya and Seas Adjacent', in *Good Words for 1881*, edited by Donald Macleod, 89–205 & 277-282, (Ibister & Co., London, 1880).

Markham, Albert H., 'Through Hudson Strait and Bay: A Naval Officer's Holiday Trip', in *Good Words For 1888*, edited by Donald McLeod, 23–8, 116–23, 187–94 & 256–64, Vol. 29 (Isbister & Co., London, 1888).

Markham, Albert H., 'Monasteries in the Air', in *Pearson's Magazine* 7, no. 41 (May 1899): 211–17 (Pearson Publishing Co., New York, 1899).

Markham, Clements R., 'Obituary: Admiral Jansen', in *The Geographical Journal: Including the Proceedings of the Royal Geographical Society. July to December, 1893*, 465–8, Vol. 2 (The Royal Geographical Society, London, 1893).

Markham, Clements R., 'Polar Regions', in *The Encyclopedia Britannica: A Dictionary of Arts, Sciences, and General Literature*, 315–30, Vol. 19, 9th ed. (Henry G. Allen & Company, New York, 1888).

Markham, Clements R., 'The Cruise of the Rosario in Melanesia', in *The Colonial Church Chronicle, and Missionary Journal*, 378 (John & Charles Mozley, London, 1872).

'Mexico Electric Tramways', in *The Electrical Engineer. A Weekly Journal of Electrical Engineering, With Which is Incorporated 'Electric Light'. From January 4, 1901, to June 28, 1901*, 828, Vol. 27 (Printed & Published by the Proprietor by Brass & Co., London, 1901).

Munroe, Charles E., 'Explosions Caused by Commonly Occurring Substances', in *Science: A Weekly Journal Devoted to the Advancement of Science. January to June, 1899*, 345–63, Vol. 9 (The MacMillan Co., New York, 1899).

'Naval Court Martial-Collision Between the "Hecla" and the "Cheerful"', in *Hansard's Parliamentary Debates, Third Series: Commencing with the Accession of William IV. Comprising the Period from the Twenty-Seventh Day of July, 1885, to The Twelfth Day of August, 1885. Eighth Volume of Session 1884–85*, 1733, Vol. 100 (Published by Cornelius Buck, London, 1885).

'Navy – Court Martial – H.M.S. "Triumph" – Case of Louis Price', in *Hansard's Parliamentary Debates, Third Series: Commencing with the Accession of William IV. Comprising the Period From the Twentieth Day of July 1883, to The Ninth*

Day of August 1883. Seventh Volume of the Session, 934–5, Vol. 282 (published by Cornelius Buck, London, 1883).

'Navy-Collision With H.M.S. "Hecla"', in *Hansard's Parliamentary Debates, Third Series: Commencing with the Accession of William IV. Comprising the Period from The Eighth Day of July, 1885, to The Twenty-Fourth Day of July, 1885. Seventh Volume of Session 1884–5*, 1516–17, Vol. 229 (published by Cornelius Buck, London, 1885).

Noel, Gerard H., 'On the Training of the Executive Branch of the Navy', in *Journal of the Royal United Service Institution*, 801–26, Vol. 33 (Published by W. Mitchell & Co., London, 1889–90).

'Obituary', in *The Gentleman's Magazine, January to June, 1861*, edited by Sylvanus Urban, 225 (John Henry & James Parker, London, 1861).

'Obituary: Admiral Sir Albert Hastings Markham, K.C.B.', in *The Geographical Journal* 53, no. 1 (January 1919): 61–3.

'Obituary: Thomas Colan, M.D.', in *The Lancet: A Journal of British and Foreign Medicine, Philosophy, Surgery, Chemistry, Public Health, Criticism, and News*, edited by James G. Wakley, 415, Vol. 2 (Published by John James Croft, London, 1885).

'Obituary: Vice-Admiral Sir George Strong Nares, K.C.B, F.R.S.', in *The Geographical Journal. January to June, 1915*, 255–7, Vol. 45 (The Royal Geographical Society, London, 1915).

Osborn, Sherard, 'On the Exploration of the North Polar Region', in *The Journal of the Royal Geographical Society* 36 (1866): 279–99.

Parkinson, Roger, 'Perceptions of Strategy in the Victorian Era', in *The Late Victorian Navy: The Pre-dreadnought Era and the Origins of the First World War*, 6–42, (The Boydell Press, Woodbridge, 2008).

Palinkas, Lawrence A. & Suedfeld, Peter, 'Psychological Effects of Polar Expeditions', in *Lancet* 12, no. 371 (January 2008), 153–63.

'Per Mare, Per Terram', in *The Navy & Army Illustrated*, edited by Charles N. Robinson, 531–4, Vol. 7 (Hudson & Kearns, London, 1899).

Pike, Herbert C., 'The Torpedo School of the Royal Navy', in *The Windsor Magazine: An Illustrated Monthly for Men and Women*, 279–85, Vol. 14 (Ward, Lock & Co., London, 1901).

'Proceedings of the Royal Geographical Society. Third Meeting, 12th December 1876', in *Proceedings of the Royal Geographical Society, Session 1876–77*, 94–120, Vol. 21 (William Clowes & Sons, London, 1877).

'Results of the Arctic Expedition, 1875–76', in *The Geographical Magazine, 1878*, 137–45, Vol. 5, edited by Clements R. Markham, (Trübner & Co., London, 1878).

Rowbotham, W.B., 'The Bombardment of Kagoshima, 15 August 1863', in *Royal United Services Institution Journal*, 108, no. 631 (1963), 273–8.

'Royal Geographical Society', in *The Artizan: A Monthly Record of the Progress of Civil and Mechanical Engineering, Shipbuilding, Steam Navigation, The*

Application of Chemistry to the Industrial Arts, edited by William Smith, 57–8, Vol. 26 (Published at the Office of 'The Artizan' Journal, London, 1868).

'Saturday, September 20th: Arctic Exploration', in *Ocean Highways: The Geographical Review*, edited by Clements R. Markham, 303–307, Vol. 1 (N. Trübner & Co., London, 1874).

Saunders, Howard, 'On some Laridae from the Coasts of Peru and Chili, collected by Capt. Albert H. Markham, R.N., with Remarks on the Geographical Distribution of the Group in the Pacific', in *The Proceedings of the Scientific Meetings of the Zoological Society of London for the Year 1882*, 520–30, (Messrs Longmans, Green, Reader, & Dyer, London, 1882).

'Second Voyage of the "Eira" to Franz-Josef Land', in *Proceedings of the Royal Geographical Society and Monthly Record of Geography*, 204–28, Vol. 5 (Edward Stanford, London, 1883).

Stein, Glenn M., 'Gunner George Porter, R.M.A.: Sledding Toward Destiny', in *Medal Collector* 60, no. 2 (March/April 2009), 3–11.

'Stephen Taroniaro: Native Catechist of the Melanesian Mission', in *Mission Life; Or Home and Foreign Church Work*, 221–2, Vol. 3 (W. Wells Gardner, London, 1872).

'The Arctic Expedition', in *The Geographical Magazine, 1875*, edited by Clements R. Markham, 171–3, Vol. 2 (Trübner & Co., London, 1875).

'The Barcelona Exhibition and Festivities', in *The Tablet. January to June, 1888*, 832, Vol. 71 ('Tablet' Office, London, 1888).

'The Canadian Government and Admiral Markham', in *The Geographical Journal. July to December 1896*, 179, Vol. 3 (Edward Stanford, London, 1896).

'The Hecla's Collision', in *The Saturday Review of Politics, Literature, Science, and Art*, 175–6, Vol. 60 (Published at the Office, London, 1885).

'The Hudson Bay Route', in *Debates of the Senate of the Dominion of Canada 1890. Fourth Session-Sixth Parliament*, 65–82 (Printed by Brown Chamberlin, Ottawa, 1890).

'The Late Admiral Jenkins, C.B', in *By-Gones Relating to Wales and the Border Companies, 1893–4*, 429–30, Vol. 3 (Elliot Stock, London, 1894).

'The Loss of the Victoria', in *The Saturday Review of Politics, Literature, Science and Art*, 34–5, (Published at the Office, London, 1893).

'The Mayor of Shrewsbury', in *Salopian Shreds and Patches, 1880–81*, 248, Vol. 4 (Printed & Published at the Office of Eddowes's Journal, Shrewsbury, 1881).

Theseus, late R.N., 'Our Sailing Navy', in *Colburn's United Service Magazine and Naval and Military Journal*, 52–62, (Hurst & Blackett, London, 1859).

'The "Victoria" Disaster', in *The United Service. A Monthly Review of Military and Naval Affairs*, 381–4, Vol. 10 (L.R. Hamersly & Co., Philadelphia, 1893).

Tomlinson, Barbara, 'Chivalry at the Poles: British Sledge Flags', in Proceedings of the XIX International Congress of Vexillology, York, July 23–27, 2001, *Proceedings*, 215–21, https://www.flaginstitute.org/pdfs/Barbara%20Tomlinson.pdf.

'Vote of Thanks to Commodore Lambert and the Officers of the New Zealand Squadron, August 18, 1869', in *New Zealand Parliamentary Debates. Fourth*

Session of the Fourth Parliament. Legislative Council and House of Representatives. Comprising the Period from the Twentieth Day of July, to the Third Day of September, 1869, 507–10, Vol. 6 (Printed for the House of Representatives, by George Didsbury, Government Printers, Wellington, 1869).

Webb, F.C., 'Old Cable Stories Retold – VII. The Red Sea and India Cable of 1859–60', in *The Electrician: A Weekly Journal of Theoretical and Applied Electricity and Chemical Physics*, 428–30, Vol. 15 (Printed and Published by George Tucker at the 'Electrician' Office, London, 1865).

Yarrington, William H.H., 'Patteson, Atkin, Stephen, Martyrs, 1871', in *Australian Verses*, 101–102, (George Robertson & Co., Melbourne, Sydney, Adelaide, 1892).

Websites

'Bottle of 140-year-old Arctic Ale beer sells for £3,300', *BBC News*, 15 June 2015, https://www.bbc.com/news/uk-england-shropshire-33122420.

Derbyshire, Tom, 'Bottle of ice-cold beer that costs you £3300', *Antiques Trade Gazette*, 25 June 2015, https://www.antiquestradegazette.com/news/2015/bottle-of-ice-cold-beer-that-costs-you-3300/.

Galbraith, Michael, 'Death threats sparked Japan's first cricket game', *The Japan Times*, 16 June 2013, https://www.japantimes.co.jp/news/2013/06/16/national/history/death-threats-sparked-japans-first-cricket-game/#.XHV7VTYo7ct.

Gamroth, Clarence J. ed., 'One-Hundred Years of Independence, Wisconsin: Bicentennial Historical Album, 1876–1976', *The Trempealeau Co. WIGenWeb Project*, http://trempealeau.wigenweb.org/histories/100independence/frontierlife.htm.

'George V to Captain Albert H. Markham, 17 February 1890', *International Autograph Auctions Ltd*, 2 April 2011, https://autographauctions.co.uk/0024-lot-731-GEORGE-V-1865-1936-King-of-the-United-Kingdom-1910-36-A-L-S-George-as-Prince-George-of-Wales?auction_id=0&view=lot_detail#?high_estimate=90000&low_estimate=0&sort_by=lot_number&catId=&ipp=10&cat_id=&lot_id=24343.

'Imperial Hats and Polar Sheep', *Scott Polar Research Institute, Department of Geography, University of Cambridge*, 6 October 2015, https://www.spri.cam.ac.uk/museum/news/collections/2015/10/06/imperial-hats-and-polar-sheep/.

'John Coleridge Patteson, A Sermon by Canon Charles Elliot Fox on the Occasion of the Centenary of the Consecration of Bishop John Coleridge Patteson, February 24, 1961', transcribed by the Reverend Dr Terry Brown, *Project Canterbury*, http://anglicanhistory.org/oceania/fox_patteson1961.html.

'Lot 139: Admiral Sir Albert Markham', *Bonhams*, 24 June 2015, https://www.bonhams.com/auctions/22714/lot/139/.

'Lot 140: Illustrated autograph journal kept by Captain Albert Hastings Markham on his tour of the United States', *Bonhams*, 24 June 2015, https://www.bonhams.com/auctions/22714/lot/140/.

'Markham Family', *Westminster Abbey*, https://www.westminster-abbey.org/abbey-commemorations/commemorations/markham-family/.

'Markham Obituaries', *The Trempealeau Co. WIGenWeb Project*, http://trempealeau.wigenweb.org/histories/trempco/vol1bsup/02-markham obituaries.htm.

Pattinson, Ron, 'Arctic Ale', *BeerAdvocate*, July 2012, https://www.beer advocate.com/articles/6920/arctic-ale/.

'Remarkable Wedding Cakes: Admiral Markham's "Arctic" Wedding Cake', *All Things Victorian*, http://www.avictorian.com/wedding_cakes.html.

'Scott's Last Expedition: Preface by Clements R. Markham', *Scott Polar Research Institute, Department of Geography, University of Cambridge*, https://www.spri.cam.ac.uk/museum/diaries/scottslastexpedition/preface-by-clements-r-markham/.

'(Wild West) Markham, Albert Hastings, Capt. Illustrated autograph manuscript journal of his tour of the United States, including the Indian Territories and Dodge City, England to the United States and back, 22 September 1877 to 8 March 1878', *The 19th Century Rare Book and Photograph Shop*. http://www.19thshop.com/book/illustrated-autograph-manuscript-journal-of-his-tour-of-the-united-states-including-the-indian-territories-and-dodge-city/.

Index

A Polar Reconnaissance: Being the Voyage of the "Isbjörn" to Novaya Zemlya in 1879, 127

A Whaling Cruise to Baffin's Bay and the Gulf of Boothia, and an Account of the Rescue of the Crew of the "Polaris", 74–5

Aborigines' Protection Society, 43

Abdülhamid II, Sultan, 145, 155

Acland, William D., 131–3, 160

Actaeon (ship), 21–2

Active (ship), 143–4

Adams, John, 50

Adams, William, 71–2

Admirals in Collision, 148, 170

Alcock, Rutherford, 69

Aldrich, Pelham, 77–8, 88
  sledge expedition, 91, 94–6, 105–106, 111
  sympathy for Markham's death, 167–8

Albert (ship), 156

Alert (ship), 68, 87, 97–8, 125, 128
  abandoned Floeberg Beach, 106–107, 109
  characteristics, 78–9
  crew, 77
  in Portsmouth before departure, 66–7
  in the Hudson Bay, 137–9, 142
  represented on Markham's wedding cake, 162
  voyage up Smith Sound, 80, 81–2, 83, 89
  winter camp, 84, 86, 88, 91, 95–6, 99, 100–102, 104–105, 110, 112
  winterised, 85

Alexander II, Tsar, 12

Alexandra (sledge), 95

Algeria (ship), 113

Amat Lodge, 164

Ambrym Island, 50

Amedeo, Prince Luigi, 112

American Civil War, 42, 114, 117

Amethyst (ship), 22

Amoy, 4, 14, 16, 18, 20

Amphion (ship), 148, 154

Ancón, Treaty of, 134

Anglo-Chinese trade, 14–15

Aniwa Island, 53

Antarctica, 127, 144, 169

Anti-Slavery Society, 43

Archer, Robert H., 77–8

Arctic (ship), 71–4, 78, 120

Arctic Circle, 80, 83, 107–108

Arctic Committee, 71, 74–5

Armistice (1918), 168

Armstrong, Joseph, 53

Arthur, Chester A., 135

Assistance (ship), 9

Atacama Desert, 128–9

Atkin, Joseph, 47–9

Aurora Island, 56

Austin, Horatio, 9

Australia (ship), 145

Australia Station, 39, 44, 61, 65, 78

Baffin Bay, 1, 71–2, 76, 135

Baggett, John, 151–3

Baird, John K.E., 144

Balaclava, Battle of, 151

Ballantyne, Robert M., 138–9

Banks Islands, 52

Baquedano, Manuel, 131–4

Barclay (captain), 32

Barents, Willem, 126

Barents Sea, 120–2, 124, 126, 128, 138

Barham (ship), 154

Baring, Evelyn, 145

Barnhill, Laura, 119

Baskerville, Thomas, 62

Beaumont, Lewis A., 77–8, 91, 106–107, 111, 168

Becca Hall, 7

Benthall, John, 10

Benthall, William, 10

Beresford, Charles Lord, 148, 160, 167

Bessels, Emil, 73, 120

Beynen, Koolemans, 120–1

Biquatenac, 139–41
  see also Tom

Birkenhead (ship), 151

Black River Falls, 38–9

blackbirders, 42–4, 46, 49–50, 55, 58, 64

blackbirding (South Pacific), 1, 44–6, 50–7, 64
    misdeeds committed, 42–3, 49, 50, 52, 58
    see also blackbirders
Blanche (ship), 39–41, 45–6, 78, 92
Bloodhound (sledge), 95–6
Borrodaile, Margaret, 34–5
Bounty (ship), 50
Bourke, Maurice A., 149–50, 152–3, 157, 159–61
Bowles, Oldfield, 7
Brackenbury, John, 153
Bradshaw, Henry B., 150–1, 158
Brenton, Reginald C., 131, 133–4
British Columbia, 131
Brompton Parish Church, 168
Brooke, Charles H., 49–50, 59
Bruce, James, 109
Budington, Sidney O., 73–4
Bulldog (sledge), 95–6
Bryan, James, 55

Caddo, 114, 117
Cagni, Umberto, 112
Callao, 128–9, 130, 131–4
Camilla (ship), 12–7, 23–5, 28
    anchored at Canton, 21
    expedition against pirates, 18–20
Camp Supply, 118
Camperdown (ship), 147–8, 150, 153–4, 157
    collison with *Victoria*, 151
Canton, 4, 14, 16, 17
    bloodshed between foreigners and citizens, 20, 21–5, 36
Cape Albert Markham, 169
Cape Isabella, 80–1, 107
Cape Joseph Henry, 85, 95–7, 102
Cape Sabine, 118, 136
Carl (ship), 52–3
Carlsen, Elling, 122
Carpenter, Kenneth J., 110
Carthaginian (ship), 137
Caswell, John E., 110
Catinat (ship), 22
Cayzer, Charles W., 162
Centaur (ship), 31, 33–6
Challenge (ship), 45–6
Challenger (ship), 70, 76, 78
Chandler, William E., 136
Charles, Richard, Lord Gillford, 149, 157, 159
Charlton, Edward F.B., 145–6
Cheerful (ship), 135
Chesapeake (ship), 29

Chester, Hubbard C., 73
Cheyenne-Arapaho Reservation, 118
China Station, 1, 12, 15, 18, 25, 27, 29, 35, 37
Chorrillos, Battle of, 131–3
Christ Church, University of Oxford, 6, 10, 46
Christian IX, King, 144
Churchill, Hudson Bay, 138–9, 141
Churchill, Winston, 113
Churchill Mountains, 144
Chusan Archipelago, 31, 33
Cinderella, 117
Clan Matheson (steamer), 162
Clapp, William H., 118
Clarke, Henry T., 40
Clarke, Woodthorpe, C., 34–5
Claron (Saxon chief), 5
Clements Markham (sledge), 94
Clifton Zoological Gardens, 74, 123
Clown (ship), 26
Codrington, Robert H., 46, 50
Colan, Thomas, 80, 87, 94–5, 128
Collingwood (ship), 8
Collingwood (Mediterranean Fleet), 148
Colomb, Philip, 160
Colvile, George T., 17, 28, 16, 25
    actions against pirates, 18–20, 22, 26–8
    career, 14
    death, 37
Colville, Stanley, 168
Commerell, Edmund, 160
Commonwealth War Graves Commission, 155
Confederate States of America, 42
Conybeare, Crawford J.M., 78
Cook (trooper), 115
Cooper, James, 57
Cooper, James F., 115
Cooper Key, Astley, 120
Coromandel (ship), 29
Crank, Sarah, 166
Cress, Thomas H., 166
Crimean War, 12, 16, 29, 68
Croft, Henry P. (wife), 165
Cross Island, 124
Crusoe, Robinson, 140
Culme-Seymour, Michael, 157, 161
Cygent (ship), 78

Daggett (chief magistrate), 46
Dalton Gang, 114
Daly, James T., 62
Davies, Thomas H.T., 134–5

Davis, George W., 135–6
Davis, John, 2, 120
Daza, Hilarión, 129
de Bruyne, A., 120–1, 125–6
de Busli, Roger, 5
de Lisle, Rudolph, 130
de Piérola, Nicolás, 130, 133
Dean of Dundee, 102
Deuchars, David, 72, 78
Digges Island, 138
Discovery (ship), 6–7, 79, 94, 105, 125
  crew, 77
  description, 78
  leaving Smith Sound, 107
  reunited with *Alert* 106
  voyage up Smith Sound, 80, 81
  winter camp, 82, 91
Disko Island, 78, 80
Disraeli, Benjamin, 75
Dodge City, 118–19
Dodge House Hotel, 119
Donald McLean (schooner), 57
Doolin Gang, 114
Doterel (ship), 135
Dreadnought (ship), 148
Duke of Edinburgh, 66
Duke of York, 6
Duminick, 87–8

Easterbrook, Bill, 57
'Eastern Question', 107
Eastman's Royal Naval Academy, 10–11
Eastough, George, 41
Edgar (ship), 148, 156
Edgell, Harry E., 28
Edinburgh (ship), 148, 153
Efate Island, 51
Egerton, George Le C., 77, 80, 84, 87, 94,
  104, 168
Elgin, Lord, 23
Ellesmere Island, 1, 69, 74, 83, 89, 91, 135,
  169
Erebus (ship), 68
Eskimo remains, 106, 108
Espiritu Santo Island, 55
Esquimalt Harbour, 131
Euclid, 18
Eugénie, Empress, 66–7, 125–6
Ever-Victorious Army, 31, 33
  see also EVA

Fan-qui (foreigners), 21
Fanny (ship), 51–2, 57
Fawkes, Guy, 88

Fearless (ship), 154–5
Feilden, Henry W., 77, 87–8, 143
Fennell, Edmund, 5–6
Ferbrache, William, 92, 101, 104
Fiji, 42, 44, 50, 52
Fitzroy, Robert, 8
Flash of Lightning (race horse), 16
Floeberg Beach, 83, 90, 105–106, 109
Fort Reno, 117–18
Fort Sill, 114, 116–17
Fortnightly Review, 160
Foxon, William N., 134
Francombe, Reuben, 92, 99, 100–101, 104
Franklin, John, 9, 76, 169
Franklin, Lady Jane, 169
Franklin Expedition, 68, 70, 109
Franz Josef Land, 122, 126–7, 169
Fraser, James C., 36
Frederick, 80
Frederick, Empress, 144
Fremantle, Sydney R., 3, 144, 161, 167
Freya (ship), 124
'Frostbite Range', 85
Fulford, Reginald B., 78

Galapagos Islands, 131
Galbraith, Michael, 36
Geldart, Herbert D., 143
George II, King, 6
Gervers, Charles T., 162
Gervers, Francis T., 162, 164
Gibson, George H.R., 165
Giffard, George A., 77, 80, 86, 88, 167
Gilford, Lord, 66
Gisborne, William, 40
Gladstone, William, 75, 129
Gliddon, James, 62
Godhavn, 80
Good Words, 121, 128
Goodenough, James G., 71
Goodwill, J., 55
Gordon, Andrew R., 136–7, 142
Gordon, Charles G., 15, 30, 33–4
Gore-Booth, Georgina, 121
Gore-Booth, Henry, 121–25
Goschen, George J., 161, 163
Gouch, 122
Gower, Abel, 34
Graham, Gerald, 15
Grant, Hope, 29
Grant, William J.A., 125
Grau, Miguel, 129
Gray, John, 17–18
Greely, Adolphus, W., 2, 112, 118, 135–6

Greely Relief Board, 135–6
Guernsey, 7–8, 12, 14
Gulf of Boothia, 71–2

Hall, Charles F., 69, 73–4, 80
Hamilton, Richard Vesey, 160
Hand, James, 106–107
Harley, Daniel, 84, 92, 101, 104
Hart, Robert, 22
Hastings, Warren, 7
Hawkes, Henry, 18–22
Hawkins, John, 92, 98–9, 100–101, 104
Hawkins-Smith, Thomas, 149, 151–2, 157, 159
Hayes River, 1, 139–40
Hazen, William B., 136
Hecla (ship), 135
Helen (ship), 56
Hendrick, Hans, 80
Henry, Prince, 144
Henry, Princess, 144
Hill, Archibald O., 62
Hill, Shuldham S.C., 56–7
Hisamitsu, Shimazu, 34
Hodson, Charles E., 77
Hong Kong, 3, 13–14, 16, 26
Hong Xiuquan, 30
Hooker Island, 169
Hope, George J., 29
Hope, James, 27, 35, 37
    30–mile campaign around Shanghai, 30–31
    attempt to capture Taku Forts, 28–9
    recommended Markham for promotion, 33
Horace, 18
Hornby, Geoffrey T.P., 160
Hornet (ship), 25
Hotham, Charles F., 156
Hough, Richard, 170
Huáscar (ironclad), 129–30
Hudson, Henry, 2
Hudson Bay, 1, 4, 136–9, 142
Hudson Strait, 1, 136–8, 142
Hudson's Bay Company, 138
Hugo, Victor, 7
Hunt, G.W., 66
Hydra (ship), 120

Ice Haven, 126
Imperieuse (ship), 137
Indian Territory (Oklahoma), 1, 114, 118
Inflexible (ship), 148
Inglefield, Edward A., 167

Inglefield, Frederick S., 3, 167
Inkerman, Battle of, 16
Isbjörn, 123
    description, 121–2
    voyage in the Barents and Kara seas, 124–6

Jack (cowboy), 118
Jackson, Benjamin, 50, 51–4, 56, 63
Jackson, Frederick G., 169
James Gang, 114
Jan Mayen, 120
Janus (ship), 26–7
Jellicoe, John, 3, 153, 162, 167–8
Jem, 139, 140–1
Jenkins, Robert, 21–2
'John Henry mange', 102, 110
Johnstone, Charles, 150
Joliffe, Thomas, 91, 101, 104
Jorgensen, Lors, 122–6
Jutland, Battle of, 3, 153

Kagoshima, bombardment of, 36
Kaiser Wilhelm Canal, 163
Kalabaka, 146
Kane, Elisha, 69, 80
Kara Sea, 124–5
Kawasaki, 34
Kay, John, 59
Kendall, E.J.C., 110
Kensal Green Cemetery, 168
Kerr, Walter T., 144
Kerr, William M., 167
Kilgallon, Thomas, 122
King, Bob, 118–19
King, George St Vincent, 12
Kiowa and Comanche Reservation, 115
Knell, James, 170
Koolan, 26–7
Kuper, Augustus L., 35–6

Lady Franklin Bay, 82, 107
Lawrence, Edward, 92, 101, 104
Leang-paou-heun, 23–4
Legg, Charles, 134
Lelson (corporal), 22
Leonidas, 145
Lepolow, 57
Lewin, Henry R., 42, 51, 58
Lie-wan-moon, 27
Lima, 128–34
Lockwood, James B., 2, 112
Lopes, Massey, 66
Lords Commissioners, 11, 33, 60, 61, 64, 77, 78, 79, 109, 161, 166

Los Angeles Herald, 155–6
Louise, Queen, 144
Lushington, Vernon, 60, 63–4, 66

Macao, 26, 27
Macbeth, 95
Mack, Frederick C., 122–3
Mackenzie, Ranald S., 114–15, 117
Maclean (doctor), 132
Malekula Island, 52
Malta, 147, 156–8, 163
Manitoba, 1, 136, 139, 142
Māori guerrillas, 40
Maple Leaves in Flanders Fields, 165
Marathon (battlefield), 145
Marco Polo (sledge), 91, 94, 96–7, 99, 105,
    112
Marcus, William, 55
Marewatta (chief), 57
Maria Christina, Queen, 144
Marion Rennie, 40, 50
Markham, Albert Hastings, 1, 2, 13, 120,
    128, 148
  ancestry, 5
  Arctic Expedition (1875–76), 66–7, 77,
    78–80, 82–3, 90, 106–12
    fall sledging expedition, 84–5
    observation halls, 86
    reaches the highest northern latitude,
      101
    spring/summer sledge expedition,
      91–100, 102–105
    wintering activities in the *Alert*, 87–9
  assigned to the *Camilla*, 12
  birth, 7
  cadet examination, 9–11
  character, 3
  China Station, 13–14, 28, 37
    expedition against Skektsing, 23–5
    on pirates in the South Seas, 15
    operations against pirates, 18–20, 22,
      26–7, 31–3
    partakes in the first cricket match in
      Japan, 36
    relationship with Colvile, 16–17
    Richardson Incident, 34–5
    Taku Forts, 29
    witnesses bloodshed in Canton, 21
  commander of the Training Squadron,
    143–4
  consulted by Americans in Greely rescue
    operation, 135–6
  death and legacy, 166–70
  Hudson Bay expedition, 137–42
  influenced by Clements Markham, 8
  involvement in the War of the Pacific
    (1878–83), 132–4
  marriage, 162
  praise of George Nares, 81
  reaction to Sherard Osborn's death, 76
  reputation as a martinet, 41, 129, 130
  role during WWI, 165
  Rosario's cruise, 44–6, 50, 51–7
    criticised, 58–65
  sightseeing the Mediterranean Basin,
    145–7
  travels to the Galapagos Islands, 131
  tours Indian Territory, 113–19
  Victoria disaster, 150–1, 160
    blacklisted by the Admiralty, 163–4
    impact on him, 152–5, 161
    rebuke from the Admiralty, 159
    support of colleagues, 156
    testified at court martial, 157–8
  view of Bishop Patteson, 49
  visits family in the United States, 38–9
  voyage to Novaya Zemlya, 121–7
  whaling cruise on the *Arctic*, 71–4
    importance to the Arctic movement,
      75
Markham, Arthur, 7, 38–9
Markham, Catherine, 7–10, 13
Markham, Clements R., 17, 71, 75–6, 91,
    120–1, 127, 147, 160, 169
  advocate for the Arctic movement, 68
  Arctic Expedition (1875–76), 78, 80
    comes to its defence, 109
    praise of expedition, 108
  background, 2, 8–9, 37, 78
  death, 166
  description of home, 113
  guest on the Training Squadron, 143–5
  helps cousin get appointed to the
    Camilla, 12
Markham, Daniel, 5
Markham, David, 6
Markham, David F., 7, 9
Markham, David W., 8
Markham, Elizabeth, 5
Markham, Elizabeth (Bowles), 7
Markham, Elizabeth (Fennell), 5
Markham, Enoch, 5
Markham, Frederick, 7
Markham, George, 5
Markham, George (Albert Markham's
    brother), 7, 11, 38–9
Markham, Georgina, 8
Markham, Gertrude, 8

Markham, John (admiral), 6
Markham, John (jun.), 7, 12, 14, 33–4
Markham, John (sen.), 7–8, 11–12, 39
Markham, Joy (McCann), 164, 170
Markham, Marianne (Wood), 7, 39, 163
Markham, Minna, 113, 120, 147, 164, 166
Markham, Ronald A., 165
Markham, Sarah (Goddard), 6
Markham, Selina, 8
Markham, Theodora (Gervers), 3, 163, 165,
    170
  condolences from friends following
      husband's death, 166–8
  marriage, 162
  wrote to Prince of Wales, 164
Markham, Warren, 8
Markham, William (jun.), 5–6, 8
Markham, William (sen.), 5–6, 8, 17
Markham, William (third), 6, 7
Markham Ice Shelf, 169
Marshall, William, 34–5
Maskell, William, 92, 101–102, 104–105
Matochkin Shar, 124–6
May, William H., 77–8, 80, 87–8, 102,
    167–8
  helps to rescue Markham's sledge crew,
      104
  sledge excursion, 84–5
McCann, William S., 170
McClintock, Francis L., 66, 78, 84
McClure, Robert, 169
McKenzie, Kenneth, 56
Mediterranean Basin, 145
Mediterranean Fleet, 144, 148, 156, 162
Mediterranean Station, 38, 78, 112, 145
Megaera (ship), 41
Melanesian Mission, 46, 58, 59
Mercury (Australian paper), 58
Milne, Alexander, 66
Milne, Peter, 51–2, 57
Minesweepers' Fund, 1, 165
Minipa, James, 47
Miraflores, Battle of, 133–4
Mizner, John K., 117
'Monasteries in the Air', 146
Montgomerie, John E., 31, 34, 39, 40, 45–6
Morning Post, 66–7
Morris, Samuel, 151
Moss, Edward L., 68, 77, 80, 87, 96,
    104–105
Moto (chief), 47
Mow-way (chief), 115
Murray, James P., 52
Mutual Benefits, Treaty of, 128–9

Nameless Bay, 124
Nanking, Treaty of, 21
Nansen, Fridtjof, 112, 167
Napoleon, 7
Napoleon III, 66, 125
Nares, George S., 66–7, 98, 101–103,
    106–107, 111
  aided rescue of Greely Expedition, 118,
      135–6
  appointed to lead Arctic Expedition
      (1875–76), 76–7
  characteristics of leadership, 81–2
  criticism, 109–10
  decides to return to England, 105
  dispatches sledge teams, 84
  experience sledge travelling, 78, 83
  on Floeberg Beach, 85–9, 95
  orders to Albert Markham's sledge teams,
      91, 93
  purchased sledge dogs, 80
  receives accolades, 108
  rescue of Markham's sledge teams, 104
Neale, Edward St John, 35–6
Nellie, 78, 80, 87
Nelson, Horatio, 2, 12, 19, 29, 149
Neville, William L., 10
New Hebrides Islands, 42, 44, 50, 52
New Hebrides Mission, 43, 51, 55
Nguna Island, 51, 54, 58–9, 60, 61–4, 161
  comes under attack, 52
  villagers murder *Fanny*'s crew, 57
Nichi, 140–1
Nicoll, John, 6
Niger (ship), 25–8
Nile (ship), 148, 153
Ningpo, 4, 14, 31, 33, 113
Nobbs, George H. (son), 46
Noel, Gerard H., 143
Nonomo, John, 47
Norcock, Charles J., 41
Nordenskjöld, Otto, 135
Norfolk Island, 46, 50, 59, 64
Norman Conquest, 5
North Pole, 66, 101, 120, 162, 167
  quest to reach it, 2, 68, 70, 73–4, 77,
      82–3, 88–9, 91, 109, 112, 127
Northumberland (ship), 7
*Northward Ho! Including a Narrative
    of Captain Phipps's Expedition, By a
    Midshipman*, 120
Northwest Passage, 9, 68, 142
Northwest Territories, 136
Norway House, 141
Norwich Naturalists' Society, 143

Novaya Zemlya, 2, 113, 120, 121–2, 127–8
  Isbjörn's voyage, 123–6
Nukapu Island, 53, 60, 61, 64, 161
  Bishop Patteson's visit, 47, 50
  comes under attack, 54–5
  in the press, 58
  losses, 62–3
  missionaries disapprove of *Rosario*'s visit,
    59
  scheduled 2021 reconciliation there, 65

Opium Wars, 1, 3, 14, 42, 46
Opossum (ship), 28–9
Osborn, Sherard, 72
  death of, 76
  praise of Albert Markham, 74–5
  urge renewal of Arctic exploration, 68–9,
    70–1
Oxford House, 139–41
Oxford Lake, 141

Pacific Station, 12, 128, 131
Page, Clarence, 33
Palinkas, Lawrence A., 86–7
Palmer, George, 41, 46–7
Palmer, William W., 164
Paparatu, Battle of, 40
Parker, James, 115–16
Parkes, Harry S., 21, 25
Parry, William E., 2, 9, 69, 91–2, 112
Patteson, John C., 50, 65
  body, 48–9
  characteristics, 46–7
  murder, 58–9, 63–4
Paul, Charles W., 107
Pearce, Alfred B., 92, 98–9, 100, 101, 104
Pearson, John, 92, 101, 104
Peary, Robert E., 112, 127
Peel, Robert, 9
Peel, William, 9
Peking, 28–30
Pelegatonga (chief), 53
Petersen, Nels C., 80, 87, 94–5
Phaeton (ship), 148, 156
Phipps, Constantine J., 2
Pirates (China), 1, 18–20, 22, 25–7, 31–2
  opponent of the Royal Navy, 15
Pitcairn Islands, 50
Plover (ship), 28
Polaris (ship), 73–4, 81
Polynesian Labourers Act, 43, 51
Pondora (ship), 107
Poppie (sledge), 95
Port de Laperriere, 138

Port Royal, 128
Porter, George, 92
  death, 103–104
  suffering from scurvy, 97–9, 100–101
Power, William, 142
Prado, Mariano, I., 130
Price, Louis, 130
Prince Imperial, 66, 125–6
Prothero, Arthur W.E., 167–8
Prothero, Reginald C., 167
Pullen, Henry W., 78, 88, 90, 95, 105

Qing, 1, 14–15, 28–30, 34
Queensland, 42–4

Radmore, John R., 92, 101–102, 104, 105,
  112
Rae, John, 142
Ravenscraig (ship), 73
Rawlings, Thomas, 92, 101, 104
Rawlinson, Henry C., 69–70
Rawson, Wyatt, 77, 94
Read, Tom B., 20
Reading Mercury, 67
Red River War, 115
Rendova Island, 40–1
Retribution (ship), 28
Richardson, Charles L., 34–7
Riwha Tītokowaru, 40
Roberjot (lieutenant), 134
Roberts-West, Philip, 153
Rodgers, Alexander K., 115–16
Ronceval (Markham Castle), 39
Rosario (ship), 44, 59, 63–4
  cruise, 46, 50, 51–7
  description, 41
  officers' testimonies, 61–2
Ross, John, 169
Rover (ship), 143
'Royal Arctic Theatre', 88
Royal Geographical Society, 9, 68–9, 71, 75,
  108, 168
Royal Naval College, 29, 38
Royck, Conde, 133–4
Ruakituri, Battle of, 40
Russo-Turkish War 1877–78, 120

Salvin, Osbert, 131
Samuel Allsopp's Arctic Ale, 80
Sanders, Francis W., 57, 62
Sans Pareil (ship), 148, 155
Santa Cruz Islands, 44
Satsuma, 35–7
Satsuma, Prince of, 36

Schley, Winfield S., 136
Schumann, Emil, 73
Scott, Mount, 115
Scott, Robert F., 143–4, 169
Scurvy, 71, 87, 124
    afflicts Markham's sledge teams, 99,
        100–102, 111, 161
    investigation by the Admiralty, 109
    outbreak among *Alert*'s and *Discovery*'s
        crews, 105–107
    the reason it affected the expedition, 110
    see also 'John Henry mange'
Second Boer War, 163
Second World War, 170
Selkirk, 141
Selwyn, George, 46
Senggelinqin, 28
Sevastopol, Siege of, 9, 16
Seymour, Edward H., 15, 162, 168
Seymour, Michael, 25, 27, 29
Shakespeare, 6, 8, 17, 95
Shanghai, 14, 30–1, 33–4
Shannon (ship), 130
Shektsing, 23–5
Sheridan, Philip H., 113–14, 118
Shirley, John, 84, 92, 101
    devises heating apparatus, 93
    suffering from scurvy, 97–100, 104
Sho-we-tat (chief), 117
Sill, Joshua W., 114
Simpson, Thomas. H., 92, 101, 104
Sinai Peninsula, 145
Smith Sound, 1, 69–70, 118, 135, 138
    Arctic Expedition (1875–76) in Smith
        Sound, 80–2, 107
    favourable travelling conditions, 73–5
Sodom and Gomorrah, 119
Solomon Islands, 40, 42, 45, 52
Sorensen (sailor), 123
South China Sea, 12, 15, 18
South Pole, 127, 144
Southern Cross (ship), 47–9
Spencer, John. P., 159, 163
Spitsbergen, 120–1, 126–7
St Jean d'Acre (ship), 12
St John, Spenser, 132–4
St Louis, 114, 117, 119
St Michael's Church, 162
Stanhope, James, 5
Stansfield, William R.C., 10
Stephenson, Henry F., 67, 77, 108, 135
Stirling, Frederick, 41, 57, 58, 64, 128, 131
    help to mediate the War of the Pacific
        (1878–83), 132–4

investigate the conduct of *Rosario*'s
    cruise, 61–3
sailing orders to *Rosario*, 44–5
Strathnavar (ship), 51
Suedfeld, Peter, 86, 87
Suez Canal, 120, 145
Sultan (ship), 78
Sutherland, Hugh, 136–7, 142–3
Symons, Robert, 88

Taiping Rebellion, 1, 3, 30, 31, 33–4, 113
Taku Forts, 28–9
Tanna Island, 51, 57–8
Taroniaro, Stephen, 47–9
Taula (chief), 47
Te Koneke, Battle of, 40
Te Kooti Rikirangi, 40
Terror (ship), 68
Tewfik, Khedive, 145
Thackeray, William M., 8
The Admiralty, 10, 11, 77, 107, 109, 126,
    130, 137, 143–4, 154–6, 163–4
    banned the use of xerotive siccative, 135
    grant Markham leave, 12, 113, 121
    inquiry of Markham's cruise, 60, 61, 63
    investigate the *Cheerful-Hecla* collision,
        135
    memo to Markham's widow, 166
    promoted Markham to lieutenant, 33
    reviewed the *Victoria* court martial, 161
    turned down Markham's service during
        WWI, 1, 165
    visit the *Alert*, 66
    see also Lords Commissioners
The Cruise of the "Rosario" Amongst the New
    Hebrides and Santa Cruz Islands, Exposing
    the Recent Atrocities Connected with the
    Kidnapping of Natives in the South Seas,
    64
The Five Civilized Tribes, 114
The Fleet (team), 36
The Geographical Journal, 76
The Great Frozen Sea: A Personal Narrative
    of the Voyage of the "Alert" During the
    Arctic Expedition of 1875–6, 76, 120
The Great Meteoron Monastery, 146–7
The Life of Sir John Franklin and the North-
    West Passage, 166
The Little Vulgar Boy, 88
The Spectator, 75
The Times, 160–1
The Voyages and Works of John Davis, the
    Navigator, 120
Thermopylae (battlefield), 145

Thompson, William A., 115–16
'Thursday Pops', 87–8
Tientsin, 29
    Treaty of, 28
Tobiesen, Sivert, 124
Torres Islands, 45
Towns, Robert, 42
Trafalgar, Battle of, 12, 29, 88
Trafalgar (ship), 145–7, 162–3
Training Squadron, 143–4
Tribune (ship), 12, 21–2
Tripoli, 148, 154
Triumph (ship), 128–31, 133–5
Tromsø, 121–3, 125–6
Tryon, George, 148, 156, 161
    reputation, 144–5
    Victoria disaster, 149–55
        culpability, 157–60
Tryon, Lady, 155
21 Eccleston Square, 113, 115, 121

Valorous (ship), 79–80
van Straubenzee, Charles T., 23–4
Vancouver Island, 131
Vanua Lava, 45
Vernon (ship), 135–6
Victoria, Queen, 1, 12, 66, 144, 164
    Arctic Expedition (1875–76), 67,
        107–108
    on blackbirding in the South Seas, 43–4
    reaction to the *Victoria* disaster, 155–6,
        159
Victoria (ship), 38, 78, 168
Victoria (city), 14
Victoria (sledge), 92, 94, 96–7
Victoria (Tryon's flagship)
    court martial of crew's survivors, 156–8
    disaster, 3, 148–55, 161, 163, 168, 170
Victory (ship), 12
Vivid (ship), 31–3
von Payer, Julius, 122

Wales, Prince of (Edward VII), 66–7, 108,
    164, 165
Wales, Prince of (Frederick), 6
Wales, Prince of (George V), 164
Wales, Princess of, 67
Wan-Chu-Ki, 22
Ward, Frederick T., 31, 33
Watt, William, 51–2
West Markham, 5
Westminster School, 6
Weyprecht, Carl, 122
Whitcombe, P.P., 166
White, George, 77, 87
Whitney, James T., 62
Wichita Reservation, 117
Wild Duck (ship), 55
Wilhelm II, Emperor, 1, 163
Willem Barents (ship), 120, 125–6
William the Conqueror, 5
Wilson, Arthur, 15
Wilson, George, 62
Windsor Castle, 108
Winnipeg, 136–7, 139, 141
Winnipeg, Lake, 141
Winnipeg and Hudson Bay Railway and
    Steamship Company, 136, 142
Winstone, George, 92, 100–101, 104
Wolseley, Garnet, 2, 15, 92
Wootton, James, 77

Xerxes, 145

Ye Mingchen, 20–1
Yokohama, 35–6
Yokohama (team), 36
Yonezaemon, Narahara, 34–5
York Factory, 137–9
Young, Ned, 50
Ypres, Battle of, 165

Zulus, 125